Seeking Spatial Justice

SEEKING
SPATIAL JUSTICE

Edward W. Soja

Globalization and Community Series

University of Minnesota Press
Minneapolis
London

Globalization and Community Series
Susan Clarke and Gary Gaile, Series Editors
Dennis R. Judd, Founding Editor

Published by the University of Minnesota Press
111 Third Avenue South, Suite 290
Minneapolis, MN 55401-2520
http://www.upress.umn.edu

Library of Congress Cataloging-in-Publication Data

Soja, Edward W.
    Seeking spatial justice / Edward W. Soja.
        p. cm. — (Globalization and community series 16)
    Includes bibliographical references and index.
    ISBN 978-0-8166-6667-6 (hc : alk. paper) —
ISBN 978-0-8166-6668-3 (pb : alk. paper)
    1. Social justice. 2. Justice, Administration of. 3. Space perception.
4. Geographical perception. I. Title.
    HM671.S675 2010
    304.2′3—dc22
                                    2009049955

Printed on acid-free paper

The University of Minnesota is an equal-opportunity educator and employer.

Contents

Prologue

Injustice anywhere is a threat to justice everywhere.

—Martin Luther King, Letter from
Birmingham Jail, April 16, 1963

A REMARKABLE MOMENT IN AMERICAN URBAN HISTORY—and geography—occurred in October 1996 in a courtroom in downtown Los Angeles. A class action lawsuit brought against the Los Angeles Metropolitan Transit Authority (MTA) by a coalition of grassroots organizations on behalf of those who depend on public transit for their basic needs was resolved in an unprecedented and momentous consent decree. It was decided that, for at least the next ten years, past decades of discrimination against the transit-dependent urban poor, those who could not afford to run a car, would be remedied by making the MTA give their highest budget priority to improving the quality of bus service and guaranteeing equitable access to all forms of public mass transit.

The direct outcome of the case of *Labor/Community Strategy Center et al. v. Los Angeles County Metropolitan Transit Authority,* also described as the Bus Riders Union (BRU) decision, was no simple slap on the hand. According to the consent decree, not only was the MTA required to purchase a specific number of new environment-friendly buses, it would also have to reduce overcrowding, freeze fare structures, enhance bus security, reduce bus stop crime, and provide special services to facilitate access to jobs, education, and health centers. If followed to the letter, these requirements would soak up almost the entire operating budget of the MTA, making it impossible to continue with its ambitious plans at that time to build an extensive fixed-rail network in keeping with the perceived view of Los Angeles as a major world city. A Joint Working Group of the BRU and MTA was also created to maintain a lasting influence of the BRU on transit policy.

As a direct attack on racist practices, the Bus Riders Union decision signaled a revival of the civil rights movement and stimulated comparisons to the famous *Brown v. Board of Education* case in 1954 on the racial desegregation of schools. Here, too, it was deemed that the rights of a particular segment of the population were being denied by the existence of two separate but unequal systems in the provision of a vital public service, in this case public mass transit. At the same time, it was also a stirring expression of the environmental justice movement, combating racial injustice and discrimination based on place of residence and affirming the view that where one lived could have negative repercussions on important aspects of daily life as well as personal health.

Nothing quite like this had ever happened before with regard to public transit services in any major American city. Giving such priority to the needs of the inner-city and largely minority working poor was a stunning reversal of the conventional workings of urban government and planning in the United States, as service provision almost always favored the wealthier residents even in the name of alleviating poverty. It also ran against the grain of American politics at the time, with its neo-conservative ascendancy, detrimental welfare reform, and weakening civil rights and antipoverty efforts. There were very few examples anywhere across the country of successful grassroots social movements affecting urban planning and governance at such a scale of financial commitment. In essence, the consent decree resulted in the transfer of billions of dollars from a plan that disproportionately favored the wealthy to a plan that worked more to the benefit of the poor.

Even more surprising was that this decision occurred in Los Angeles, historically not known to be a progressive urban environment for either labor or community organizations. Los Angeles had been the focal point for two of the bloodiest racial justice–based urban uprisings in U.S. history, in 1965 and 1992, after both of which there was relatively little success in alleviating the problems causing the riots in the first place, from extensive poverty and discrimination to racist police violence. By the mid-1990s, public attention had shifted toward an ambitious but costly fixed-rail building program that fed local pride and the desire to join the list of great world cities with advanced subway-tube-metro systems. With a few minor exceptions, however, rail construction ended soon after the BRU decision and the accompanying loss of public support for the expensive and problem-filled rail project.

The two key organizations behind the successful class action lawsuit were the Bus Riders Union itself and the lead plaintiffs in the case, the Labor/Community Strategy Center (L/CSC), which initiated the court action and spearheaded the creation of the larger coalition. The Bus Riders Union/Sindicato de Pasajeros is not a traditional labor union but rather an assertively multiracial and antiracist mass organization of the transit dependent aimed at improving the public transportation system and the lives of the more than 400,000 predominantly minority and female working poor of Los Angeles. It forms a branch of the L/CSC, or Strategy Center, an activist organization founded in 1989 as, in its own words, an antiracist, anticorporate, and anti-imperialist think tank/act tank focusing on theory-driven practice. It aims at generating mass campaigns of the working class and oppressed nationalities, in particular black and Latino workers and communities. The Strategy Center runs a National School for Strategic Organizing and publishes *Ahora Now,* a bilingual political magazine.

After the consent decree was announced, the victorious BRU and Strategy Center organizers proclaimed their achievements in deservedly epochal language. They were "driving the bus of history," producing "billions for buses" in an ongoing struggle for justice at the "intersection of mass transit, civil rights, and the environment," creating "a new vision for urban transportation" and "a new theory of urban insurgency in an age of transnational capitalism." In an article published in the *Socialist Register* in 2001, Eric Mann, director of the Strategy Center, described their effort as "a race struggle, a class struggle, a women's struggle all at once." For more on the Strategy Center and additional references, see "Notes and References" following chapter 6.

Hollywood too noticed the significance of the decision. Activist and Academy Award–winning cinematographer and director Haskell Wexler spent three years with the BRU and produced a feature-length film detailing its visionary efforts, adding to his earlier works on labor issues (*Matewan*, 1987), the Vietnam War, torture in Brazil, and the uprising in Chiapas, Mexico. While rooted in the local milieu, the BRU victory took on a global significance, enhanced by the international ambitions of its leaders.

Defining Transit Equity and Justice

Many factors figured into the stunning court decision in 1996. In part, it reflected the recognition that any investment in alternative forms of mass transit (such as fixed rail or subway construction) that compromised vital bus services, especially for the inner-city poor, was discriminatory and unjust. In specific legal terms, it violated Title VI of the Civil Rights Act of 1964, the generative act that defined and propelled the civil rights movement. The transit needs of the poor and racial minorities were never ignored entirely by the transportation planners, but it was argued that they were systematically subordinated to the needs and expectations of those living well above the poverty line. A massive redistribution of resources and a major shift in public policy were deemed necessary to redress decades of systematic geographical and racial discrimination.

This long entrenched form of discrimination in meeting the mass transit needs of the poor was rooted in an even larger pattern of discriminatory investment that had shaped the geography and built environment of Los Angeles and other major metropolitan areas throughout the twentieth century. I refer here to the pronounced investment gap between the building and maintenance of roads and freeways on the one hand, and the construction of all other means of mass transit on the other. The outcome of this socially and spatially discriminatory process was an unjust metropolitan transit geography, favoring the wealthier, multicar-owning population in the suburban rings over the massive agglomeration of the immigrant and more urgently transit-dependent working poor in the inner core of the urban region.

By the time of the consent decree in 1996, the five-county Los Angeles urbanized area had become the densest in the United States, with more than five million predominantly immigrant and largely Latino/a workers packed into the teeming inner city and many more spilling out into the new cities forming in what had been classical suburbia. Some estimates claimed that 40 percent of the population was living at or below the poverty line, with a growing proportion consisting of women and children. A United Nations report published after the riots of 1992 claimed that the gap between rich and poor in Los Angeles and New York City was the widest in the developed world and was approaching that in Karachi, Bombay, and Mexico City.

Economic restructuring, increasing poverty and social polarization, and the rise of the so-called New Economy had worsened the problems of the transit-dependent poor and minority households concentrated in the inner city. Nearly every low-wage worker held multiple jobs, both sequentially and simultaneously, and in most cases these jobs, as domestics, gardeners, cleaners, nannies, home-care specialists, were multilocational, requiring travel to many different sites scattered around the city. The simple hub-and-spoke spatial structure of the proposed and partially built fixed-rail system could never serve the inner-city working poor as effectively as the dense mesh of a flexible bus network.

Other local factors entered into the court decision. After what some called the Justice Riots of 1992, confidence was shattered that local, state, or federal governments could deal with the magnitude of problems facing Los Angeles. While some progressive activists withdrew from politics, others recognized the necessity to foster new kinds of collective and connected social movements that would challenge neoliberal and neoconservative power. In the 1990s, many new campaigns and labor–community alliances were developed around Justice for Janitors, the need for a living wage, the differential effects of public investment, the availability of affordable housing, and what the Los Angeles Alliance for a New Economy (LAANE) called development with justice. The successful and committed organizing effort of the Strategy Center and its allies, however, stands out from the rest.

Building on deeper roots, going back to struggles against the closure of automobile assembly plants in an earlier period of deindustrialization (see in particular Eric Mann's *Taking On General Motors,* published in 1987), the Labor/Community Strategy Center from its founding in 1989 was among the early leaders in the antiracist environmental justice movement in the United States and continues to be an important actor today. It played a key role in making connections between the attack on environmental racism and the struggles for transit equity and justice, with the Bus Riders Union as perhaps the most successful grassroots organization to grow out of these efforts.

In addition to the BRU and Strategy Center, there were many other actors involved in the court case. On the side of the accused was above all the MTA, a relatively new public authority formed in 1992 with the merger of the Los Angeles County Transportation Commission (LACTC) and the county Rapid Transit District (RTD). Although there were exceptions, on the whole the LACTC tended to be supportive of large-scale rail transport and countywide "regional" interests. One must remember that the City of Los Angeles is just one of nearly ninety municipalities interspersed with extensive unincorporated areas that make up the County of Los Angeles, reputed to be one of the largest local government units in the world. In 1990, the county had a population of more than eight million, less than half residing in the very oddly shaped City of Los Angeles.

Also countywide, the RTD controlled the huge but fractious bus system as well as several rail lines. The merger created a new organization that almost surely had a majority of decision makers that favored rail and conventional transportation planning practices, but there was also a minority that preferred the flexibility of bus transit and maintained serious concerns for issues of transit equity and justice. The MTA Board of Directors consisted of a mix of rail and bus advocates but also reflected a competitive division between what might be called the county regionalists and the city centrists, the former led by the five county supervisors, and the latter by the mayor and city council of the City of Los Angeles. The thirteen-member board consisted of the five supervisors, the L.A. mayor and three of his appointees, and four others from other parts of the county chosen by a county selection committee.

The opposing coalition led by the BRU and the Strategy Center also included the Korean Immigrant Workers Advocates (KIWA), a nonprofit community services organization that played a key role in improving relations between African American and Korean communities after the conflicts of 1992 and in continuing struggles for immigrant and workers' rights; the Southern Christian Leadership Council of Greater Los Angeles County, the national civil rights organization that supported Rosa Parks in her efforts to stop racial segregation in buses and other public facilities; and thousands of individual plaintiffs representing the "class" of transit-dependent bus riders. The chief attorneys for the case came from the Western Regional Office of the NAACP Legal Defense and Education Fund (LDF), with some support also from the American Civil Liberties Union Foundation of Southern California and the Environmental Defense Fund.

The LDF is a public interest law firm that has played a major role in the national civil rights movement. Its most well-known success was the 1954 Supreme Court decision of *Brown v. Board of Education* ending school segregation, a case that would eventually involve the political and symbolic importance of buses. The LDF has been specifically committed to building coalitions aimed at social and environmental justice and was active in earlier efforts to influence MTA policies in favor of the working poor. Its commitment to the plaintiffs was unquestionable, although the more radical BRU–L/CSC persistently and vigorously asserted its own priorities even when the LDF was not in total agreement. Despite some divergent viewpoints, it is hard to imagine a stronger team of advocates for the lawsuit that was formally initiated in 1994.

The interaction between opposing political and professional interests during the lead-up to the final court decision and, one might add, after the consent decree was issued was unusually intense and controversial. Perhaps as significant as anything else in these debates was the exposure of the general public to the significant racial, class, and geographical biases that are embedded in all forms of public planning. It was almost as if the writings of critical geographers on the injustices that characterize the normal functioning of the modern metropolis were coming vividly into public awareness in Los Angeles.

The court case was characterized by a clash between two contrasting views of equity and justice. The MTA felt it was committed to transit justice, but its concept of equity was quite different from the BRU's. As a county authority strongly influenced by the generally very conservative and predominantly white and suburban Board of Supervisors, it defined equity primarily in administrative and territorial terms. If every supervisorial district had equally efficient mass transit and served in some way the needs of the poor, then the system was considered to be equitable. This territorial district view of equity and transit justice was rooted in a "flat" geographical perspective and also ignored the markedly uneven geography of transit need. The importance of the downtown core of the county and region was always recognized, as were such key activity locations as the international airport of LAX and the twin ports of Los Angeles and Long Beach, but the boundaries that mattered most reflected above all the political interests of the Board of Supervisors and its associates.

A constitutional principle of nondiscrimination guaranteed some degree of transit justice, but as in the U.S. Senate and House of Representatives this was assured mainly by not favoring one territorial district or constituency over another in the distribution of benefits (with the disguised exception of pork barrel allocations for the most influential politicians). This made it seem unconstitutional to pay special attention to certain areas and not others. Not every individual in the MTA thought this way, but simple district-to-district equity tended to dominate the overall political culture, and its logic was used in the court case to defend MTA policies and decisions against what were perceived as essentially incomprehensible and unwarranted charges of racial discrimination.

This form of thinking is deeply engrained in conventional planning practices. If policies, whether involving rail or bus, favored the City of Los Angeles over the rest of the county, this would be considered by many to be unacceptably discriminatory. Racial and ethnic minorities could be recognized as deserving special attention, but the MTA argued with mountains of data that every segment of its planned system of mass transit would carry large, if not majority, numbers of minorities and poor people. If a few segments, such as the light-rail Metrolink system that served the expansive San Fernando Valley or the Blue Line link to Pasadena, carried mainly white suburban passengers, this was only fair in this something-for-everyone logic of planning. How could there be claims of racial and spatial discrimination?

The coalition entered the battle with a very different strategic perspective. They argued, with abundant incriminating data, that there was a long historical record of discrimination through disproportional investments and attention to mass transit facilities that served the relatively wealthy, while those most transit-dependent in their everyday lives and densely clustered in what was defined as the inner city remained seriously and systematically underserved. At one point it was shown that each Metrolink rail trip was subsidized at a rate of more than $21 while the figure was a little over $1 per bus trip. It was made clear that when the needs of the transit-dependent poor are given priority, a very different view of justice and discrimination emerges, one that calls for significant changes in public policies and planning practices.

The court deliberations revealed the deeply embedded biases in urban transportation planning that shaped not just the actions of the MTA but practically every planning agency in the country. The bias was not just a matter of overemphasizing simplistic cost-benefit analyses but more so of intrinsically privileging the non-poor automobile driver, and because of this, actively discriminating against those residents who had little choice other than to use public transit for journeys to work, school, health services, shopping, and entertainment.

This car-centered ideology seemed highly rational to the majority of professional planners. Aiming to provide the best possible service for the population as a whole focused attention on the majority of riders and their needs, a seemingly admirable strategy. In all metropolitan regions of the world that, like Los Angeles, are not served with existing and well-used metro rail/subway systems, the majority of travel trips are done by automobile. This usually means that the private (and highly individualized) transit sector outweighs the public or mass transit sector in levels of investment both in absolute and per capita terms, especially when all public costs for street and freeway construction and maintenance as well as automobile prices, insurance, and so on are measured in.

When well-intentioned transportation planners approach mass transit issues on these terms, especially when making the choice between rail and bus, the bus will lose out almost every time. Even if fixed-rail systems such as BART or any of the more recently built systems never reach the overly optimistic goals of their promoters with regard to substituting for private automobile trips, there will always be thousands of car trips avoided. Buses can also take riders out of their cars but will continue to keep street traffic gridlocked and contribute more pollutants to the air unless extraordinary investments are made. When the majority rides in cars, or when this is perceived to be the case by transportation planners, rail investment will tend to be more attractive than improving bus transit. And for the most part, the urge to become more like New York, or London, or Paris will intensify this bias and add to the pressure to make rail investment appear both efficient and equitable.

Once the specific and immediate needs of the transit-dependent poor are clearly recognized, however, everything changes. Los Angeles, once considered the most suburban of cities, provided an especially visible expression of transit injustice in the 1990s, with its massive agglomeration of the immigrant working poor in the dense corona surrounding the downtown business district. With many of the transit dependent holding multiple jobs and with each form of employment typically requiring movement between multiple locations, flexible, multinodal, and densely meshed bus networks will nearly always be preferable, and urgently so, to fixed-rail systems, whether light or heavy, above- or underground.

As was shown for Los Angeles and can probably be demonstrated in almost every U.S. city, transit discrimination or transit injustice has prevailed as normal practice, almost entirely unconstrained and unquestioned, for at least the past eighty years, or since the beginning of the age of Fordism. Maintaining these automobile-driven discriminatory practices does not require evil people intentionally making racially biased decisions, just well-trained experts following conventional procedures to make decisions and plans that will almost always favor the wealthier and more powerful segments of urban society. That this ideology-bound system of transit discrimination was successfully challenged and judged to require enormous and immediate remedial action was among the most extraordinary accomplishments of the case of *Labor/Community Strategy Center et al. v. Los Angeles County Metropolitan Transit Authority*. The significance of the decision would not go unnoticed.

Aftermath and Implications

For all its local roots, the BRU victory had implications that extended well beyond the Los Angeles region. If allowed to expand to its potential limits as a legal precedent, it could have led to radical changes in urban life throughout the country. Imagine the possibilities. Any plan by any public authority, whether for public transit or health policy or for the location of schools and fire stations, could be subjected to a "justice test" to determine whether the distributional pattern proposed was fair and equitable for all areas and communities affected, with fairness based on the different needs of the rich and the poor as well as majority and minority populations. Similar legal tests could potentially be applied to tax policies, electoral districting, hospital closures, school building programs, the health effects of air and water pollution, the siting of toxic facilities, practically every planning and policy decision influencing urban life. Not surprisingly, the consent decree triggered vigorous reactions. The MTA and other major planning authorities, reinforced by more conservative as well as some liberal political voices, mobilized in a determined effort to reverse or sabotage the decision. Legal appeals were made (and rejected). Hints of a "red scare" similar to that which destroyed public housing efforts in Los Angeles in the 1950s were floated in the local media. When these fears did not take hold, there were more direct personal attacks on the BRU leaders.

Reactions were not confined to Los Angeles. The radical potential of the BRU decision and consent decree was not lost in Washington and in the Bush administration, especially in the wake of the Bush–Cheney regime's infusion of presidential power into the judicial system. The federal effort to prevent the potential spread of the BRU legal precedent came to a head in 2001. In the case of *Alexander v. Sandoval,* based on a challenge to the federal Department of Transportation (DOT) raised in Alabama over driving license exams being given only in English, the U.S. Supreme Court in effect blocked further legal application of the BRU precedent. In a five to four decision, it not only ruled that intent to discriminate had to be proved, drawing on earlier decisions that seriously weakened the entire civil rights movement, but also went further to state that private parties cannot sue the DOT or any other federal agency based on disparate action claims, that is, on the basis of alleged discriminatory practices. There were other efforts to limit the impact of cases such as the BRU based on the need to show intent, but none went as far as *Alexander v. Sandoval* in protecting public authorities against all antidiscrimination lawsuits.

The Sandoval decision built a legal barrier around attempts to extend the BRU victory beyond its immediate local impact, although efforts continue to encourage the spread of the BRU organizing and strategic model to other cities. The local impact, however, has been impressive. According to the BRU Web site, more than $2.5 billion were redistributed to serve bus riders in the ten-year period 1996–2006. The largest clean-fuel fleet in the country was created, replacing more than 1,800 diesel buses. At least a million annual bus service hours were added, more than eight hundred "green" and unionized jobs were created, bus ridership increased by 12 percent, and many rapid bus lanes were added to major surface streets. There are probably no other metropolitan areas in the country where bus services have improved more significantly over the past fifteen years.

On May 1, 2006, the BRU and L/CSC helped organize the "Great American Boycott," or in Spanish, El Gran Paro Estadounidense (the Great American Strike), when perhaps as many as two million people marched peacefully for immigrant rights and against the rising national tide of anti-immigrant feeling. Even after the consent decree came to an end on October 29, 2006, the strategic coalition has, if anything, broadened and intensified its efforts in protesting against environmental racism, police mistreatment of minorities, all new plans for rail construction, proposed bus fare increases, and larger issues such as the war in Iraq. As indicated on its current Web page, the Strategy Center and its allied groups have been promoting extensions of the BRU model to other cities, such as Atlanta, protesting vigorously against recent regressive shifts in MTA policy, and expanding their publication and multimedia programs. In 2009, the Strategy Center published a map-rich *Clean Air Economic Justice Plan*, presenting a new bus-centered model for urban transportation, environmental justice, and economic development that would build on federal funds arising from the Obama government's economic stimulus package.

There is a great deal to learn from the accomplishments of the strategic coalition behind the BRU decision and its continuing struggles. For social movement activists and progressive scholars everywhere, it stands out as an exemplary model of successful urban insurgency in the search for racial, environmental, and spatial justice. With some degree of strategic optimism, one can see the possibility that the BRU along with the other resurgent coalitions that have been developing in Los Angeles over the past two decades can become effective springboards for a much larger movement seeking to erase injustices wherever they may be found. All that follows in *Seeking Spatial Justice* is aimed at encouraging this possibility.

Introduction

Questions of justice cannot be seen independently from the urban condition, not only because most of the world's population lives in cities, but above all because the city condenses the manifold tensions and contradictions that infuse modern life.

—Erik Swyngedouw, *Divided Cities*, 2006

Just as none of us is beyond geography, none of us is completely free from the struggle over geography. That struggle is complex and interesting because it is not only about soldiers and cannons but also about ideas, about forms, about images and imaginings.

—Edward Said, *Culture and Imperialism*, 1993

THE BUS RIDERS UNION CASE provides an evocative beginning for a wide-ranging exploration of spatial justice as a theoretical concept, a focal point for empirical analysis, and a target for social and political action. Guiding the exploration from the start is the idea that justice, however it might be defined, has a *consequential geography*, a spatial expression that is more than just a background reflection or set of physical attributes to be descriptively mapped. As suggested in the above quotations, the geography, or "spatiality," of justice (I will use the two terms interchangeably) is an integral and formative component of justice itself, a vital part of how justice and injustice are socially constructed and evolve over time. Viewed in this way, seeking spatial justice becomes

1

fundamentally, almost inescapably, a *struggle over geography,* to use the phrasing of Edward Said.

This definitive struggle over geography can be best understood from an assertive spatial perspective, one that emphasizes what can be described as the explanatory power of the consequential geographies of justice. Stated differently, these consequential geographies are not just the outcome of social and political processes, they are also a dynamic force affecting these processes in significant ways. As I hope to demonstrate, an assertive and explanatory spatial perspective helps us make better theoretical and practical sense of how social justice is created, maintained, and brought into question as a target for democratic social action.

This forceful approach is more than just a claim that "space matters," as geographers like me have been arguing for decades. It arises more ambitiously from a deeply held belief that *whatever your interests may be, they can be significantly advanced by adopting a critical spatial perspective.* Spatial thinking in this sense cannot only enrich our understanding of almost any subject but has the added potential to extend our practical knowledge into more effective actions aimed at changing the world for the better. Reaching this potential for innovative theoretical and empirical discovery as well as successful practical application defines the particular promise and premise of *Seeking Spatial Justice.*

Putting into the foreground such an assertive spatial perspective deserves further explanation, for to a public as well as to an academic audience, emphasizing the affective or explanatory power of space is relatively unfamiliar and for some quite controversial. Most social scientists not surprisingly emphasize a sociological and historical rather than geographical perspective. Primary attention is given to social processes and social consciousness as they develop over time in comparison to what might be called spatial processes, spatial consciousness, and spatial development. Indeed, to most readers, I suspect, attaching *spatial* to the words processes, consciousness, development, and, more specifically, justice, democracy, and human rights may seem quite jarring. Rather than being seen as a significant force shaping social action (and hence influencing the search for social justice), the spatial dimension has traditionally been treated as a kind of fixed background, a physically formed environment that, to be sure, has some influence on our lives but remains external to the social world and to efforts to make the world more socially just.

For at least the past century, thinking about the interrelated historical and social aspects of our lives has tended to be much more important and widely practiced than emphasizing a pertinent critical spatial perspective. Thinking historically somehow has been made to feel more intellectually stimulating than thinking spatially or geographically. There may be no justifiable reason for privileging history over geography or, in more abstract terms, time over space, but such privileging persists in mainstream social science and philosophy as well as in more radical or socialist theory and practice. It also powerfully shapes the popular imagination.

In recent years, however, the way we interpret the relation between the social, the historical, and the spatial aspects of our lives has begun to change in significant ways. A new and different approach to thinking about space and spatiality has been emerging in conjunction with what some have described as a *spatial turn* affecting nearly all the human sciences. As discussed in chapter 1, the spatial turn is still in its early stages, but enough has happened to suggest that a rebalancing is beginning to occur between social, historical, and spatial perspectives, with no one of the three ways of looking at and interpreting the world inherently privileged over the others.

The main impetus for this resurgence and diffusion of spatial thinking and spatial theory came initially from critical human geographers but has been carried forward in recent years by scholars from many different disciplines, ranging from archaeology, art, and anthropology to law, theology, and economics. While the privileging of the historical and the social still persists, perhaps never before in the past 150 years has a critical spatial perspective been so widespread and influential. As the effects of consequential geographies become more widely understood, many different concepts and subject matter that had hitherto been rarely seen from a critical spatial perspective, such as social capital and social justice, are being significantly spatialized in terms of both causes and effects.

Driving this transdisciplinary diffusion of spatial thinking have been two fundamental ideas that have already been touched on. The first is the promising possibility that applying an assertive spatial perspective, using approaches that have been relatively neglected in the past, can open up new sources of insight and innovative practical and theoretical applications. Complementing this expectation is the idea that there exists a mutually influential and formative relation between the social and the spatial dimensions of human life, each shaping the other in similar ways. In this notion of a *socio-spatial dialectic,* as I called it some time ago, the spatiality of whatever subject you are looking at is viewed as shaping social relations and societal development just as much as social processes configure and give meaning to the human geographies or spatialities in which we live. Taken together, these two ideas help to understand what is meant by consequential geographies, an assertive spatial perspective, and the explanatory power of spatial thinking.

There continues to be significant resistance to this emphatically spatial approach, and not just from those who consider a sociological or historical perspective to be superior and unchallengeable. Many geographers, for example, see the so-called spatial turn as little more than a passing fad promoting in other disciplines a superficial spatial perspective lacking the rigor and depth of their own well-developed and long-established ways of thinking and writing about space. Some of these critical geographers may claim they accept the basic idea of a socio-spatial dialectic, but nearly all tend nonetheless in their writings to give greater stress to how social processes such as class formation, social stratification, or racist or masculinist practices shape geographies than to how geographies actively affect these social processes and forms.

This persistent asymmetry between social and spatial explanation reflects in part a long-standing disciplinary precaution among geographers against giving too much causal power to the spatiality of social life for fear of falling into the simplistic environmental determinism that plagued geographical thinking in the past. Thinking in this overly cautious way, however, misses too much, making almost invisible the political and other forces emanating from the geographies we have created and in which we live out our lives. In this more cautious spatial perspective, space tends to be seen as little more than a receptacle. Things happen to it and in it, helping us to explain the formation of more- or less-just human geographies but blocking from view how space is actively involved in generating and sustaining inequality, injustice, economic exploitation, racism, sexism, and other forms of oppression and discrimination.

Arising out of these disciplinary entanglements and controversies has been a peculiar bias against actually using the specific term *spatial justice.* Up to the turn of the twentieth century, for example, there was only one short journal article, one pamphlet, and not a single book published with the specific words in the title. It has even been difficult to find the phrase *spatial justice* used in any twentieth-century text, even when the subject has to do with the relation between justice and geography or social justice and the city. When the question of justice is addressed from a spatial perspective, other terms are typically used, such as territorial justice, environmental justice, the urbanization of justice, or simply the geography of social justice.

To emphasize the consequential spatiality of social justice and its connections to related notions of democracy and human rights, I pay particular attention to the explicit use of the term *spatial justice* in all that follows. Highlighting the socio-spatial dialectic, I also adopt from the start the view that the spatiality of (in)justice (combining justice and injustice in one word) affects society and social life just as much as social processes shape the spatiality or specific geography of (in)justice. Given the persistent constraints to thinking in this way, I return in each of the first three chapters to clarify further what is meant by an assertive spatial perspective and to explore the new spatial consciousness that has been emerging over the past ten years from its more widespread application. I apologize in advance to those readers who, whether in agreement or not, find these arguments repetitively familiar and perhaps unnecessarily elaborated. For all readers, however, my objective is clear: to stimulate new ways of thinking about and acting to change the unjust geographies in which we live.

Before moving on, a few additional points of clarification need to be made. It is important to stress that seeking spatial justice is not meant to be a substitute for or alternative to the search for social, economic, or environmental justice. It is intended instead as a means of amplifying and extending these concepts into new areas of understanding and political practice. Calling it spatial justice is not meant to imply that justice is determined only by its spatiality, but neither should spatial justice be seen as just one of many different components or aspects of social justice to be comparatively gauged for their relative strength. This relativist view misses the point of the socio-spatial dialectic, that not only does the social comprise the spatial, it is also comprised by it. In the view taken here, everything that is social (justice included) is simultaneously and inherently spatial, just as everything spatial, at least with regard to the human world, is simultaneously and inherently socialized.

I will not provide a simplified "cookbook" definition of spatial justice but allow its meaning to evolve and expand chapter by chapter from its initial description as what arises from the application of a critical spatial perspective to what is more familiarly known as social justice. I also want to make clear that exploring the spatiality of justice and its expressions in struggles over geography is not just an academic exercise but has more ambitious political and practical objectives. Seeing justice spatially aims above all at enhancing our general understanding of justice as a vital attribute and aspiration in all societies. It seeks to promote more progressive and participatory forms of democratic politics and social activism, and to provide new ideas about how to mobilize and maintain cohesive coalitions and regional confederations of grassroots and justice-oriented social movements.

Reflecting the introductory comments of Erik Swyngedouw, urbanization and the urban condition will figure centrally in *Seeking Spatial Justice*. It should be emphasized, however, that the impressive impact of urbanization is not confined to the formal administrative boundaries of the city. The urbanization process and along with it what can be called the urbanization of (in)justice are generated primarily in and from dense urban agglomerations, but in the present age of accelerating globalization the urban condition has extended its influence to all areas: rural, suburban, metropolitan, exurban, even wilderness, parkland, desert, tundra, and rain forest. In this sense, the whole world has been or is being urbanized to some degree, making the search for spatial justice relevant at many different geographical scales, from the most global to the most local, and everywhere in between.

This broader view of the urbanization process links the search for spatial justice to struggles over what has been called the *right to the city*, a politically charged idea about human rights in an urban context that was originally developed more than forty years ago by Henri Lefebvre, perhaps the twentieth century's most creative urban spatial theorist and philosopher. Lefebvre's original concept was packed with powerful ideas about the consequential geography of urban life and the need for those most negatively affected by the urban condition to take greater control over the social production of urbanized space. Fighting for the right to the city seen in this way, as a demand for greater control over how the spaces in which we live are socially produced wherever we may be located, becomes virtually synonymous with seeking spatial justice.

In recent years, the right to the city idea has been politically revived in global, national, regional, and urban social movements, stimulating a mutually reinforcing convergence between these two versions of the struggle over geography: for spatial justice and for democratic rights to urbanized space. This convergence is addressed in several different ways. In chapter 2, it enters into the discussion of the urbanization and globalization of (in)justice as they are empirically expressed at various geographical scales. In chapter 3, the right to the city idea is treated in more detail as part of the development of a spatial theory of justice. Particular attention is given to the original ideas of Lefebvre and the evolving, more contemporary reconceptualizations of David Harvey, perhaps Lefebvre's closest rival as a leading urban spatial theorist. Seeking spatial justice in terms of the right to the city is returned to in chapter 4, which deals with the resurgence of innovative forms of coalition building in Los Angeles over the past forty years. At the end of the last chapter, the struggles for spatial justice and the right to the city are briefly reexamined in light of the current financial crisis.

I approach the active search for spatial justice and more democratic rights to the city with a sense of strategic optimism, and I hope that a similar feeling will affect those who read what I have to say. Such optimism comes partially from necessity, for there is an urgent need to find some sources of hope in a world of eroding civil liberties and degraded participatory democracy. Strategic pathways for reclaiming and maintaining an active and successful democratic politics, the foundation for achieving justice and reducing oppression and exploitation of all kinds, must be found and kept radically open to new and innovative ideas. This is especially important as the world economy plunges into serious financial crisis and deepening recession, as was the case at the time this introduction was written.

A few words are needed regarding the specific term *justice,* for it too has been experiencing a revival of sorts as a mobilizing force and strategic objective in contemporary politics. From the global to the local and at every geographical scale in between, variations on the stirring demand for jobs with justice, peace with justice, development with justice are pressuring governments to deal more effectively with worsening problems of economic inequality, intercultural conflict, political polarization, and environmental degradation. We hear more and more about the need for environmental justice, justice for workers, for youth, for all who feel the negative effects of social and spatial discrimination based on race, class, gender, sexual preference, and many other axes of unacceptable inequality. Renewed attention, it seems, is being given to both parts of the concept of spatial justice.

The literature on justice and democracy is enormous, and I do not intend to delve as deeply into it as I do with the spatial and geographical literature. Some key works on the theory of justice are discussed briefly, but the main emphasis is on how justice is being used politically and strategically in social movements of all kinds. My aim is to reach out to an audience of actual and potential activists by adding a challenging and politically useful spatial perspective to these justice debates and to the strategies and tactics of the diverse organizations aimed at achieving greater justice and more egalitarian democracy.

Seeking Spatial Justice is divided into six chapters, followed by an extensive notes and references section containing full bibliographic references and further commentary. Chapter 1 presents brief synopses of such topics as why and how spatial thinking as well as the search for justice in the broadest sense have been receiving increasing attention in the contemporary world, and why and how Los Angeles has emerged as an influential center for strategically spatial labor–community coalition building and for the practical application of spatial theory. As another kind of preview, the first chapter concludes with a discussion of how the specific term *spatial justice* has begun to be referred to and used over the past ten years, after more than a century of almost complete neglect. Chapter 2 outlines and illustrates the comprehensive scope and scale of spatial justice. It is intentionally eclectic and wide-ranging, a kind of tasting menu presenting concrete empirical examples of the many different ways unjust geographies are produced and responded to by political actors of various kinds.

Spatial (in)justice is situated and contextualized in three overlapping and interactive levels of geographical resolution. The first results from the external creation of unjust geographies through boundary making and the political organization of space. Examples range from

South African apartheid and other forms of colonial control to more subtle efforts at spatial manipulation such as electoral district gerrymandering and the privileging of private property rights under the law. At a more local scale, unjust geographies arise endogenously or internally from the distributional inequalities created through discriminatory decision making by individuals, firms, and institutions. In such cases as exclusionary zoning, the siting of toxic facilities, and restrictive forms of racial segregation, discriminatory geographies have been challenged in the courts and become the focus for a rich literature on law and space. How race, space, and the law interact is discussed, along with a brief look at the environmental justice movement. The third scale of geographical resolution is more regional, or mesogeographical, and is rooted in the injustices associated with geographically uneven development and what is described as the globalization of injustice. Geographically uneven development is given particular attention as a general process underlying the formation of spatial injustice at the meso, or "middle," scale, between the urban and the global. Seeking spatial justice is expanded here to include regional coalition building, the search for regional democracy, and the development of new action strategies such as community-based regionalism.

Following this illustrative exploration of concretely produced unjust geographies, chapter 3 turns more specifically to theorizing spatial justice and tracing how the concept has evolved over time and in the relevant literature. Building a spatial theory of justice begins with a theoretical look at theory itself, as a means of distinguishing between normative, positive, and critical perspectives. This is followed by an excursion into the highly abstract realm of ontology, aimed at rebalancing how we think about the existential spatiality, historicality, and sociality of life. I encourage even those readers averse to such abstract discussions to persevere, for I believe that such ontological rethinking is necessary to comprehend the power and meaning of a critical spatial perspective and to understand the new spatial consciousness that has been emerging in recent years.

The chapter continues with a critical assessment of how justice has been theorized in itself, highlighting the work of John Rawls and Iris Marion Young. This is followed by a discussion of how the theory of justice was given a spatial dimension through three intersecting streams of thought: one focused specifically on spatial justice as such; another focusing on the urbanization of social injustice, with both liberal and Marxist variants; and the third revolving around the right to the city. Theorizing spatial justice is brought up to date in a critical evaluation of the historical and contemporary contributions of David Harvey and Henri Lefebvre, and how both and others have been stimulating a political revival of the right to the city idea, especially from a multiscalar and/or regional perspective. Also included is another round of discussion of the new spatial consciousness, tracing it back to its early roots in the innovative spatial thinking of Lefebvre and Michel Foucault.

The final chapters shift attention from theory to practice and to a detailed exemplification of the resurgence of labor–community coalition building in Los Angeles. Chapter 4 starts with a backdrop to these developments, seen through a synthesis of local research on urban and regional restructuring and the radical changes that have been taking place in cities all over the world in the past thirty years. Particular attention is paid to the rising income inequalities and social polarizations that have intensified social and spatial injustices at many different scales. The chapter continues with a discussion of the transformations that have occurred in the Los Angeles urban region.

The second half of chapter 4 focuses on the development of labor and community-based organizations in Los Angeles from the Watts Riots in 1965 to the events of September 11, 2001. Highlighted are the innovative achievements in community-based unionism influenced by such organizations as the United Farm Workers, the formation of diverse community development corporations, the vigorous rent control movement, early examples of the struggles over environmental justice, the emergence of the Justice for Janitors movement and the successful living wage campaign, the expansion of workers' justice struggles, and the more recent development of spatial justice–oriented labor–community–university coalitions such as the Los Angeles Alliance for a New Economy (LAANE) and Strategic Action for a Just Economy (SAJE).

Chapter 5, covering the same time period, presents a connected discussion of the role of the faculty and students in the UCLA Department of Urban Planning in the history of social movements in Los Angeles and in encouraging theoretically informed social and spatial action. My objective here is to present a case study illustrating how productive ties can form between the university and the wider urban community, and to describe how these ties played a role in the resurgence of labor–community coalition building discussed in chapter 4. Helping to explain how specifically spatial theory and spatial practice became so effectively intertwined in Los Angeles, I also describe, with some personal detail, the formation of the influential research cluster of geographers and planners based mainly at UCLA whose writings have led some, often rather controversially, to call it a distinctive L.A. "school" of critical urban and regional studies.

The final chapter begins with a discussion of the national and global extension of social movements for spatial justice in Los Angeles after 9/11. Included are the expanding application of Community Benefits Agreements, one of the most innovative forms of local government planning to emerge in recent years; the struggles over Wal-Mart superstores exemplified in the battle for Inglewood; the complex story of the South Central Farm captured in the 2008 Oscar-nominated documentary film *The Garden;* and the recent formation of what is now a nationally representative Right to the City Alliance. The chapter and book conclude with a short commentary on spatial justice and struggles over geography and the right to the city today in light of the economic meltdown of the neoliberal capitalist credit bubble in 2008.

In these pages, I do not focus narrowly on the labor movement, nor do I discuss in any detail community-based organizations or ethnic or religious groups on their own terms. My emphasis throughout is on coalition building, on how diverse organizations unite in cooperative struggles for social and spatial justice. It is in this coming together of activist groups and social movements where the spatiality of justice is most relevant. I concentrate on Los Angeles not only because I know more about it than other places but because there are good reasons to believe that the Los Angeles experience over the past twenty years has something special to say to activists and theoreticians everywhere. Focusing on Los Angeles is not intended to exclude examples from other cities and regions but rather to invite such comparisons and mutual learning. What ties everything together is an assertive spatial perspective.

Why Spatial? Why Justice?
Why L.A.? Why Now?

> [A] kind of paradigm shift is occurring; we are perhaps
> now acceding to a new, invigorated sense of looking at the
> struggle over geography in interesting and imaginative
> ways.
>
> —Edward Said, *Edward Said's Culture and*
> *Imperialism,* 1994

Putting Space First

As I hope I have made clear, spatial justice is not a substitute or alternative to other forms of justice but rather represents a particular emphasis and interpretive perspective. I have also argued that foregrounding
a critical spatial perspective and seeing the search for social justice as
a struggle over geography increase the possibility of opening up new
ways of thinking about the subject as well as enriching existing ideas and
practices. The discussion continues here with a more detailed look at
the resurgence of interest in a critical spatial perspective that has been
developing in recent years, and how it is provoking and being provoked
by new modes of thinking about the spatiality of (in)justice and the
(in)justice of spatiality.

The Spatial Turn

Foregrounding the spatial aspects of justice is one of many "spatializations" that are being generated by what scholars are now calling a *spatial
turn,* an unprecedented diffusion of critical spatial thinking across an
unusually broad spectrum of subject areas. An emphasis on space and

spatiality has traditionally been given particular attention in only a few disciplines, mainly geography, architecture, urban and regional planning, and urban sociology. Today, it has reached far beyond these spatial disciplines into such fields as anthropology and cultural studies, law and social welfare, postcolonial and feminist critiques, theology and bible studies, race theory and queer theory, literary criticism and poetry, art and music, archaeology and international relations, economics and accounting.

Often these applications of a spatial perspective are superficial, involving little more than a few pertinent spatial metaphors such as mapping this or that or using such words as cartography, region, or landscape to appear to be moving with the times. In some fields, however, such as in current debates in urban archaeology and development economics, radically new ideas have been emerging from an understanding of socio-spatial causality, the powerful forces that arise from socially produced spaces such as urban agglomerations and cohesive regional economies. What can be called the stimulus of socio-spatial agglomeration is today being assertively described as the *primary* cause of economic development, technological innovation, and cultural creativity, one of the strongest claims ever made for urban spatial causality. (For more on this, see Notes and References.)

Whether affecting mainstream thought or more peripheral subject matter, this spatial turn and the new spatial consciousness it has engendered are beginning to reverse a century and a half of relative neglect of spatial thinking. Moreover, a critical spatial perspective has also begun to extend its influence beyond the academic world into a wider public and political realm, as exemplified by the increasingly active search for spatial justice and the right to the city. Perhaps never before has the spatial organization of human society, particularly as it takes shape in the modern metropolis and the expansive global economy, been as widely recognized as an influential force shaping human behavior, political action, and societal development.

A critical spatial perspective of some sort has become increasingly relevant to understanding the contemporary condition, whether we are pondering the increasing intervention of electronic media in our daily routines, trying to understand the multiplying geopolitical conflicts around the globe, or seeking ways to act politically to reduce poverty, racism, sexual discrimination, and environmental degradation. What you are reading is a product and an extension of this transdisciplinary diffusion of a critical spatial perspective from its original academic confines into social and political theory and practice. From local and urban contexts to the regional, national, and global scales, a new spatial consciousness is entering into public debates on such key issues as human rights, social inclusion–exclusion, citizenship, democracy, poverty, racism, economic growth, and environmental policy.

As I view it, the spatial turn is signaling what may turn out to be a profound sea change in all intellectual thought and philosophy, affecting every form of knowledge production from the abstract realms of ontological and epistemological debate to theory formation, empirical analysis, and practical application. In particular, it represents a growing shift away from an era when spatial thinking was subordinated to historical thinking, toward one in which the historical and spatial dimensions of whatever subject you are looking at take on equal and interactive significance, without one being inherently privileged over the other. This rebalancing of spatial and historical perspectives deserves further explanation.

Space and time, along with their more concrete and socially constructed extensions as geography and history, are the most fundamental and encompassing qualities of the physical and social worlds in which we live. For most scholars and across the wider public, however, thinking historically about society and social relations is more familiar and has tended to be seen as potentially if not inherently more revealing and insightful than thinking spatially or geographically. Few would deny that understanding any subject, in the past or present, will be significantly advanced by adopting an inquisitive historical perspective. After all, we are essentially temporal beings. Our biography defines our individual lived time. Time brings us to life, tempers our existence, makes us unalterably and irreversibly contemporary, and, in the end, unavoidably temporary.

It is over time that we also create our collective selves, construct the societies and cultures, polities and economies within which our individual experiences are expressed and inscribed. Time and its socially produced outcome, history, almost self-evidently define human development and change, create problems and solutions, motivate, complicate, expand, and eventually extinguish our being. Although only under conditions given to us from the past, we make our histories, transform society, move from tradition to modernity, produce justice and injustice as social attributes, and so much more.

The larger significance of the spatial turn and the resurgence of interest in critical spatial thinking arise from the belief that *we are just as much spatial as temporal beings,* that our existential spatiality and temporality are essentially or ontologically coequal, equivalent in explanatory power and behavioral significance, interwoven in a mutually formative relation. Human life is in every sense spatio-temporal, geo-historical, without time or space, history or geography, being inherently privileged on its own. There is no a priori reason to make one more important than the other. Yet despite this relational equivalence, the interpretive balance between space and time, spatial and historical perspectives, has for the most part tended to be distorted, at least in Western social thought, with time and history taking precedence and privilege in virtually every field of knowledge formation, academic theory building, and public consciousness.

That such intellectual discrimination persists was brought home to me when I saw the film *The History Boys,* based on the autobiographical writings of Alan Bennett and an award-winning play of the same name. If you have seen it, you will remember that the title refers to the eight brightest students at a grammar school in northern England who are assiduously educated to obtain entry to Oxford or Cambridge. They share a deep interest in history and debate its merits and complexity with great skill, assisted by the history instructor, seemingly the most balanced and perceptive of the teaching staff. The primary villain in all this is a sniveling headmaster who basks in the students' accomplishment but is deeply jealous of their cleverness. While interviewing someone he hopes can help the students spice up their test essays, he grudgingly admits that he did not go to Oxford or Cambridge. "It was the fifties after all," he says. "It was a more adventurous time. I was a geographer and went to [the University of] Hull." One could almost hear the audience snigger, especially when composed of largely British viewers: a geographer at a minor university being almost as far away from the intellectual status of the history boys as one can be. It was the almost unquestionable matter-of-factness of the historian's superiority that came through most vividly.

The spatial turn has emerged against the grain of this continued privileging of the historical over the geographical imaginations. Its most ambitious objective is to bring about a restoration of sorts, a complementary rebalancing of historical and geographical thinking and interpretation. Achieving this, at least for the present moment, involves some degree of foregrounding if not a strategic but temporary privileging of the spatial perspective over all others. This means inverting the usual order, putting space first as the primary discursive and explanatory focus, as is intended in spatializing such concepts as justice, development, politics, and planning.

Putting space first does not mean that spatial thinking should be practiced alone, divorced from life's social and historical realities. I cannot emphasize enough that foregrounding a spatial perspective does not represent a rejection of historical and sociological reasoning but an effort to open them up to new ideas and approaches that have been systematically neglected or marginalized in the past. Driving the spatial turn forward is the expectation of significant theoretical and practical payoffs, for this strategic foregrounding of the spatial flexes interpretive muscles that have not been well developed or widely applied in the past. This in turn raises new possibilities for discovering hidden insights, alternative theories, and revised modes of understanding, such as has been occurring in the aforementioned discovery of the generative effects of urban agglomeration and in the search for spatial justice.

Toward a New Spatial Consciousness

Moving the argument further, it is important to realize that spatial thinking today has evolved in several new directions that make it different from the way space was conventionally conceptualized and studied. When space is referred to here, it is more than just a physical quality of the material world or an essential philosophical attribute having absolute, relative, or relational dimensions. These physical and philosophical features of space have dominated the historical discourse on space for the past century, especially among geographers. They remain relevant to our contemporary understanding of the spatiality of human life, but focusing exclusively on them can lead us away from a cogent, active, and critical understanding of human geographies.

Although some may think this to be too obvious to mention, the spatiality of human life must be interpreted and understood as fundamentally, from the start, a complex social product, a collectively created and purposeful configuration and socialization of space that defines our contextual habitat, the human and humanized geography in which we all live out our lives. Such socialized lived space, constructed out of physical and natural spatial forms, mentally and materially intertwines with our socialized lived times to create our biographies and geo-histories. Human life is consequently and consequentially spatial, temporal, and social, simultaneously and interactively real and imagined. Our geographies, like our histories, take on material form as social relations become spatial but are also creatively represented in images, ideas, and imaginings, to take us back to Edward Said's incisive opening comments.

Building on this foundational starting point are other defining principles of critical spatial thinking. As intrinsically spatial beings from birth, we are at all times engaged and enmeshed in shaping our socialized spatialities and, simultaneously, being shaped by them. In other words, we make our geographies just as it has been said that we make our histories, not under conditions of our own choosing but in the material and imagined worlds we collectively have already created—or that have been created for us. In this way, our lives are always engaged in what I have described as a socio-spatial dialectic, with social processes shaping spatiality at the same time spatiality shapes social processes. Stated another way, our spatiality, sociality, and historicality are mutually constitutive, with no one inherently privileged a priori.

Here too there has been a great imbalance in our intellectual traditions. Much greater emphasis continues to be given to how social processes shape spatial form as opposed to the reverse relation, how spatiality and spatial processes shape social relations of all kinds, from the immediacy of interpersonal interaction to relations of class and social stratification to long-term patterns of societal development. To emphasize again, this is not to say that spatial processes are more important than social processes or to suggest a simplistic spatial determinism. As with the relations between space and time, the social and the spatial are dialectically intertwined, mutually (and often problematically) formative and consequential.

This perspective and the new spatial consciousness that is arising from it strive to rebalance the spatial, the social, and the historical dimensions of reality, making the three dynamically interactive and equivalent in inherent explanatory power. The actual production of useful knowledge will almost surely emphasize one of these interacting modes more than the others, but there should be no predetermined disposition to subordinate any one of the triad to the others, as has arguably been the case when the spatial is reduced to physical form or a mere reflection or background environment to social and historical processes. Emphasizing the spatial does not mean simply reversing the biases of the past to create a new spatial determinism, but neither should there be a continued acceptance of the space-blinkered social historicism that has prevailed in nearly all the human sciences to this day.

Activating this strategically foregrounded spatial perspective and extending its reach from theory into practice is the even bolder recognition that the geographies in which we live can have both positive and negative effects on our lives. They are not just dead background or a neutral physical stage for the human drama but are filled with material and imagined forces that affect events and experiences, forces that can hurt us or help us in nearly everything we do, individually and collectively. This is a vitally important part of the new spatial consciousness, making us aware that the geographies in which we live can intensify and sustain our exploitation as workers, support oppressive forms of cultural and political domination based on race, gender, and nationality, and aggravate all forms of discrimination and injustice. Without this recognition, space is little more than a background complication.

Leading us closer to the search for spatial justice is still another fundamental realization. Since we construct our multiscalar geographies, or they are constructed for us by more powerful others, it follows that we can act to change or reconfigure them to increase the positive or decrease the negative effects. These efforts to make changes in our existing spatial configurations, whether they involve redecorating our homes, fighting against racial segregation in our cities, creating policies to reduce income inequalities between the developed and developing countries, or combating global warming do not express innocent or universally held objectives. They are the target and source of conflicting purposes, competing forces, and contentious political actions for and against the status quo. Space is not an empty void. It is always filled with politics, ideology, and other forces shaping our lives and challenging us to engage in struggles over geography.

Translating these ideas as a template for this book, it can be said that

- justice and injustice are infused into the multiscalar geographies in which we live, from the intimacies of the household to the uneven development of the global economy;
- the socialized geographies of (in)justice significantly affect our lives, creating lasting structures of unevenly distributed advantage and disadvantage;
- these geographies and their effects can be changed through forms of social and political action.

It becomes clear then that seeking spatial justice is a vital political objective but not an easy task, as it is filled with countervailing forces aimed at maintaining existing geographies of privilege and power. With this reformulated critical spatial perspective in mind, we look next at the concept of justice, for it too is being redefined and reasserted in the contemporary context.

Seeking Justice Now

Justice has several dictionary definitions. With a capital *J* it refers to the department of national government (federal in the United States) responsible for enforcing the country's laws. A related definition describes the public official authorized to decide questions brought before a court of law, such as a justice of the Supreme Court or, at a much lower level of authority, a justice of the peace. Still within a legal framework but moving closer to how it will be discussed here, justice in the practice of the law refers to the act of determining rights and assigning rewards or punishment. Here a key link is made to the concept of human rights and to the etymological root of the word "justice," from the Old French *justice,* derived from the Latin *jus,* meaning both law and right. The French word *droit* carries this double meaning of law and right.

Although never completely uprooted from the law and legal adjudication, the concept of justice obtains a much broader meaning as the quality of being just or fair. In this sense of justice as fairness and in conjunction with the establishment of rights under the law, the concept expands in scope to apply to many other conditions of social life and everyday behavior. It links the active notion of seeking justice to other broad concepts referring to the qualities of a just society: freedom, liberty, equality, democracy, civil rights. Seeking to increase justice or to decrease injustice thus becomes a fundamental objective in all societies, a foundational principle for maximizing human dignity and fairness.

All these related terms have been used as mobilizing and consciousness-raising political symbols, but it seems that seeking justice has obtained a stronger hold on the contemporary public and political imagination than its alternatives. Seeking freedom has added increasingly conservative overtones, as in the unbridled idealization of the freedom of choice; liberty feels somehow outdated; equality as such is often made to appear unattainable; and even the demand for universal human rights has connotations of excessive abstraction and lack of attachment to particular times and places. For many today, a new, more grounded and inclusive *justice politics* is emerging to mobilize and guide collective action.

Although difficult to prove conclusively, I am suggesting here that justice in the contemporary world tends to be seen as more concrete than its alternatives, more oriented to present-day conditions, more open to a multiplicity of interconnected perspectives and hence to more successful coalition building and connections between different social movements. Seeking justice today seems to be imbued with a symbolic force that works more effectively across cleavages of class, race, and gender to foster a collective political consciousness, create a sense of solidarity based on shared experience, and focus attention on the most challenging problems in the contemporary world in ways that span large segments of the political spectrum.

The search for justice has accordingly become a powerful rallying cry for contemporary political movements of many different kinds. Achieving specifically social and economic justice has long been at the core of debates on liberal democracy and a focus for social activism and political debate. In recent years, however, the mobilizing force of the concept of justice has been extended into many new political arenas. In addition to familiar social and economic modifiers, many new terms now define particular types of justice struggles and activism: environmental, racial, worker, youth, global, local, human, community, peace, monetary, border, territorial, and, of particular relevance here, spatial. To illustrate the widening use of justice as a mobilizing concept, a partial list of current national and regional organizations and action campaigns in the United States with *justice* specifically in their title is presented in Notes and References.

Why growing attention seems to be given to justice as a political objective has several possible explanations. Particularly relevant has been an increasing awareness of the negative social, political, cultural, and environmental effects arising from globalization and the formation of the New Economy. Many have benefited from globalization, economic restructuring, and the new technologies, but it is also clear that these developments have magnified many existing inequalities in contemporary society, such as between the rich and the poor, between men and women, and between different racial and ethnic groups. They have also accentuated other forms of social and political polarization, such as the clash between domestic and immigrant populations over resources, state policies, and civil rights. Cities such as Los Angeles, New York, and London now have income disparities that rank among the highest in the world, and it is no surprise to see new justice movements arising with particular force in these highly globalized city regions.

Globalization has also been associated with state restructuring and challenges to the political domination of the nation-state as the exclusive political space for defining citizenship, legal systems, and hence justice itself. Struggles for justice, more than ever before, stretch across political scales, from the global to the local, as the feminist political theorist Nancy Fraser observes in her recent book *Scales of Justice: Reimagining Political Space in a Globalizing World* (2008). Her key point is that the theory of justice needs to be reconstituted in a "post-Westphalian" world, referring to the origins of the now outdated nation-state system. All struggles over democracy, solidarity, and the public sphere revolve around rethinking the concept of justice.

Also affecting the attention being given to justice have been environmental factors. Growing problems of global warming, erosion of the ozone layer, the health dangers of hazardous wastes, and destruction of the rain forests have expanded the scope and intensity of the environmental justice movement beyond what David Harvey (2000) and others have called merely "militant localism." The increasingly urgent need to deal with famine, genocide, Third World debt, weapons of mass destruction, the devastating wars in Iraq and Afghanistan, and multiplying threats to world peace has at the same time invigorated a global justice movement, which, like the environmental justice movement, often focuses on explicitly spatial strategies and objectives.

These social and spatial movements have spread the politicization of justice to many different arenas or scales of social activism. Labor unions, NGOs, community-based organizations, and urban civil society more generally have increasingly adopted the cause of achieving socio-economic, environmental, and global justice to further their own local objectives. This has created a new kind of multiscalar embeddedness for worker-, community-, and neighborhood-based activism, in which local-ized justice struggles are connected to larger urban, regional, national, and global contexts and campaigns. Particularly relevant here and in later chapters discussing the new labor–community coalitions emerging in Los Angeles is the mobilizing concept of *community-based regional-ism,* the notion that local efforts at community development can be fostered by adopting a regional perspective and recognizing how the regional economy shapes local events. Also relevant has been the cre-ation of a World Charter for the Right to the City, discussed in more detail in chapter 3.

Further encouraging the emergence of justice as a unifying force for social activism has been the shift away from a traditional binary, or we/they, politics of economic equality, attached to rigidly defined and often exclusionary channels of oppositional resistance based on class, race, gender, or sexual preference. In the development of what some call the new cultural politics of difference, simply achieving equality or destroying the dichotomous relations between labor and capital, black and white, male and female, gay and straight is not the singular goal or the only driving force. Instead, the emphasis is on an inclusive and com-binative rather than exclusive and narrowly channeled political mobi-lization, one that is radically open to new bases of support and aimed at building effective coalitions between different social movements and organizations. Achieving greater justice here becomes a more encom-passing, inclusive, and above all feasible goal than achieving full equality or fomenting revolutionary transformation.

Justice in the contemporary world has been developing a political meaning that transcends the defined categories of race, gender, class, nationality, sexual preference, and other forms of homogeneous and often exclusive group or community identity. In doing so, it helps to bring together the diverse movements built around each of these specific axes of unequal power relations in a common project. Concluding this first look at the concept of justice as it is being used today is another key point guiding the forthcoming chapters, that adding spatial to justice, collectively seeking an explicitly spatialized form of social and economic justice, can be particularly effective in providing an organizational and motivational adhesive, or "glue," that can encourage and maintain heterogeneous and pluralistic association and coalition building. All who are oppressed, subjugated, or economically exploited are to some degree suffering from the effects of unjust geographies, and this struggle over geography can be used to build greater crosscutting unity and solidarity.

Foregrounding Los Angeles

Seeking justice as an organizing strategy and political objective has been particularly prominent and effective in Los Angeles over the past twenty years. Leading the way has been the Justice for Janitors movement (J4J) and related struggles for a living wage for all workers. The J4J experience also significantly influenced the events of spring 1992 in Los Angeles, when banners proclaiming "No Justice—No Peace" were prominently displayed in what many now call the Justice Riots. Justice continues to be the focus today for local struggles over jobs and urban regeneration, as activist groups punctuate their demonstrations at strategic locations with demands not to stop all new development but to achieve "Development with Justice."

Growing out of these justice struggles has been a remarkable resurgence of the labor movement, driven largely through new coalitions between union locals and a wide range of community-based organizations. Innovative organizing strategies, especially with regard to immigrant workers, and a series of successful justice-oriented campaigns have helped to transform what was once considered an intensely antilabor environment into what some national observers today see as the most vigorous and effective urban labor movement in the United States.

Accompanying and to some extent driving this resurgence of the labor movement has been the rise of local and neighborhood consciousness and place-based politics. What was once a notoriously "placeless" urban world, where local communities rarely impinged on people's lives, has now become a hive of community-based organizations and grassroots activism that rivals what can be found in any other major urban region. Springing from this place-based politics has been an integrative regional consciousness, an awareness of how the regional economy significantly shapes local conditions. A strategic community-based regionalism has entered the activists' agenda and has facilitated coalition building and the formation of what might be described as regional confederations or networks bringing together diverse organizations that in the past would rarely work together.

These local and regional achievements are even more remarkable given the deteriorating economy, huge job losses, and declining union power that have characterized most of the rest of the country over the past thirty years. Describing how this dramatic change took place, why it happened in Los Angeles of all places, and specifically examining the role played by strategically incorporating the spatiality of (in)justice in organizational mobilization and action will be the focus for the last three chapters.

Linked into the history of labor–community coalition building has been an important university connection. Particular attention is given in chapter 5 to how students and faculty in urban planning at UCLA have contributed to the translation of theoretical developments and empirical research into social activism and effective coalition building. These university–community connections have been especially effective in such organizations as the Los Angeles Alliance for a New Economy (LAANE), Strategic Action for a Just Economy (SAJE), and the recently formed Right to the City Alliance.

Suggested in these discussions is the idea that a critical spatial imagination entered the world of political practice earlier and more deeply in Los Angeles than in almost any other major metropolis in the country. Also implied is the argument that this early development was at least in part a reflection of the emergence at UCLA and later other local universities of an exceptional cluster of scholars specialized in making theoretical and practical sense—from an explicitly spatial perspective—of the dramatic changes that were taking place in cities around the world over the past forty years. This spatially oriented research cluster built their more general theorizations primarily on empirical studies of urban restructuring in the region of Los Angeles.

As noted earlier, I do not intend to resolve the issue of whether or not these developments deserve to be described as a unified "school," but whatever one's position on this debate, there is little doubt that a remarkable expansion of academic research and writing on Los Angeles occurred after the mid-1970s and that it had a significant influence on urban and regional studies around the world. While many contributed, this research was most densely and creatively generated from faculty and students in the urban planning and geography departments at UCLA and revolved primarily around new ways of thinking about urban and regional development and change. It will also be argued that these achievements fed off an unusually stimulating two-way flow of ideas and experiences between the university and local and regional social activists and labor and community-based organizations.

Contemporary Applications

Before the turn of the twentieth century, the specific term *spatial justice* was almost entirely absent from the literature, at least in English. As will be discussed in more detail in chapter 3, one journal article (Pirie 1983) and a pamphlet on "interdictory space" (Flusty 1994) were the only publications to use spatial justice in their titles. Since 2000, however, the use of the term has become much more widespread. The following discussion continues to add new elements to the evolving definition of spatial justice and illustrates how the term is currently being used.

References to spatial justice appear throughout my book *Postmetropolis* (2000) and its broad examination of the crisis-generated restructuring processes that have been reconfiguring the modern metropolis over the past forty years. To balance the rather bleak picture of the new urban forms that were emerging in Los Angeles and other large urban regions, with their deepening economic inequalities and rampant social polarization, I concluded the book with some glimmers of hope and optimism in a section entitled "New Beginnings: Struggles for Spatial Justice and Regional Democracy." I looked with hopeful expectation to the Bus Riders Union, the Los Angeles Alliance for a New Economy (LAANE), and other successful local organizations as inspirational models for the future and added regional democracy to the struggle for spatial justice, reflecting a new regionalism that was emerging at the time in the local academic discourse as well as in the community-based regional coalitions that had formed in the 1990s (Pastor, Benner, and Matsuoka

2009). In essence, *Seeking Spatial Justice* was initiated in these concluding eight pages.

Mustafa Dikec, a doctoral student in urban planning at UCLA at the time, took the lead in publishing a more elaborate and explicit theorization and discussion of the concept of spatial justice in "Justice and the Spatial Imagination." Starting with a quote from G. H. Pirie, whose article "On Spatial Justice" was published in 1983 in the same journal, *Environment and Planning A,* Dikec (2001) reviewed the relevant literature and developed his own "dialectical formulation of the spatiality of injustice and the injustice of spatiality." He described the spatiality of injustice as focusing on how injustice is embedded in space, while the injustice of spatiality emphasizes how injustice is created and maintained through space.

Without belaboring this distinction, Dikec goes on to draw some significant political conclusions and allusions, anticipating the growing connections between seeking spatial justice and struggles over the right to the city. He calls for the development of new urban spatial sensibilities and a new ideological discourse that will activate struggles for spatial justice (mentioning the Bus Riders Union as an example) informed by the idea of the right to the city and the related rights to difference and resistance. In his subsequent research, Dikec took these ideas into the world of French urban policy to assess the injustices embedded in the formation of the now immigrant-dominated *banlieues,* the dense inner suburbs of Paris and other large French cities, which exploded in 2005. I will return to his work on the *banlieues* in the next chapter, as an example of how spatial injustice is produced top-down through the political organization of space.

The most comprehensive and focused publication of the decade was a special double issue on spatial justice of *Critical Planning,* the UCLA student-managed and refereed journal of urban planning, published in 2007. A list of the articles that contained spatial justice in their titles appears in Notes and References. Here are some brief excerpts from the editorial note:

> [T]he renewed recognition that space matters offers new insights not only to understanding how injustices are produced through space, but also how spatial analyses of injustice can advance the fight for social justice, informing concrete claims and the activist practices that make

these claims visible. Understanding that space—like justice—is never simply handed out or given, that both are socially produced, experienced, and contested on constantly shifting social, political, economic, and geographical terrains, means that justice—if it is to be concretely achieved, experienced, and reproduced—must be engaged on spatial as well as social terms.

Thus, those vested with the power to produce the physical spaces we inhabit through development, investment, planning—as well as through grassroots embodied activisms—are likewise vested with the power to perpetuate injustices and/or create just spaces. . . . What a just space looks like is necessarily kept open, but must be rooted in the active negotiation of multiple publics, in search of productive ways to build solidarities across difference. This space—both process and product—is by definition public in the broadest sense; the opportunity to participate in inscribing its meaning is accessible to all. . . . Justice is therefore not abstract, and not solely something "handed down" or doled out by the state, it is rather a shared responsibility of engaged actors in the socio-spatial systems they inhabit and (re)produce.

An exhibition on Just Space(s) was held in fall 2007 at the Los Angeles Contemporary Exhibitions center (LACE) to coincide with the publication of the special issue of *Critical Planning*. The exhibits and panel discussions were intended not just to show what is unjust about the world but also to encourage active participation in producing more just space(s).

In March 2008 the first international conference on spatial justice ("Justice et Injustice Spatiales") was held at the University of Paris X–Nanterre, the site where the Paris uprising of May 1968 first erupted almost exactly forty years earlier. The university, located near one of the dense *banlieues,* was also where Henri Lefebvre, the French philosopher who originated the concept of the right to the city, taught for many years and for whom the main auditorium where the plenary sessions took place was named. Various panels examined spatial justice and its relation to urban and regional planning, globalization, segregation, environmental politics, and cultural identity. The main conference organizer was Philippe Gervais-Lambony, a professor at Nanterre and a specialist on South Africa.

The concept of spatial justice had already appeared in French urban studies and geography. The geographer Alain Reynaud's *Societé, espace et justice: inégalités régionales et justice socio-spatiale* was published in 1981, and Lefebvre's writings on the closely related concept of the right to the city continued to be influential, although somewhat muted, in the closing decades of the twentieth century. Growing out of the conference and under the leadership of Gervais-Lambony is a new journal, with the bilingual name *Justice Spatiale/Spatial Justice*.

Among those present at the conference were Peter Marcuse and Susan Fainstein, two prominent figures in urban planning and planning theory and promoters of a parallel discourse to spatial justice and the right to the city revolving around the normative search for what they call a "just city." This discourse is preeminently normative, reflecting the strong utopian tradition among planning theorists. It rarely adopts a critical spatial perspective, although the intrinsic appeal of its underspatialized concept of justice has attracted many geographers and others who prefer not to emphasize a more forceful form of spatial explanation. As such, it has captured increasing attention in contemporary theoretical and practical debates on spatial justice and the right to the city.

In recent years, the specific concept of spatial justice has begun to enter university curricula and research institutes as well as undergraduate textbooks. For example, Social Well-Being and Spatial Justice is now a research and teaching cluster in the Department of Geography, University of Durham, UK; Social Exclusion and Spatial Justice is a course in the Department of Geography, Newcastle University, UK; and Spatial Justice in the United States is taught in the Department of Geography, University of Vermont. An online teaching module with the title Global Theme II: Spatial Justice forms part of an introductory text in human geography written by Sallie Marston and Paul L. Knox. They provide a basic definition of spatial justice and prepare students for an exercise in how spatial injustices produce and aggravate local, national, and global health problems related to increasing obesity.

Although they do not use the specific term, also worth mentioning with regard to teaching related to spatial justice are two additional initiatives. The inaugural Summer Institute for the Geographies of Justice (SIGJ), organized by *Antipode: A Radical Journal of Geography* in conjunction with the International Critical Geography Group (ICGG), was held in Georgia, United States, in 2007, and another was scheduled to occur in 2009 in Manchester, UK. Topics studied include activist geographies and scholar activism, producing relevant public geographies, locating the boundaries of the geographies of justice, working with and researching social movements, and mapping the future of radical/critical geographies. The second initiative is exemplified by a working paper by the geographer Heidi Nast, "Statement of Procedure in Developing a Certificate Program in International Spatial Justice and GIS," part of a series sponsored by the People's Geography Project based at Syracuse University and directed by Don Mitchell, author of *Right to the City: Social Justice and the Fight for Public Space* (2003) and journal articles on the geography of injustice and scales of justice. While these activities relate closely to the concept of spatial justice as defined here, the seemingly determined avoidance of the specific term by many radical geographers, especially those influenced by the writings of David Harvey, is significant, as I will explain further in chapter 3.

Clearly, the concept of spatial justice has entered the contemporary agenda in a variety of areas. At the same time, a cluster of associated and overlapping concepts and discourses has also emerged. Some, like the ideas about the right to the city, add significantly to the evolving definition of spatial justice, while others, such as the "just city" discourse, tend to draw attention away from the core arguments about the innovative possibilities that arise from applying an assertive and explicit spatial perspective. I will continue to address at least some of these alternatives to the specific notion of spatial justice in chapter 3. I turn next to the many different ways unjust geographies are produced and reproduced.

2

On the Production of Unjust Geographies

AS BOTH OUTCOME AND PROCESS, seeking spatial justice can be studied at multiple scales and in many different social contexts. Stretching the concept to its maximum scope, we can speak of unjust geographies involving the human body, as in debates about abortion, obesity, stem cell research, the transplantation of body parts, sexual practices, or the external manipulation of individual behavior. At the other extreme, the physical geography of the planet is filled with spatially defined environmental injustices, some of which are now being aggravated by the uneven geographical impact of socially produced climate change and global warming. These two extremes, the corporeal body and the physical planet, usefully define the outer limits of the concept of spatial (in)justice and the struggles over geography but will not be discussed any further here.

Instead, we look next at how consequential geographies are produced in the spaces in between these outer limits, ranging in scale from what Michel Foucault once called the "little tactics of the habitat" to the regional, national, and global expressions of geographically uneven development. Focusing in on specific examples of where and how (in)justice takes place helps to ground the search for spatial justice in socially produced contexts rather than letting it float in idealized abstractions and too easily deflected calls for universal human rights or radical revolution.

Of particular importance here is the urban context and condition. Given that the majority of the world's population now lives in cities, contextualizing spatial (in)justice becomes to a significant degree a matter of locating it in the specific conditions of urban life and in the collective struggles to achieve more equitable access of all residents to the social resources and advantages that the city provides. As noted in the introduction, however, the specifically urban condition and the justice/injustice associated with it are not confined to or by a particular territorial scale. Urban life is nested within many different geographical contexts above and below the administrative space of the city itself.

This gives to the search for spatial justice a regional, national, and global dimension as well as a localized and more immediate and intimate expression. This *multiscalar view of the city* is not a familiar one but is key to understanding the scope and interpretive power of a critical spatial perspective and pivotal in the development of a spatial theory of justice and injustice. In this chapter, I explore the conceptual and empirical scope of the spatiality of (in)justice by selecting pertinent examples of the diverse ways unjust geographies are produced, reproduced, and responded to at three different but overlapping arenas of social action, roughly definable as exogenous or top-down, endogenous or bottom-up, and mesogeographical or regional, conceived as the in-between spaces where the macro and the micro, the global and the local, converge. The intent is not to present extensive details on the specific topics mentioned but to use them to illustrate the multifaceted nature of the struggles over geography and to exemplify the range of contexts that can be explored from a spatial justice perspective.

Exogenous Geographies and the Political Organization of Space

Viewed from above, every place on earth is blanketed with thick layers of macrospatial organization arising not just from administrative convenience but also from the imposition of political power, cultural domination, and social control over individuals, groups, and the places they inhabit. These exogenously generated geographies range in scale from the global divisions of power associated with what we have called First, Second, and Third Worlds, to the internal governmental structures that have evolved within sovereign nation-states, to the dense web of state-created political and administrative districts and boundaries that impinge on practically every daily activity wherever one is located. At every scale, these superimposed or exogenous geographies of power define and contextualize particular geographies of (in)justice.

The Banlieues of Paris

Building on his conceptual discussion of spatial justice in "Justice and the Spatial Imagination," Mustafa Dikec has focused his empirical and interpretive work on the spatial injustices implicitly embedded in the immigrant-impacted *banlieues* surrounding Paris. These dense inner suburbs have been the sites of major urban uprisings, the most explosive of which took place in autumn 2005. In his book he calls these sites of contextualized immigrant struggles and urban insurgency the "badlands of the republic" (2007a). These real and imagined badlands provide a revealing first look at the many material and symbolic framings—the taking place—of what Dikec has called the spatiality of injustice and the injustice of spatiality.

The term *banlieue* is temptingly translatable in a literal sense as "banned place" but actually derives from the ancient notion of the bann. Surviving today almost entirely in church-announced banns of matrimony, banns in medieval times were pronouncements often placed at the entrance to the city telling newcomers what proper "civilized" or "urbane" life was about. Banns were boundary markers of urban civilization and ranged in subject matter from how to dispose of refuse to what were an urban dweller's political rights. In more recent times, however, the *banlieues* came to refer to the inner suburbs that ringed the outer edge of the city, often where city walls were formerly located. To some degree, they continue to mark the edge of specifically urban culture.

The *banlieues* surrounding Paris have had a particularly interesting geo-history. For the most part, they formed a densely settled and largely high-rise ring of inner suburbs after World War II, when the majority of the Parisian working class moved out of the central city. Observers have argued that this was largely part of a process of fragmenting working-class political control in the central city and making central Paris more amenable to the local middle classes and to global tourism. This "cleansing" or "decanting" of the working class from the Parisian urban core was in many ways as dramatic a spatial transformation as that induced by the nineteenth-century strategic boulevards designed by Baron Hauss-mann, overtly for efficiency of movement but with the additional effect of creating improved spatial systems of social control, especially over the poor populations of the city. Postwar economic development and further efforts at urban spatial restructuring led to major changes in the *banlieues*. As the prospering French domestic population moved farther out to expanding middle-class suburbs, they were replaced in the worst left-behind high-rise hous-ing by immigrants and ex-colonial citizens, creating a volatile geography of increasing economic exclusion, public neglect, and cultural and polit-ical polarization. As these changes were taking place, the increasingly unjust urban geography of Paris exploded with unrest. The riots and demonstrations of May 1968 began in Nanterre, one of the rapidly changing inner suburbs located near the imposing new business node of La Defense.

These deteriorating conditions were aggravated by French urban policies both before and after 1968. While superficially filled with what seemed to be democratic ideals and principles, including lip service to Lefebvre's notion of *le droit à la ville,* the right to the city, they were actually constrained by persistent republican values that refused to recognize differences in the socioeconomic and spatial configuration of the city, seeing everyone as equal under French law, *le droit*. In an exaggerated sense, there were no minorities and majorities, immigrants and native born, rich and poor. Promoting the right to the city in French urban policy became little more than a matter of police- and state-maintained security, what in the United States would be called "law and order."

From this deeply rooted cultural and ideological perspective, it was improper to discriminate negatively or positively based on race, class, or location in space. As a result, the problems of geographically concen-trated poverty, unemployment, and social exclusion were made virtu-ally invisible or at least very difficult to address directly in public policy, thereby contributing to the increasingly volatile conditions. The even-tual irruption of violence in 2005 and continuing unrest in Paris and other large French cities, expressing what Dikec describes as insurgent citizenship and unarticulated justice movements, brought to the surface these underlying problems of spatial injustice.

Such episodes of explosive urban unrest are often moments when the deprivation and injustices that are buried under normalized or taken-for-granted geographies burst to the surface and into the public eye, exposing deep structures of privilege based on race, class, gender, and other forms of social discrimination and oppression. A long list of such revelatory moments can be identified for Paris alone, from the revolutionary storming of the Bastille in 1789 and the uprisings of 1848 to the Paris Commune in 1871, to the paradigmatic events of May 1968, to the immigrant insurgency of 2005.

The list can be extended to include many other cities as well. Particular attention will be given in later chapters, for example, to what are now being called the Justice Riots of 1992 in Los Angeles. This peak moment of urban unrest in U.S. history was one of the earliest examples of violent protests against the negative socio-spatial effects of neoliberal globalization and the New Economy of flexible capitalism. It was followed by a period of intensified surveillance and an accelerated retreat by those who could afford to move into more defendable spaces such as gated communities and high-security buildings. At the same time, however, it also stimulated grassroots coalition building and the translation into practice of specifically spatial theories of justice and injustice.

The problems associated with the tightly bounded immigrant populations in the *banlieues*—and the analogous badlands of all cities—vividly illustrate the relevant spatiality of urban injustice (as outcome) and the active infusion of injustices (as process) into the geography of the city by corporate interests and the local and national states. Seeking spatial justice was not explicitly referred to in mobilizing the Paris uprisings or organizing grassroots efforts in 2005, nor was there a conscious struggle over *le droit à la ville* as occurred in 1968. Although achieving spatial justice was not the primary motivating force, interpreting what happened through a critical spatial perspective and its wide-ranging geographical imagination adds significant insight and understanding to conventional commentaries. The specific case also opens up a wider exploration of other empirical expressions of the multiscalar search for spatial justice.

Colonial and Postcolonial Geographies

"None of us is completely free from the struggle over geography," writes the Palestinian cultural critic Edward Said, a struggle that he describes as not just about expressions of military power but also about ideas, about our images and imaginings. Said's writings on culture and imperialism, the politics of dispossession, and the profound imprint of colonial and postcolonial geographies supply one of the richest sources for conceptualizing how spatial injustice is socially produced through the intrusive process of organizing specifically political geographies.

Among the leading cultural critics and postcolonial thinkers of the twentieth century, Said stands out for his exceptionally creative and insightful applications of a critical spatial perspective, weaving into his historical, anticolonial, and autobiographical narratives a brilliantly conceived and incisive geography. In exposing the "imaginative geographies" associated with Eurocentric orientalism, Said brings into focus the powerful spatial strategies of territorial dispossession, military occupation, cultural domination, economic exploitation, and reactive popular resistance that have permeated East–West relations and defined the colonial condition everywhere in the world. As he writes, "Imperialism and the culture associated with it affirm both the primacy of geography and an ideology about control of territory."

Said develops his concept of imaginative geographies drawing on Michel Foucault, who played a major role in the formation of Said's (and many other scholars') critical spatial imagination. Foucault's probing inquiries into the microgeographies of power and social control, both as a mode of dominating and governing political subjects and as a pathway for enabling and encouraging political resistance and action, inspired Said's personal, political, and explicitly spatial approach to analyzing the starkly ambivalent relations between the colonizer and the colonized. As Said argues, it is impossible to conceive of colonialism and imperialism without significant attention to the material forms and imaginative processes associated with the acquisition, subordination, and intrusive political organization of space. This holds true just as forcefully for the social production of (in)justice.

For Said, colonizing power and the imaginative geographies of Eurocentric orientalism, the cultural construction of the colonized "other" as subordinate and inferior beings, are expressed poetically and politically in defined and regulated spaces. These colonizing spaces of social control include the classroom, courthouse, prison, railway station, marketplace, hospital, boulevard, place of worship, even the private household and home, practically every place used in everyday life. The spaces of social control extend on to a larger scale as well in geopolitical arrangements, the drawing of administrative boundaries, and the politics that arise over the location of public buildings and the allocation of land. The resulting real and imagined geographies, the material, symbolic, and hierarchically organized spaces of colonial occupation along with the processes that produce them, contextualize enclosure, exclusion, domination, disciplinary control.

Said's contributions expand on and explain how the political organization of space, through its material manifestations as well as representational imagery, produces oppressive and unjust geographies. Following Foucault and giving hope to the postcolonial condition, Said also recognizes that these unjust geographies of political power can also be enabling, creating the foundations for resistance and potential emancipation. It is important to remember this double-sidedness, how the spatiality of (in)justice can be both intensely oppressive and potentially liberating, as we move on to other examples.

Gerrymandering

A much more innocent but easier to grasp example of how the political organization of space produces and reproduces spatial (in)justice has to do with the drawing of boundaries defining electoral districts in a representative democracy. Electoral districts are socially constructed and easily manipulated spaces whose effects can range from fair and just to the highly discriminatory and unjust. The ideal solution to drawing fair and democratic boundaries would be a set of roughly equal-sized, compact, and contiguous districts that reflect the overall distribution and demographic makeup of the population and assure that every individual vote counts much the same as any other, the familiar one person–one vote principle. But when there is electoral competition, as there is likely to be in every democratic election, hierarchical differences in political power enter the picture to create distortions and deviations from the ideal condition, some of which will be expressed in purposeful manipulations of the political organization of space.

Perhaps the best-known example of such undemocratic distortions in the political organization of space is gerrymandering, illustrated in the well-known map of a congressional district signed into law by Elbridge

Gerry, governor of Massachusetts from 1810 to 1812. Designed to favor the Republican Party versus the Federalists, the district as depicted in a newspaper cartoon resembled a wriggling salamander-like (hence Gerrymander) monster with a dragon's head and extended arms and legs. A series of Supreme Court decisions in 1842, 1962, and 1985 ruled that such spatial strategies of drawing electoral district boundaries were unconstitutional and unfair (unjust in our terms) when they favored one individual or one political party over another. This did not stop such maneuvering; it just became more sophisticated and deceptive, especially with the creation of computer programs capable of designing district geographies to maximize any purposeful (spatial) advantage.

Three microtechnologies of empowerment, to use a heavy Foucauldian phrase, have been identified—and used—in drawing spatially unjust congressional constituency boundaries. The excess vote, or "packing," strategy concentrates the voting power of oppositional parties (or certain racial groups) in just a few districts. A wasted vote, or "cracking," strategy dilutes the vote of the opposition by distributing it across all constituencies. Stacking the vote is still another form of gerrymandering, creating bizarrely shaped districts to favor one party or group over the other. All are unconstitutional and democratically unfair, but actual examples are constantly under examination in the courts, and perhaps will always continue to be, for the ideal solution may be impossible to reach. There will always be some degree of unfairness and injustice embedded in electoral geographies, and these injustices are usually intensified the more culturally and politically heterogeneous the voting population.

As is often the case in the political organization of space, there is a complicated double-sidedness to electoral geographies. Boundaries can be redrawn to serve both positive and negative purposes, giving greater or lesser representation to certain population groups on a kind of sliding scale of inequality. Sometimes positive and negative objectives are combined in a tenuous balance, making it even more difficult to decide whether the results are spatially just. Take, for example, the recent efforts of the state of Texas to allow the state legislature to redraw and gerrymander districts as often as they would like to favor one political party over another, as long as they maintain the equitable voting rights of racial and ethnic minorities. Although seemingly unconstitutional and undemocratic, the practice was upheld for the most part by the conservative U.S. Supreme Court majority in June 2006 based primarily on the absence of increased racial and ethnic bias.

South African Apartheid

Standing at another extreme in the process of creating unjust geographies is apartheid, the system of spatial or territorial control associated with the formerly racist regime of the Republic of South Africa and now a symbolic reference to all forms of cultural domination and oppression arising from spatial strategies of segregation and boundary making. The story of apartheid revolves paradigmatically around struggles over geography. Through legislation, ideological rationalization, and violent political action, the political organization of space in South Africa was reshaped starting in 1948 into a hierarchy of territorially segregated and tightly bounded areas that persisted up to the remarkably peaceful breakdown of the system of domination in the mid-1990s.

Apartheid as it was expressed at the national level involved the creation of separate administrative regions for the dominant white elite, mostly in the best-developed areas, and the assignment of the majority African population to peripheral reservations, or "homelands," which functioned economically as enclosed labor reserves. A finer grain of spatial discrimination at the local scale within white-controlled cities partitioned urban space down to the street level, displacing and spatially dispossessing long-established African, Coloured (mixed race), and Asian residents when deemed necessary for achieving racial-spatial purity. Ideologically rationalized as separate but equal, the South African "badlands," to use Dikeç's term for the Parisian *banlieues,* rigidly confined daily life and urban, regional, and national politics in multiscalar straitjackets of spatial control.

The lasting effects of the apartheid system are vividly expressed in contemporary urban landscapes of the independent and African-led Republic of South Africa. In Johannesburg today, residential spaces in the wealthy and formerly entirely white suburbs, now sprinkled with a black elite, are still fortressed with high walls and guarded entranceways running continuously block after block, street after street, like a massive agglomeration of residential citadels signaling obsessive protection against a perceived threat of invasion. At the opposite end of the economic spectrum, Soweto, a name derived from the exclusionary South West Township designed to contain the African population, lives on as a displaced city-within-the city, marginalized yet central, suburban in some senses yet densely urbanized in others, creatively surviving in its poverty and isolation, both inside and outside Johannesburg. There is nothing quite like this polarized cityscape of fortressed urban extremes in any other city I know, although nearly every major world city today has its growing citadel–ghetto metro-polarities.

This socially produced geography of institutionalized racial segregation that was apartheid pushed to an extraordinary level spatial strategies and processes that were commonly used in colonial situations as a means of population control and assuring disproportionate economic advantage for the colonizers versus the colonized. This was not only a matter of divide and rule in an abstract and theoretical sense, it was a sophisticated strategy specifically designed to produce beneficial geographies for the hegemonic few while creating spatial structures of disadvantage for the rest. Even the voracious demands of capitalism adjusted to this colonial geography, and powerful though they may have been, they were probably not the primary force shaping the spatiality of social life in South Africa and most other colonies as well.

The imposition of these powerful colonial geographies, rationalized through ideological variants of orientalism that dehumanized the colonial "other," was an integral part of what critical scholars called the development of "underdevelopment." Seen from a critical spatial perspective, underdevelopment processes actively involve the creation of discriminatory urban and regional built environments and a restrictive political organization of space that fix in place a persistent geography of dependent development, cultural domination, and efficient economic exploitation. This has been at the heart of the relations between the First World and the Third World, the core and the periphery, since the beginnings of colonialism. Even after independence, these concretely embedded and imaginatively maintained unjust geographies of underdevelopment and colonial control linger on as stubborn continuities, almost impossible to erase entirely, virtually defining what has come to be called the postcolonial condition.

Occupying Palestine

Colonial and postcolonial geographies of control and domination continue to be produced today, perhaps nowhere as vividly and deliberately as in Israeli-occupied Palestine. Reflecting the volatile and violent current events in the wider region, the Arab–Israeli borderlands have become an unusually fertile and ideologically charged contemporary milieu for creative research on oppressive geographies and the production of spatial injustice. One of the best of these contemporary researchers is Eyal Weizman, an architect, designer, and critical spatial analyst. In *Hollow Land: Israel's Architecture of Occupation* (2007) and other writings, he shows how the Israeli military has literally and figuratively penetrated into the built environment, bulldozing "overground tunnels" into the existing walls and through the living rooms of Palestinian homes and settlements while at the same time building new walls and barricades to keep people apart, what Yiftachel and Yacobi (2005) call "creeping apartheid."

Demonstrating that this battle over space and territory is not just about soldiers and guns but also about ideas and imagery, Weizman has filmed Israeli military officers at their leisure discussing the latest philosophical writings of Gilles Deleuze and Félix Guattari, as well as other specialists in urban and spatial theory, including Edward Said, to enhance their ultrasophisticated and technologically advanced strategies of social and spatial control in territories that are nominally Palestinian. Disturbingly obvious here is the realization that spatial theories and spatial strategies can be used both to reinforce oppression and control as well as to stimulate resistance and enhance the search for spatial justice.

Observing these spatial tactics and strategies makes one realize that the occupied territories would essentially remain under the control of the Israeli military even with the creation of an independent Palestinian state. Almost invisible microgeographies of power, surveillance, and control, as well as the intentionally overt construction of barrier walls and guarded settlements, infuse the spaces in and around the state of Israel with an array of multilayered injustices more subtle and sophisticated in their colonizing effect and spatially organized system of control than ever achieved by apartheid. One lesson is clear: once spatial injustice is inscribed into the built environment, it is difficult to erase.

These borderlands strategies and their spatially unjust effects echo around the world wherever boundaries separate contrasting and/or combative cultures and nation-states. An especially cruel and violent example has emerged in recent years along the fluid boundary between the United

States and Mexico, where drug cartels have carved out "plazas" of territorial control and superhighway-like corridors in and under the twinned border cities to channel the flow of drugs. Here the insidious geography is maintained through the murder of thousands of individuals connected either to public authorities or to the cartels themselves. As with all these inflections of what Michel Foucault described as the intersection of space, knowledge, and power, it is important to remember that the inscription of oppressive geographies can also create potential spaces of resistance and enablement, as occurred in the unexpectedly nonviolent struggles against South African apartheid. And it is equally important to recognize that opening up these spaces of hope hinges on the development of a critical spatial consciousness as a motivating and mobilizing political force. Without such spatial awareness, the creation and maintenance of unfair geographies are likely to remain invisible and unchallenged.

Security-Obsessed Urbanism

The findings of such spatially informed scholars as Said, Dikec, and Weizman can be extended into many other contemporary debates, especially with regard to the geographies of political control and the relations of power embedded in the political organization of the restructured modern metropolis. Particularly noteworthy is the rampant expansion of what Mike Davis in *City of Quartz* (1990) described as security-obsessed urbanism, a defensive fortressing of urban life and urban space built on a pyschogeography (he calls it an ecology) of fear and aimed at protecting residents and property against real or imagined threats of invasion.

The rich have always lived behind protective walls of various kinds, physical as well as institutional and psychological. However, over the past thirty years and in many ways linked to the uneven effects of globalization and economic restructuring, fortressing the urban and suburban built environments has spread almost everywhere. Not only are residences becoming increasingly gated, guarded, and wrapped in advanced security, surveillance, and alarm systems, so too are many other activities, land uses, and everyday objects in the urban environment, from shopping malls and libraries to razor-wire protected refuse bins and spiked park benches designed to stave off incursions of the homeless and hungry.

Microtechnologies of social and spatial control infest everyday life and pile up to produce a tightly meshed and prisonlike geography punctuated by protective enclosures and overseen by ubiquitous watchful eyes.

The best known of these defensive enclosures is the gated community, a fortressed housing compound often protected by armed guards and various visible and invisible indications that trespassers will be shot. These security-obsessed islands can be found in many cities around the world but have become especially numerous in the United States. Some of the earliest gated communities were established on the Palos Verdes peninsula south of Los Angeles, where today whole municipalities exist comprised entirely of these insulated enclosures. Are these gated communities spatially unjust? Or are they extreme expressions of democratic individualism and freedom of choice? Perhaps the main problems arise from answering yes to both questions.

The gated and guarded community, however, is only the tip of a much larger iceberg of change in the political geography of the city, at least in the United States. Driven both by fear and voluntary preference, growing numbers of people, predominantly from the upper quintile of the income ladder (called by some the fortunate fifth), are in many ways withdrawing from urban public life and civil society to live in insular "privatopias," as the political scientist Evan Mackenzie called them in his 1994 book. This trend has created a growing number of privatized residential governments embedded in and often disconnected from the larger public realm. This centrifugal movement away from the city and urban responsibilities is very different from the back-to-the-city movement and the so-called gentrification process in its lack of commitment to urban living.

What we are seeing in all these pervasive and privatizing reconfigurations of urban life is another form of spatial colonization, less overtly dominated by the state but not entirely different from the blunt institutional expressions of territorial power associated with apartheid or the more technologically advanced spatial tactics of the Israeli military in controlling occupied Palestine. Fear of potential invasion and violence by what the more powerful perceive as threatening "others" drives all these processes of spatial control. This almost endemic and security-obsessed sense of fear has been reaching a fever pitch over the past thirty years of profound urban restructuring, hastening the fortressing of urban space and the drenching of the city with surveillance cameras.

The globalization of capital, labor, and culture, along with the formation of a New Economy and the accompanying explosion of transnational and intranational migration flows, has resulted in the concentration of the richest and the poorest populations of the world in around five hundred megacity regions of more than one million inhabitants. Although it is again impossible to prove conclusively, it is probably safe to say that those city regions with the largest concentrations of the urban poor, especially when they differ in culture and ethnicity from domestic populations, are where security-obsessed urbanism and its associated carceral geography are most advanced. In this sense, the more localized "City of Quartz" described by Mike Davis looking at Los Angeles has exploded globally into his more recent depiction of a "planet of slums" (2007). This deepening chasm between the rich and poor populations of the world is perhaps the most emphatic life-threatening expression of spatial injustice at a global scale.

Public Space and Private Property

Hidden behind the florid materiality of gated communities and privatopias is a more intricate web of spatial injustice deeply rooted in the naturalized sanctification of property rights and privileges. Every square inch of space in every market-based economy has been commodified and commercialized into parcels of valued land that are owned by individuals, corporations (usually considered as individuals under the law), or by the state (considered to be representative of the public at large). Direct social or collective ownership of land or common spaces has almost disappeared as the three-sided ownership model (individual/family, corporate, and state/institutional) has been accepted virtually without question, even when it leads to and sustains the production and reproduction of profound injustices.

This property blanket is the underlayer of a thick sedimentation of bounded spaces that powerfully shape our everyday life. Above (and below) each of us is a stratification of almost innumerable and virtually invisible spatial authorities. Decades ago, it was noted that looking out from the top of the Empire State Building in New York City one could see, if boundaries were visible, more than 1,500 governments. If we could see further into the thick layers of spatial regulation that enmesh us, the numbers would zoom even higher, boggling our geographical imaginations. Every movement we make crosses some boundary whether we are aware of it or not. Understanding how unfair geographies are formed requires some attention to this underlying blanket of property rights.

The property ownership model upon which American and other capitalist societies have been built originated thousands of years ago in the ancient city-states, was filtered through feudalism, and constituted anew in the aftermath of the American and French revolutions as integral to emerging notions of liberal democracy aimed at combating the influential effects of more radical socialist thought. What became legitimized if not sanctified in this later process was the inalienable right to own property as the central principle in defining the capitalist nation-state, its system of laws, and its revised definition of citizenship. Human rights in general and such specific claims as the right to the city become subordinated to the primacy of rights to property. As a result, a finely grained netting of recorded but usually invisible boundaries was thrown over the earth's surface, creating a perpetual tension between private and public ownership and between private and public space that is played out in everyday life all over the world.

For some the essential starting point in the search for spatial justice is the vigilant defense of public space against the forces of commodification, privatization, and state interference. It is widely contended that public space has been rapidly eroding in contemporary cities, as neoliberal policies of deregulation remove the microspatial structures that maintained our "civil liberties" in place, literally and figuratively. Waves of privatization have been flowing into formerly public arenas of all kinds, compromising freedoms of speech, association, and political expression. Although seeking spatial justice should not be confined only to struggles over public space, such struggles are vital and can be extended in many different directions in the search for justice and the right to the city.

For example, we can see public space as a localized urban expression of the notion of common property or, as it was once called, the commons. These democratic spaces of collective responsibility extend to involve many geographical scales, starting with the microspatial mesh of property ownership itself. All the publicly maintained streets of the city as well as crossroads, plazas, piazzas, and squares are part of the commons, and so too are the mass transit networks and the buses and trains (if not the automobiles) that move across the city. Think not just of the Bus Riders Union case but also of Rosa Parks demanding her democratic spatial rights to sit anywhere on a public bus. Are sidewalks also part of the commons? Are beaches and parks? Are forests and wilderness areas?

Actually, all these are zones of contention between public and private property rights and focal points for social action aimed at assuring residents' rights to the city, in the sense of collective access to the common pool of public resources the city provides. Extending these arguments to the scale of the metropolitan or city region is relatively straightforward, creating the foundation for what some now call community-based regionalism, regionwide coalition building for local community development and environmental justice. The mobilizing idea of the commons can be extended still further to larger regional, national, and global scales, building on the strategies defined in struggles over the regional right to the city and associated demands for access to public goods and services no matter where they may be available. Raising the scale to national and global levels makes it possible to expand the notion of the collective commons to include all natural and cultural resources that are shared by all the world's inhabitants, from clean air and water to sites of natural beauty, ecological significance, and cultural heritage. It does not take much to see how local struggles for spatial justice and the right to the city can be connected to global movements for planetary sustainability and universal human rights. The scales of spatial justice are not separate and distinct; they interact and interweave in complex patterns.

My purpose making these cross-scalar connections is not to attack property rights and private property ownership in themselves, or to call for a revolutionary transformation into collective ownership as the only solution to the problems involved, but to use a critical spatial perspective to open up a fresh look at the subject of public versus private space and to explore the possibilities for developing new strategies to achieve greater socio-spatial justice. The aim is to heighten awareness of the powerful grip on our lives that comes from the political organization of space as it is imposed from above as a form of social control and maintained by the local state, the legal system, and the land market.

Endogenous Geographies of Spatial Discrimination

The whereness or taking place of spatial justice is not only shaped from above by the exogenous drawing of territorial boundaries and the impositions of hierarchical power. It is also configured from below through what can be broadly called endogenous processes of locational decision making and the aggregate distributional effects that arise from them. In this sense, spatial justice and injustice are seen as the outcome of countless decisions made about emplacement, where things are put in space.

Distributional Inequalities and Discriminatory Geographies

Distributional inequality is the most basic and obvious expression of spatial injustice, at least when emphasizing geographical outcomes rather than the processes that produce them. Take, for instance, the distribution of doctors, hospitals, clinics, and other health services. In every urban region, some effort is made to distribute health facilities in ways that will provide equal access to the entire population, but when seen from a spatial perspective, such equal access is virtually impossible to achieve. Some distributional inequality is inevitable, in part because of the differential effects of relative location and distance friction on consumers and in part due to the locational decisions made by individuals producing the services. Budget requirements, institutional inefficiency, personal greed, racial bigotry, differential wealth and social power, and a host of other factors add to this basic distributional inequality, creating locationally biased and hence discriminatory geographies of accessibility to health services and perhaps more seriously to public health itself.

Similar distributional inequalities arise with regard to all basic needs of urban life, ranging from such vital public services as education, mass transit, police and crime prevention, to more privatized provisioning of adequate food, housing, and employment. The end result is an often self-perpetuating interweaving of spatial injustices that, at least after passing a certain level of tolerance, can be seen as a fundamental violation of urban-based civil rights and legal or constitutional guarantees of equality and justice. This is what came to the surface in the Bus Riders Union case and underlies nearly all struggles for spatial justice.

Distributional inequalities are the more visible outcome of deeper processes of spatial discrimination set in place by a multitude of individual decisions made by many different, often competing actors. Urban geographies have been shaped by such decisions from the very beginnings of the industrial capitalist city, mostly to the advantage of the rich and powerful. As Engels noted for Manchester and the Chicago School codified in its models of urban ecology, industrial capitalist cities tend to develop concentrically around a dominant center with radial wedges of wealth and poverty that work to produce and maintain geographies that proffer greater advantage and higher status to the wealthier versus the poorer residents. While never as rigid as racial apartheid or as restrictive as ethnic enclaves and ghettoes, which have also always characterized the industrial capitalist city, the social geography of class has been and continues to be spatially unjust and open to democratic challenge in nearly every city in the world, whether fully capitalist or not.

Challenges can occur, however, only when such discriminatory geographies are recognized as being socially constructed (rather than naturally given) and therefore open to being changed through concerted social action. It is no surprise that such critical spatial awareness has not been widespread. Rather than being seen as modifiable injustices or violations of civil rights, distributional inequalities have most often been buried under claims that they are the normal, expected, and unavoidable consequences of urban living. For some observers, they may even be viewed as ultimately contributing to the greater public good as products of individualized freedoms of choice, as noted for the multiplication of gated communities. This has ingrained in the industrial capitalist city and, one might add, in many socialist cities as well, deep and unquestioned *structures of privilege and spatial advantage* based on differential wealth and power.

David Harvey in *Social Justice and the City* (1973) was one of the first to uncover and expose to fuller examination this hidden urban geography of injustice and discrimination. More will be said about Harvey in the next chapter, but for the present discussion I refer mainly to his "liberal formulations," where he delves deeply into the everyday operations and processes of locational decision making that work to create and sustain unjust urban geographies. Focusing on the normal functioning of labor, housing, and real estate markets as well as the locational decisions of planners, banks, developers, and retailers, Harvey argues that the net effects of these normalized activities tend to lead consistently to the redistribution of real income in favor of the rich. In other words, the industrial capitalist city itself functions day to day as a machine for the manufacturing and maintenance of distributional inequalities and what Harvey terms territorial injustice. Even when intervention into this discriminatory geography occurs, the wealthiest tend to win out in the competition for locational advantage, another vivid example of what Said described as the inescapable struggle over geography. Harvey's early liberal formulations remain today among the most important and insightful contributions to understanding the inherent qualities of what can be called the *urbanization of injustice.*

Spatial Discrimination and the Law

Many additional discriminatory biases, from patriarchy and heterosexism to cultural nationalism and racism, accentuate spatial injustices and provide ample opportunities to raise legal and/or constitutional challenges and claims of civil rights violations. Indeed, almost every effort to achieve spatial justice seeks some form of legal or legislative judgment. Yet such claims of spatial discrimination, speaking primarily of the United States, are rarely brought to court. Why this is true has many explanations, the most pertinent to emphasize here being the absence of a cogent understanding of the spatiality of (in)justice both in the wider public and in the U.S. legal system itself. Without the insights of a critical spatial perspective, the maldistribution of vital public services and all other available resources of urban life tends to be considered as naively given and normalized outcomes, possibly inconvenient for some but unintentional in their causes and consequences. To submit them to legal scrutiny and democratic process is often perceived as opening up a Pandora's box of chaotic consequences and indeterminate claims.

The U.S. legal system also has built-in defenses against claims of spatial injustice. Avoiding the particularities of place, it defines the provisioning of justice at a strictly "universalized" national scale, available in theory to all inhabitants equally. It aims to supply justice to everyone equitably, at least in principle, and attempts to respond to demands for justice on egalitarian terms as well, but for the most part the law ignores the unfairness of the processes creating unjust outcomes in the first place. In particular, justice is almost entirely blind to the concept of unfair geographies and specifically spatial injustice. I say almost, because occasionally such explicitly spatial claims of injustice break through to open up new possibilities for remedying the problems involved.

One such breakthrough took place in 1975 in *Southern Burlington County NAACP v. Mount Laurel Township,* the so-called Mount Laurel decision. Mt. Laurel is a municipality located about ten miles from Camden, New Jersey, one of the poorest cities in the country. Mt. Laurel itself was settled early by freed slaves and has had a long and rich African American heritage. In the original court case, the township authority was challenged over what came to be called exclusionary zoning after regulations were introduced that made the production of affordable housing highly restricted. The plaintiffs directly challenged "home rule," or the rights of local government units to decide on how to regulate land use within their territory, a legally sanctioned responsibility similar to states' rights in the U.S. Constitution. Against all odds, the New Jersey Supreme Court ruled in favor of the plaintiffs. In 1983 the court reinforced its decision that affordable housing needed to be constructed (Mt. Laurel II), triggering the creation of the New Jersey Fair Housing Act in 1985 and the subsequent spread of similar court cases to other municipalities in and outside New Jersey.

Called "communistic" by a seated governor, the Mt. Laurel decision played an important role in civil rights struggles over housing throughout the country, embedding the distinction between exclusionary and inclusionary zoning into the legal system and adding the provision of fair and affordable housing to the responsibilities of local government. As was the case with the Bus Riders Union decision in 1996, the implications of this precedent were potentially far reaching. The Mt. Laurel decision could have led, for example, to legal recognition that location in space is a source of discrimination in itself. This would be based not only on race/ethnicity but on meeting fundamental human needs, with everyone having the right of fair access to affordable housing and health services as well as to other location-related advantages arising from state actions, including all public investment and subsidy. It could have also created a legal principle of territorial or spatial responsibility in which all municipal governments recognize the negative spillover effects of local decision making on at least the immediately surrounding areas. Pushed to its limits, this precedent of spatial responsibility could have formed the basis for coordinated intrametropolitan regional welfare planning in the absence of other governmental structures.

The Mt. Laurel decision stimulated optimistic activism among housing advocates and planners and became linked directly into the broader civil rights movement, but it would never reach its full potential. Some efforts were made to test and extend legal principles of locational discrimination and territorial responsibility, but nearly all were unsuccessful. Resistance to these extensions, based on constitutional and other arguments, became increasingly powerful, especially from a more openly conservative federal government and judiciary. As would be the case for the civil rights movement as a whole, local tactics along with state and federal court decisions during the Reagan era constrained the impact of the more radical efforts, echoing what happened to struggles for greater racial justice after the desegregation of schools induced by the *Brown v. Board of Education* decision in 1954. It seemed that the harder the breakthrough precedents were pushed, the stronger the reactionary resistance.

During the period of increasingly restrained school desegregation, the location of elementary and high schools and the attendance areas of students in the United States were experiencing one of the largest-scale spatial reorganizations of public services ever attempted anywhere in the world. School district consolidation used tools that were forerunners of present-day geographical information systems (GIS) and ideas taken from central place theory and other formulations of professional geographers. The capacity was there, it would seem, to have planned and promoted the desegregation of schools in a fair and democratic manner, but the will and awareness were not.

It is tempting to argue that the primacy of the struggles against institutionalized racism in the civil rights movement as opposed to a broader attack on discriminatory geographies deflected any possibilities for a spatial justice movement to emerge as a complementary and supportive force. In any case, eventually the civil rights movement in all its manifestations, from inclusionary zoning and school desegregation to affirmative action and antipoverty programs, was institutionally and constitutionally blunted in its continuing impact. With the Bush administration's penetration of the Supreme Court and its constraints on the judicial system as a whole, many of its major achievements have been reversed.

Particularly influential in the derailment of the civil rights movement and the reduced national impact of such legal victories as the Bus Riders Union consent decree was the series of legal decisions that either protected the courts from hearing any complaints from private individuals or groups about any form of discrimination or, alternatively, required that plaintiffs prove that discrimination was intentional, an almost impossible task. The use of the legal system in the struggles for racial and spatial justice and the right to the city has not been entirely closed off, however, and will continue to be of major importance, especially as legal scholars increasingly adopt a critical spatial perspective.

Race, Space, and Environmental Justice

As the civil rights movement waned and the opportunities for legal recourse with regard to racial and spatial discrimination were shrinking, one new opening occurred that played an important role in the long-term search for spatial justice. It too was blunted in its impact by similar institutional and constitutional resistance, but it nevertheless raised widespread public consciousness about spatial discrimination, unjust geographies, territorial responsibility, and democratic rights to the city. I refer here to the environmental justice movement (EJM).

Reflecting the ongoing struggles for civil rights, the EJM began as an attack on what was called environmental racism, the tendency for poor and minority populations, especially African Americans, to suffer disproportionately from air and water pollution and the siting of hazardous or toxic facilities. To some extent, racial issues, at least at first, obscured the spatial issues, as they did in the civil rights movement, but the search for environmental justice did as much to raise consciousness about the spatiality of (in)justice as any other development in the last decades of the twentieth century. Its lasting effects include opening up the concept of civil rights to a broader spatial scope, especially by adding locational bias to more conventional notions of racial, class, and gender discrimination and encouraging new forms of progressive coalition building among all those who suffer from the geography of unequal spatial advantage.

Given that practically everything that happens in cities can contribute to hazardous environmental conditions, the EJM has over the years been connecting more closely with movements for spatial justice and democratic rights to the city. As with the Bus Riders Union, this convergence has created opportunities for mutual learning and shared strategies but has also led to some confusion and divergent interests, largely due to different underlying philosophies and theoretical frameworks. The alternatively radical and romantic environmentalism that often drives the EJM markedly contrasts with the critical spatial perspective that is behind the struggle to create more just geographies.

Rather than an explicitly spatial perspective, many forms of passionate environmentalism tend to emphasize physical or natural causality, leading to such overly idealized notions as the sanctity of Mother Earth and to activism that focuses on narrowly defined targets and highly localized and unique cases of discriminatory environmental impacts. David Harvey (1996) used the term "militant localism" to describe this narrowed focus of the EJM and its fragmenting effect on larger class and labor struggles. That the Bus Riders Union assertively maintained the connections between environmental and transit justice and wider struggles over race, class, and gender discrimination was among its most important achievements.

To be clear, this is not meant to say that environmental justice advocates or the issues they address are not spatial: everything on earth is spatial whether recognized as such or not. Nor does it suggest that the EJM has not contributed significantly to the struggles for spatial justice and democratic rights to a just city. Similar to struggles over public space, the search for specifically environmental justice has been and must continue to be a vital part of the larger justice struggle. Environmental and spatial justice, however, should not be too easily conflated. Environmental justice may be best considered and conceptualized as a subfield of spatial justice focusing on geographical discrimination with regard to negative environmental impacts, ranging from the location of a toxic waste facility to the uneven regional and national impact of global warming and climate change.

As such, the EJM can benefit significantly from a greater awareness of the interactive and multiscalar geographies of place-based discrimination that shape environmental justice and provide opportunities for intervention in between the global and the local. For example, although global warming and climate change have now been conclusively linked to human agency, it is useful to see that such human agency works through the production and reproduction of unfair geographies and global structures of spatial advantage and disadvantage. This calls for political responses at multiple and interacting scales.

Similarly, regarding environmental limits to growth, it can be argued that enough is produced today to feed, clothe, shelter, and entertain the entire world population without significant environmental degradation. What prevents this (and induces potentially unstoppable and disastrous climate change) is the globally unjust geography of production and consumption, with an overconcentration in some favored places and spaces and serious scarcity in others. The persistent extremes of polarized geographical development create not so much a challenge to do something about the environment per se but rather a political challenge to struggle for redistributive spatial justice at multiple scales, focusing less on outcomes than on the processes producing them.

Rephrasing Martin Luther King, spatial injustice anywhere, at any geographical scale, is a threat to justice everywhere. Even more cogently and specifically, this suggests that large-scale phenomena such as climate change have a global geography of effects but also affect individual nation-states, subnational regions, intrametropolitan areas, and local communities and neighborhoods in highly differentiated ways. The same can be said moving across scales in the other direction, linking a localized event such as the breaking of the dams and levees along the Mississippi River by Hurricane Katrina to a critique of national economic and science policy and to how global climate change has increased if not the incidence at least the ferocity of extreme weather phenomena all over the world. Everything is connected to everything else, as the environmentalists say, but not just in a flat horizontal ecosystem or biosphere. These connections also extend vertically through a socially produced layering of bounded geographical scales extending from the planet to the body.

Segregation and Spatial Justice

Whether imposed from above or generated by spatial decision making from below, segregation or the confinement of specific populations to specific areas seems clearly to be connected to the production of spatial injustice. Unjust segregation has been discussed in several different ways thus far, from the imposed structures of apartheid to the local creation of racially segregated schools, and there can be no doubt that segregation forms an integral part of the spatiality of injustice and the injustice of spatiality. But here again, as with all forms of locational discrimination, the issue is complicated by the interplay of endogenous and exogenous influences and by the complex relations between *geographies of choice and geographies of privilege.*

Not all examples of residential segregation are entirely unjust. To some degree, residential segregation can be voluntary and beneficial, with people of similar background choosing to live together for many different purposes, from creating identity and community to eating preferred food and obtaining other forms of nourishment and cultural sustenance to helping new arrivals to find jobs and housing. Segregation becomes a problem, however, when it is rigidly imposed from above as a form of subjugation and control, as with apartheid and racial ghetto formation; or when it emerges less intentionally from below as an oppressive by-product of unregulated "freedoms" of choice operating within persistent spatial structures of advantage.

It may be useful here to distinguish between two extreme forms of segregation, the discriminatory and disadvantaged ghetto versus the enclave created for largely positive reasons. I say extreme forms because there are some positive advantages to ghetto formation, such as serving to create a shared consciousness of oppression that can generate concerted resistance; and there are negative effects that can occur in the most culturally adaptive enclave. Segregation, like so much about the spatiality of (in)justice, is in itself not automatically evil and bad, nor are attempts to promote greater cultural or economic integration always positive and beneficial to the people involved.

Segregation, like the erosion of public space, seems initially to be a fundamental feature of the production and urbanization of (in)justice, and hence a principal target in justice struggles, and at different times and places this is certainly the case. The point being made here, however, is that these surface expressions of injustice are more complex than they initially appear. Rather than being inherently characterized as good or bad, they need to be seen contextually as arising from underlying spatial structures and structurings of locational advantage and disadvantage. It is the task of theoretically informed spatial practice to bring these structures of privilege, whether based on race, class, gender, ethnicity, sexual preference, disability, or any other form of hierarchical control and domination, more clearly and cogently to the surface, to greater public awareness.

Mesogeographies of Uneven Development

In between the global and the local are many regional scales: metropolitan, subnational, national, supranational. At each of these scales, much like what has been described for the internal geography of the city, geographically uneven development inscribes significant spatial or territorial inequalities. When these intrametropolitan, intranational, and international inequalities are maintained over time, as with the long-standing division between First and Third Worlds, or the lasting income differentials between north and south in Italy, England, and the United States, they become another context or arena for seeking spatial justice.

In addition to illustrating these multiscalar dimensions of seeking spatial justice, critical regional thinking has become a focal point for a more general theorization of geographically uneven development, a primary force behind the production and reproduction of unjust geographies. These theories have been central to the development of an applied field of welfare-oriented regional planning aimed specifically at reducing regional inequalities and achieving what can be called regional justice and regional democracy. Exploring these regional worlds of (in)justice opens up new avenues for strategic spatial thinking and action.

Uneven Development at the Global Scale

Perhaps the most obvious example of the search for macrospatial justice involves what is popularly known as the global North–South problem, the gaping differences in societal development and quality of life between rich and poor countries. Such terms as North–South, First–Second–Third Worlds, the international division of labor, core and periphery, developed-industrialized versus developing-industrializing countries express the unfairness, inequality, and injustice of global geographies, although I hasten to add that these great divisions are typically seen through historical and sociological rather than spatial lenses.

This organized system of global inequality did not always exist. Some degree of geographically uneven development has always been present in the human occupation of the earth, but it was only in the second half of the nineteenth century, in an age of imperialism and global colonization, that more deeply ingrained structures of privilege and spatial advantage consolidated their hold over the entire world population. A global core-periphery structure emerged at that time and persisted without many changes until the late twentieth century, when a significant but selective reconfiguration of the old world order began to occur.

After 1989 and the end of the cold war, the so-called Second World of socialist and communist countries led by the Soviet Union disinte-grated. Beginning decades earlier, a growing number of newly industri-alized countries (NICs) in the old Third World, led first by the so-called Asian Tigers and most recently by China and India, developed rapidly to join the advanced industrialized countries, while at the same time much of the rest of the world sank into deeper relative poverty. While there was a significant shuffling about in the old international division of labor, geographically uneven development proceeded apace in these decades of neoliberal globalization. Although it is difficult to prove, the global distribution of wealth and power today is almost surely more polarized (and unjust) than ever before, with growing numbers of the superrich concentrated in a few favored spaces and places while a billion or more people live, often strikingly adjacent, in increasingly compacted slums.

We can speak here of the *globalization of injustice and the injustice of globalization* in much the same way that we discuss the urbanization of injustice and the injustice of urbanization. Both arise primarily from geographically uneven development and the formation of lasting struc-tures of privilege favoring the inhabitants of some areas and disfavoring others. An argument can also be made that, like the normal workings of the industrial capitalist city, the normal functioning of the global market economy in terms of international trade and flows of capital, informa-tion, and people tends, without significant intervention, to lead to the continuing redistribution of wealth from the poor countries to the rich, from the periphery to the core. Recognizing the cross-scalar connections between globalization and urbanization and acting to change their inter-dependent spatial injustices are a vital product of a critical regional or mesogeographical perspective.

Further comparisons can be made between the urbanization and globalization of (in)justice. Building on the findings of underdevelopment and dependency theory, it can be said that the unjust global geography is the product of two interdependent but fundamentally different processes of capitalist development. One operates primarily to favor the rich and powerful, while the other, more truncated and haphazard and with fewer resources, mainly serves the poor. A similar separate-and-unequal argument was made at a different scale in the Bus Riders Union case, in efforts to combat racial segregation in the schools of the U.S. South, and for all forms of apartheid, which in Afrikaans means "separate development." Emphasizing the point is necessary, for it is too easily forgotten by the world's major decision makers. Meeting the basic needs of the poor countries is almost always relatively neglected, whether through market mechanisms or governmental policies, in comparison to filling the much greater but less urgent consumption needs of the richest and most powerful, whether speaking of nations or neighborhoods. This produces fundamentally unjust geographies across many scales and demands significant remedial action.

Continuing the global–urban comparison, the Third World, even with its recent changes in composition, can be seen as a kind of global ghetto arising from a combination of immobility, individual choice, and imposed spatial discrimination and external control. The Third World, or the global periphery, in this sense is similar to a redlined zone in a city, an area of purposeful disinvestment and superexploitation. Like urban redlining, global redlining is not necessarily the product of greedy capitalists conspiring to drain out wealth from a certain area by drawing a red no-go line around it. Redlined zones emerge primarily from the normal, everyday operations of the market and the competitive search for maximum profits. Although it may shift about over time, there will always be some area of a city that is virtually redlined, where local savings and residential income are drained away to other areas and to external interests, based largely on the perception that the affected area is dangerous, unsettled, or simply an unattractive place to do business. Investments that directly benefit the local population tend to be reduced in comparison to investments that facilitate the transfer of physical and human capital out of the area for the benefit of others. To the degree that there will always be redlined areas in a market-dominated urban economy, one might also say that without significant and persistent intervention there will always be a Third World or its equivalent in the capitalist global division of labor.

There are important differences, however, between the global and urban scales. One major example involves structures of government, which are much weaker at the global level in comparison to the power of the national and local states. It has become rather easy to blame the World Bank, the International Monetary Fund, the World Trade Organization, and even the United Nations for the persistence of global inequalities and widening income gaps, but they for the most part follow the insistent logic of the market rather than intentionally leading the way into poverty. The sources of geographically uneven development are much deeper than the superficial operations of global institutions, although they are certainly not blameless.

Deepening inequalities and worsening injustices at all geographical scales have stimulated a growing global justice movement mobilized, at least in part, around notions of environmental and spatial justice. The main targets tend to be highly generalized: neoliberal globalization, environmental degradation and global warming, nuclear proliferation, threats to world peace and universal human rights, and the perceived evils of capitalism itself. Nearly every effort to deal with these issues, however, faces regional specificities and the fundamental problems associated with the double-sidedness and related complexities of geographically uneven development and spatial injustice, especially the mixing together of the geographies of privilege and the geographies of choice.

One important manifestation of this search for global spatial justice is the World Charter for the Right to the City, created in 2005 after a series of meetings of the World Social Forum. Drawing on the key writings of Henri Lefebvre on *le droit à la ville* and long-standing struggles for universal human rights, the charter is indicative of the synergies emerging from the synthesis of ideas operating at different geographical scales. Grounding the global justice movement in the right to the city creates more tangible and achievable targets than simply organizing against neoliberal capitalism, globalization, or global warming, especially as all three are primarily generated from and made concrete in the major city regions of the contemporary world.

Some might argue that focusing on the right to the city excludes large portions of the world population who do not live in large cities. From a regional or mesogeographical perspective, however, the urbanization process and the spread of urban-based industrial capitalism have been an integral part of the globalization of capital, labor, and culture. Just as one can say that every square inch of the earth's surface has to some degree felt the effects of globalization, very thinly in some areas but much thicker and deeper in others, so too can it be claimed that urbanization and everything that accompanies it have also spread, unevenly to be sure, everywhere on earth. As the whole world becomes urbanized and globalized to some degree, the urbanization of injustice and the globalization of injustice reinforce one another to create what are probably the greatest spatial inequalities of wealth and power the world has ever seen. Seeking spatial justice and the regionalized right to the city become more urgently needed than ever before.

Supranational Regionalism and the European Union

Another aspect of the new global geography that has been forming over the past forty years has been an expansion in supranational regionalism, inspired in large part by the emergence of the European Union as the first quasi-confederation—or coalition—of advanced industrial countries and now in the midst of a significant expansion absorbing most of the countries of Eastern Europe. If one adds to this the national and regional transformations evolving in China, Russia, and other parts of the former Second World, it might seem as if the contemporary world is moving in two very different directions, toward socialism and capitalism simultaneously. It may be more accurate (and strategically optimistic), however, to say that these seemingly divergent movements and the greater ideological complexity they create are generating new possibilities for creative admixtures or hybridities of capitalism and socialism, rather than maintaining them in their conventional dichotomous opposition.

In many ways, and especially with regard to the treatment of spatial injustice and the advocacy of regional democracy, the European Union is already somewhat of a creative hybrid of socialism and capitalism. Often described as the Europe of the Regions, the EU has played a particularly innovative role in seeking spatial justice through the promotion of progressive forms of regional and spatial planning. From the beginnings of the EU, the Regional Fund has invested in reducing regional inequalities and related forms of social and economic exclusion within and between the member states. One of its success stories, at least up to the present crisis, has been the transformation of Ireland from an epitomizing example of the underdeveloped European periphery to the Celtic Tiger, one of the two or three richest European countries.

Although it has not yet had many tangible effects, there is another, more recent policy development in the EU that signifies a new approach to seeking spatial justice at the interurban and regional scale. I refer to the European Spatial Development Perspective, now an integral part of EU policy in all its member countries (Faludi and Waterhout 2002). The name itself is significant, at the very least as an expression of the importance of a critical spatial perspective. Thirty years ago, putting the words spatial + development + perspective together would have been nearly inconceivable and for most incomprehensible. Today, spatial development planning and policy, aimed at reducing spatial inequalities as well as fostering sustainable development of the social and natural environments at many different scales, have become central to the objectives of the EU.

The European Union has also led the way to the formation of a growing number of regional trading blocs, each aimed at achieving greater market size and power in the competition for global resources. Among the most prominent are the North American Free Trade Association (NAFTA), MERCOSUR (common market for virtually all of Latin America), and APEC (Asia-Pacific Economic Cooperation). These and other special purpose groupings of states such as OPEC, OECD, and BRIC (the recently created informal alliance between Brazil, Russia, India, and China), along with an even larger number of giant global corporations, have partitioned the world in a thick layer of multinational or transnational organizations. Once relatively empty of examples, this supranational but subglobal organizational scale is now becoming rapidly filled. Most of the trading blocs remain highly specialized, relatively incohesive, and purely economically motivated, but if the EU model continues to have an effect, they have the potential to play a larger role in the future of the global justice movement and in reducing international inequalities.

Regional Inequality within Nations

Intranational regionalisms and struggles over what might be called regional justice have been exploding in the past twenty years. Examples include the disintegration into subnational regions of Yugoslavia, the

Soviet Union, and Czechoslovakia; innovative forms of regional devolution in Spain (Catalonia and the Basque Country), the United Kingdom (Scotland, Wales, the Greater London Authority), and Canada (Quebec); and secessionist movements of varying intensity and success in Eritrea, southern Sudan, northern Italy, Flemish Belgium, Sri Lanka, Tibet, Kashmir, Aceh, Kurdistan, Chechnya, and Chiapas. For some, these subnational movements added to the rise of supranational regionalisms have signaled a weakening of the once unchallenged sovereignty of the nation-state. For others, however, the nation-state is seen as engaged in a significant restructuring and "rescaling" of its territorial powers (Brenner 2005), reaching upward in scale to remain the primary player in the global economy while at the same time extending its scalar power downward through controlled decentralization.

However one interprets the changing role of the nation-state, intranational regional development inequalities remain a political problem as a form of persistent spatial injustice. Efforts to achieve greater regional justice are expressed in many different ways. In some cases, cultural separatism leads to movements for secession; in other situations with "nations within nations" such as Catalonia in Spain and Quebec in Canada the struggle is primarily over degree of actual and symbolic autonomy. In every case, the established national order and the homogeneity of nationalist feeling and identity come under challenge.

Cultural separatism and struggles for regional justice are often closely associated with the pattern of geographical uneven economic development. The politics of regionalism that arises from this coincidence of spatial differences tends to move in opposing directions. The richest regions often feel they are bearing a disproportionate or unfair share of the burden in dealing with poorer regions, while the poorest regions demand even greater attention to their severe problems of poverty and unemployment. This polarized politics of uneven regional development can occur even when there are no pronounced cultural and linguistic differences between the regions. Again, there is no escape from unjust geographies. They are the battlefield for struggles over spatial justice at every scale from the global to the local.

Unfortunately, just as regional inequality and injustice at the intra-metropolitan, intranational, and global scales have been reaching unprecedented levels, state restructuring and national policies around the world, especially when strongly influenced by neoliberal ideology, have led to a weakening of welfare systems and significant reductions in central government funding for social and antipoverty programs. As a result, welfare-oriented urban and regional planning has declined, and more entrepreneurial approaches have taken over the planning process, creating vicious competition between cities and regions for global economic advantage. In this worsening context, promoting democratic regionalism and the recovery of welfare-oriented regional planning and governance becomes a major goal in the struggles seeking spatial justice.

Toward a Geographical Theory of Uneven Development

Understanding the dynamics behind geographically uneven development, why one area and its people develop faster than another, may be one of the greatest challenges facing contemporary scholarship. Yet, specifically geographical notions of uneven development have rarely been addressed directly, reflecting again what has been described earlier as the long-standing bias against giving geography a significant causal force in explaining social relations and societal development. The best available attempt to formulate a comprehensive theory of uneven development from a critical spatial perspective can be found within the field of regional development theory. The relevant literature is highly repetitive and not widely recognized or accepted by most contemporary development scholars, but a series of fundamental principles can be distilled from it that can add to our understanding of the production and reproduction of spatial (in)justice.

The starting point is the recognition that development, however it is defined, never takes place uniformly over space. All social processes have geographically uneven effects. This may sound obvious, but it was largely overlooked in the liberal social sciences and especially neoclassical economics until the 1950s, when the work of such prominent scholars as François Perroux and Gunnar Myrdal brought the discussion of economic development off the head of a pin, as some described it, and into a spatial world of cities and regions. They also took this first principle further, arguing that uneven development arises for the most part from geographical concentration, from dynamic and expansive urban agglomerations that persistently build on their own initial advantages. Spatial agglomeration or polarization, the emergence of developmental poles of growth, was therefore seen to be the primary driving force behind geographically uneven development.

Few advances were made in understanding the dynamics of spatially polarized development until relatively recently, when economic agglomeration theory was revived by a new breed of spatially aware economists and geographers. In one of the most pathbreaking extensions of the spatial turn, it is now becoming recognized that urbanization and the economic force that arises from spatially organized urban and regional habitats are the primary generators of all aspects of societal development. One of the earliest explorations of this stimulating effect of urban agglomeration was Jane Jacobs's *The Economy of Cities* (1969), ridiculed and misunderstood in its time but now the inspiration for major new ideas about urban spatial causality. For more on Jacobs's contributions to the new economic geography, see the notes and references for chapter 1.

While not advancing very far in understanding the inner workings of these development poles and how their economic forces are created and maintained, the early regional thinkers did take an important next step. In a very broad sense, they recognized that there were both positive and negative forces emanating from urban agglomerations, a double-sidedness that is related to the simultaneous production of justice and injustice, as discussed earlier. Myrdal (1957) called these two forces and their effects *spread* and *backwash,* while Albert Hirschmann (1958) termed them *polarization* and *trickle down.* In many ways, this was the first recognition of what was later described in underdevelopment and dependency theory as two distinct development processes operating at a global scale, one favoring the advanced industrialization of the core countries and the other leading to the "development of underdevelopment" in the peripheral Third World.

Myrdal added the notion of circular and cumulative causation to the theorization of geographically uneven development, an idea he first applied in his analysis of the cycle of poverty in Black America. Once an initial advantage or disadvantage was established, he argued, it would tend to build on itself, leading implicitly to growing inequalities between rich and poor regions and countries. Other theories emerged showing that urban industrialized regions had inherent advantages over rural agricultural regions, leading to ever widening differential growth patterns, building up political pressures between core and periphery that would have potentially explosive results if left unchecked. This was not unlike Harvey's analysis of the redistribution of real income in an urban system. These arguments made it appear that regional development planning and policy making were essential not just for efficient economic growth but also for reducing the problems associated with burgeoning economic inequalities or, in other words, seeking regional equity and justice.

What planners needed to do was clear. They needed to find ways to enhance the positive spread effects while reducing the negative backwash through efforts at "concentrated deconcentration," locating propulsive growth poles in relatively backward areas. How to accomplish this, however, was for the most part beyond their reach. The challenge of discovering how to redirect the powerful forces of geographically uneven development to achieve greater economic equality and spatial justice advanced little beyond these initial but rather superficial conceptual breakthroughs. Regional development theorists at the time did not help the planners very much, simply repeating the old arguments with an occasional change in terminology.

Part of the deterioration of the debates on geographically uneven development arose from a significant break and reorientation in the evolution of regional development theory beginning in the early 1970s, linked mainly to the rising force of neoliberal globalization and economic restructuring. Over the last three decades of the twentieth century, progressive forms of regionalism aimed at reducing spatial inequalities almost disappeared. As mentioned earlier, they were replaced by a neoliberal or, perhaps more accurately, neoconservative regionalism that was essentially entrepreneurial and dominated by intensified pressures to compete for a place in the global economy rather than dealing directly with issues of poverty and uneven development.

City marketing and regional image making took over the reins of planning and policy making, leading to a vicious territorial competitiveness to attract investment and the attention of global tourism, now the world's largest industry. Reducing regional inequalities was sacrificed to a rampant consumerism and the assumed need to reorganize urban and regional space to meet global market demands. With cruel irony, during a period when income inequalities and social polarization were reaching unprecedented levels, regional welfare planning almost disappeared.

Fortunately, however, there have been signs of a revival in association with what some are now calling a New Regionalism.

Spatial Justice and the New Regionalism

In part influenced by the spatial turn that has been spreading spatial thinking, and hence growing attention to urban and regional issues, a New Regionalism has been slowly emerging since the mid-1990s, with some promise of restoring the progressive ambitions of the welfare regionalism of the past and reconnecting with the justice movements operating in between the global and the local scales. The New Regionalism has sparked several innovative developments in the search for spatial justice. There is today an active and increasingly spatially conscious global justice movement aimed not only at environmental justice at a global scale but more specifically at democratic rights to the city. The European Union, especially through its Spatial Development Perspective, is reasserting the importance of multiscalar spatial planning to reduce spatial inequalities and social and economic exclusion. New developments in agglomeration theory and urban and regional economics are stimulating a radical rethinking of our notions of geographically uneven development and provoking renewed attention to regional approaches to planning, governance, and policy making at many different scales.

Of particular interest here are the new regional approaches developing at the metropolitan scale and in conjunction with the growing importance of megacity regions in the global cultural and political economy. Coalitions of local activists have begun to adopt regional approaches, connecting the local and the global, the micro and the macro, local knowledge and global strategy. The right to the city idea, for example, is being regionalized in such terms as regional rights to the city or the right to the city-region; new ideas are emerging about regional democracy and democratic regionalism at the metropolitan scale (Orfield 1997); and perhaps most surprising has been the emergence of community-based regionalism, connecting community development activists with progressive regional planners in ways never dreamed of before (Pastor, Benner, and Matsuoka 2009). How these regional approaches have developed in Los Angeles is discussed in chapters 4 through 6.

3

Building a Spatial Theory
of Justice

FROM THIS BROAD CONTEXTUAL LOOK at the production and reproduction of spatial (in)justice, we move next to the task of theorizing
spatial justice and reviewing the various ways scholars have approached
this theory-building process. Building a spatial theory of justice follows
six steps:

- Theorizing theory itself
- Building a new ontology of space
- Theorizing justice
- Examining the historical debates on spatial justice
- Focusing on David Harvey and the urbanization of injustice
- Developing and extending Henri Lefebvre's ideas about the right to
  the city

Theoretical Foundations

Theory building is one of at least five modes or levels of knowledge formation. Theory itself forms a bridge between the more abstract realms
of ontology and epistemology, which respectively make statements about
the essence of human being-in-the-world and develop ways to assure
that our knowledge of the world is reliable; and the increasingly concrete modes of empirical analysis and practical application or praxis, the
transformation of knowledge into action, theory into practice.

Before going any further, I want to emphasize the interconnectedness and equal importance of these five forms of knowledge. Practice is not intrinsically better than theory, nor is theory better than ontology. Similarly, concreteness is not inherently superior to abstraction. They all play a role in the production of knowledge and need to be seen as interdependent. I focus here on theory and its extensions, for the movement from theory building through empirical application to actual practice and social action is of primary importance in understanding the meaning of spatial justice. But this portion of the sequence rests on ontological and epistemological foundations that make the translation of theory into practice possible.

Epistemological discussion relates to methods and approaches and especially to how we can affirm that our knowledge (or our theories, empirical findings, and practices) can be confidently relied on. Theories themselves are attempts to explain as much as possible about specific aspects of the actual world we live in. They are a form of generalized explanation and are developed from particular epistemological methods. Theories can be constructed deductively, drawing on and extending existing forms of general explanation, or inductively, building on new empirical and practical information. Some theories are more speculative and hypothetical than others, but as a bridge between the abstract and the concrete, theory rests on the reliability of ontological and epistemological assumptions. Good theory never floats on its own terms without any reasonable substantiation.

How this reasonable substantiation is defined is a key epistemological question and relates to the differences between normative, scientific or positive, and critical theory. Rather than being tested in a direct way, normative theory rests on the power of logical reasoning backed by moral or ethical objectives. It builds on statements of what ought to be, what is desirable or undesirable. Scientific theory makes positive (hence positivist) statements about what is, what actually exists, and seeks empirical verification or falsification based on some form of the scientific method. For the most part, the scientific method, given the need for empirically testing the truth value of the knowledge it produces, draws only on our observational senses and perceptions. Finding the boundary between what is knowable and what is not has been a heated area of debate in the philosophy of (positive) science.

Critical theory, as I adopt it through a critical spatial perspective, is primarily concerned with usefulness in praxis, especially with regard to achieving freedom from oppression and domination. Although its epistemology is practice rather than norm or truth oriented, it is never entirely divorced from either normative or scientific theory. By its very nature, however, critical thinking leads to some questioning of all established epistemologies and to a search for their weaknesses and flaws. Although I do not reject scientific or normative thinking and try to combine rather than choose between materialist and idealist epistemologies, my approach to theory building works both toward practical application and back to ontology and the necessary assumptions about what the world must be like in order for us to know anything about it, that is, to obtain any knowledge in the first place.

New Ontological Beginnings

All theories are rooted in ontological assumptions about human existence and the nature of the world in which we live. These assumptions about human being-in-the world, what ontologists call *Dasein* or *être-là*, being there, are like axioms. They are not tested against reality but logically asserted to define what it is that all humans share in just being alive. Familiar to everyone is the notion that we are essentially social beings. Human existence is not solitary by nature but always embedded in social contexts and relations. How we behave in these relational contexts, how they vary and change over "real" time and place, and other particular qualities of human social being or sociality are not ontological. They are particularized contingencies that arise from the fundamentally social nature of our existence. Nonetheless, the accumulation of knowledge about the actual playing out or performance of these contingencies is almost unconsciously shaped by ontological assumptions. In some ways they are a kind of DNA of our thinking processes, a taken-for-granted template from which we gain knowledge and understanding of our life worlds.

The Need for Ontological Restructuring

I give so much attention to this highly abstract world of ontology because I think it is the source of what for the past century at least has been a fundamental bias in knowledge formation, distorting to some degree our epistemologies, theories, empirical analyses, and social practices. Identifying this ontological distortion and presenting a better alternative are essential to the task of developing a useful critical theory of spatial justice. An outline of this ontological restructuring has been presented earlier and can be summarized in easily understandable terms: human being-in-the-world as well as what the ontologists call "becoming," the living out of our lives, are essentially social, temporal, and spatial. At this very basic level, everything else in life is contingent on this spatio-temporal sociality of human existence.

As discussed earlier, it can be argued that most of our social theories and their associated epistemologies have been based on and shaped by almost subliminal assumptions that focus attention primarily on the social and temporal or historical aspects of being and much less emphatically on life's fundamental spatiality. This ontological distortion, as I have called it, did not always exist. According to Michel Foucault (1986), the tendency to see time as dynamic and developmental, and space as relatively fixed and dead background arose in Western thought in the last half of the nineteenth century and continued, almost entirely unrecognized, to shape our thinking up to the present. As Foucault noted, there is no good reason to presuppose that our existence as social and historical beings is axiomatically more important, more basic, than our existence as spatial beings, yet nearly all streams of philosophical thought, from the social sciences to Marx's scientific socialism, privilege the social and historical nature of reality over its fundamental spatiality.

I must repeat, for fear of being misunderstood, that I do not mean to privilege the spatiality of human life over its just as fundamental sociality and historicality. Nor do I want to diminish the importance of the social and historical imaginations. My argument, following the earlier ideas of Foucault and Lefebvre, is that there are three rather than two fundamental or ontological qualities of human existence, from which all knowledge follows: the social/societal, the temporal/historical, and the spatial/geographical. Despite this "triple dialectic," nearly all the knowledge that has been accumulated over the past century or so has been based primarily on a twofold ontology linking dynamically and dialectically the social and the historical dimensions of individual and societal development, with the spatiality of our sociohistorical being relatively neglected.

The time has come, so to speak, to rebalance this ontological triad, to see that all forms of knowledge production, from epistemology to theory formation, empirical analysis, and practical application are always simultaneously and interactively social, historical, and spatial, at least a priori. Different emphases may arise in forming specific knowledge about a given topic or theme (here the emphasis is decidedly spatial with regard to the concept of justice), but the assumption of a three-way ontological balance must always be kept in mind. This essential balance is difficult to achieve, for it runs against the grain of how nearly everyone reading this has been educated, but it is a vital starting point for understanding the nature of a critical spatial perspective and the new spatial consciousness that has been emerging in recent years.

Arising from these new ontological beginnings is a critical awareness that we are spatial beings from birth, our primordial occupation of space. Throughout our lives, we are enmeshed in efforts to shape the spaces in which we live while at the same time these established and evolving spaces are shaping our lives in many different ways. We are thus inescapably embedded in the geographies around us in much the same way as we are integral actors in social contexts and always involved in one way or another in the making of our individual biographies and collective histories.

Geographically Uneven Development and Spatial Justice

From this triple dialectic can be derived several additional principles describing the spatiality of human life. One that brings us closer to the theorization of spatial justice is the omnipresence of geographically uneven development and its associated spatial inequalities. As noted earlier, no social process takes place uniformly over space; there will always be some unevenness in the geographies we produce, just as there are always some variations between individuals in their sociohistorical development. The (social) inculcation of injustice into our geographies (and histories) arises in a most basic way from the inequalities that are produced from the uneven geographical effects of every individual action and all social processes.

In this sense, there can never be perfect equality across geographical space in any meaningful attribute of human existence. There will always be some degree of variation, although not all these variations and inequalities are of social significance. Living on the surface of the earth is the existential source of uneven development, in the first instance because of our being constantly subjected to the frictional effects of distance. The friction of distance and related physical properties not only make it impossible for two material objects to occupy exactly the same place at the same time, they induce unevenness in other ways. Human action and the collective social contexts that frame human activities literally "take place," they occur in particular places and spaces, and in so doing they tend for the most part to cluster, to seek proximity and propinquity to reduce the time and energy costs of traversing distance.

Although often out of our conscious awareness, distance-minimizing behavior is a fundamental part of our spatial being and our socially produced geographies. Relating to the theorization of (in)justice, this means that whatever we do will very rarely, if ever, be distributed perfectly evenly or randomly over space. Our actions and activities will tend more or less to be nodal, focused around particular centers or agglomerations, and this centering or nodality will generate unevenly distributed advantages and disadvantages depending on location and accessibility with respect to the center or node. These fundamental or ontological features of human spatial organization give rise to more complex and unjust empirical geographies.

The key point being made in these ontological and theoretical observations is that geographically uneven development, whatever its particular source, is a contributing factor to the creation and maintenance of individual and social inequalities and hence to social and spatial injustices. Only when we abstract away from or ignore the spatiality of human life can we conceive of a situation in which individuals and collectivities are perfectly equal no matter how such equality is defined. Whether it be occupying a favored position in front of a television set or shopping for food or finding a good school or choosing to live close to a job or achieving greater wealth and prosperity or finding a location to invest billions of dollars or, indeed, seeking greater spatial justice, human activities not only are shaped by geographical inequalities but also play a role in producing and reproducing them.

There are several important implications for the conceptualization of spatial justice that follow from this. The geographies that we have produced will always have spatial injustices and distributional inequalities embedded within them. Stated somewhat differently, location in space will always have attached to it some degree of relative advantage or disadvantage. Some of this geographical differentiation will be of little consequence, but in other cases it can have deeply oppressive and exploitative effects, especially when maintained over long time periods and rooted in persistent divisions in society such as those based on race, class, and gender. This difference between inconsequential and consequential forms of spatial injustice is vital to any collective efforts to achieve greater justice and to any workable concept of democracy.

Whether considered consequential or not, every example of unequal individual or collective advantage and opportunity can be seen as spatial injustice. Conceiving the spatiality of justice in this all-encompassing way, however, has some practical and theoretical problems. The first can be described as the loss of specificity. When spatial justice and injustice are seen as an inevitable and ubiquitous part of our lives, achieving a more just society or reclaiming our right to the city can become an overwhelming, if not impossible, task. It may be true, as Martin Luther King announced from the Birmingham jail, that injustice anywhere is a threat to justice everywhere, but this should be seen more as an invitation to recognize the salient spatiality of (in)justice rather than a call to identify and respond to every instance of injustice we can find.

This does not mean that the ubiquity of spatial (in)justice should be ignored or set aside, but rather that a first step in defining a robust political practice seeking spatial justice requires a more specific examination of the uneven geographies of power and privilege to determine which forms of spatial injustice warrant the greatest attention. How then can we avoid overgeneralization or selecting impossible-to-achieve objectives, and begin to differentiate between the consequential and inconsequential, as well as the feasible and unfeasible, in seeking spatial justice? Attempting to answer this important question leads us from the theorization of space to the theorization of justice.

Theorizing Justice

Justice defined and theorized in a narrow legal sense typically involves the notion of fair judgment of guilt or innocence under the law, and subsequent debate on what constitutes a fair punishment for the guilty. Justice in this legal sense usually refers to individuals and involves a specific event or action. A broader approach, one that is emphasized here, opens up the concept of justice to more general statements about its attributes and meaning within a given social order. Although still often rooted in an established legal system, this broader concept of justice expands beyond the boundaries of the law to discuss general principles of fairness and democracy, and the rights and responsibilities attached to being a member of a particular social group, whether or not they are legally defined as such.

Theorizing social rather than criminal justice is always to some degree a normative exercise, a rational search for what ought to be and therefore what is worth fighting for. Complete justice, however, like complete equality, is unachievable. What this realization does is shift attention to the production of injustices and the embeddedness of this production process in the social order. Combining a normative, scientific, and critical theorization of injustice as a social product leads directly to debates about democracy, citizenship, and fundamental human rights. At least from a Western intellectual perspective, this takes us back to the foundational philosophy of justice that emerged in ancient Greece.

Urban Origins

The development of a general theory of justice has deep and distinctive roots in Western culture. Most conventional accounts trace its origins to the formation of the Greek city-state, or polis, and especially to Athens in the era of Pericles, around 600 BC, when many Western writers claim that democratic society was first widely practiced. There is growing evidence that democratic principles and sensitivity to notions of social justice began much earlier in the city-states of Southwest Asia, and, strictly speaking, democracy and justice in the Athenian polis were significantly limited. The majority of the population, consisting of slaves, nearly all women, simple artisans, and others who did not qualify as citizens, were excluded from the democratic order. What did develop, however, was a thoughtful philosophical discourse on participatory democracy, the rights and obligations of citizenship, and the meaning and significance of social justice as a democratic principle.

Justice, democracy, and citizenship came to be defined as rights to participate in the politics of the city-state as well as its social, cultural, religious, and economic activities. The polis was seen as a privileged space in comparison to elsewhere, filled with advantages, opportunities, and accompanying obligations for all who qualified as citizens. After centuries of royal, theocratic, and imperial domination, citizenship rights were expanded in the Athenian city-state to include the growing merchant and landholding classes, as new institutions (and relevant bureaucracies) emerged to assure and maintain a functioning (if socially and spatially limited) democracy.

Early ideas about justice thus revolved around urban-based "civil" rights and the actions of a citizenry in what came to be known as civil society, or a public realm involved in deciding how best to maintain equitable access to urban resources for all those who qualified. It can be argued that these ideas represent one of the earliest notions of specifically spatial justice, that is, a conception of social justice in which geography matters in significant ways. For most of the next two thousand years, justice and democracy were embedded in the distinction between city and countryside, urbanity and rurality. Place of residence defined individual rights and responsibilities and became a key political framework for achieving social justice.

Universalizing (and Despatializing) Justice under the Law

These ancient urban-based spatial conceptualizations of justice, democracy, and citizenship tended to be displaced or given relatively little weight in the later development of Western theories based in the nation-state, even when discussing ancient Greece and Greek philosophical traditions. This distorting submergence of the urban spatiality of justice was associated with attempts to universalize justice as a "natural" right sustained primarily by a "blind" (in the sense of being unbiased) legal and/or constitutional system that defined citizenship not in terms of rights to the city but as rights and obligations determined by the nation-state.

A key turning point in the development of this universalized and statist concept of justice occurred in the late eighteenth century, with first the American and then the French revolutions, both founded on the need to guarantee the rights of all citizens to life, liberty, and the pursuit of happiness, to *liberté, egalité, fraternité,* and to what would later be promised in the American Pledge of Allegiance: liberty and justice for all. In the Anglo-American and French traditions at least, justice and liberal democracy became associated with generic "human rights" under the law, often with a presumptive emphasis on property rights in particular. While citizenship at first depended on property ownership of some kind, seeking "justice for all" was attached almost entirely to the legal system.

Condensing a rich history to move closer to the present, the development of a comprehensive liberal democratic theory of justice reached a major milestone with the publication in 1971 of *A Theory of Justice* by the critical legal scholar John Rawls. Ever since, Rawls has been at the center of nearly all discussions and debates on the nature of justice and liberal democracy, and the critical response to his work played a key role in stimulating the development (or rediscovery?) of specifically geographical theories of justice.

Rawls presented a theory of distributive justice that was intended to be universally applicable no matter where and when it might be applied, almost as if the theory reflected a natural law. A universal and normative-scientific theory of justice, built on reason and rational thought, is necessary, he argued, to avoid a wide range of biases based on class, gender, race, place of residence, or any other particular positioning of relative power and influence within a given social order. What actually generates the injustices to be dealt with by law was thereby submerged and subordinated to the alleviation of legally defined "unacceptable outcomes" and the pursuit of what constitutes the immediate wider good. How this wider good was defined, at least in Rawls's original formulations, tended to reflect existing conditions, with all their built-in and built-up unfairness and socio-spatial inequality.

Rawls's fundamentally aspatial and ahistorical notion of justice is primarily associated with unfettered egalitarian ideals and the fair distribution of valued goods such as liberty, opportunity, wealth, and self-respect. Justice reaches its ideal level when, as Rawls describes it, the prospects of the least fortunate are as great as they can be (under given circumstances), and when the more advantaged are contributing to meet the expectations of the least advantaged, assuming an acceptable democratic social order to begin with. Striving to achieve something close to this ideal condition lies at the core of the liberal democratic concept of social justice. What is deemed to be socially unacceptable injustice is determined entirely through and by appeal to the legal system upheld by the state.

Given Rawls's universalizing emphasis, distributive justice becomes focused on the immediate moment or condition for individuals and therefore can only be weakly spatial and historical in a collective sense. In terms of theorizing justice under the law, where one is located geographically does not matter in any significant way. Distributional inequalities are largely abstracted from geographical space into a naively given and purely social structure of stratification, usually defined in terms of income rather than the more contentious notions of class. With regard to time, the forces that may have created inequalities in the first place are not challenged, nor is intrinsic importance given to whether inequalities are increasing or decreasing at any given moment. Justice is judged in terms of existing outcomes, when they are seen as unacceptable departures from an idealized liberal democratic notion of a fair distribution.

Critiquing the Rawlsian Version

Rawls's liberal egalitarian theorization of justice has received a long sequence of vigorous criticisms both from the right and the left, and Rawls has responded with a number of modifications of his original ideas. For most conservative thinkers, the concept of distributive justice was seen almost by definition as sacrificing too many individual rights and liberties, especially with regard to private property and ownership. Justice in this sense is considered too social, if not socialist, and warranted relatively little attention except as related to the maintenance of law and order. For nearly all radical critics, again almost by definition, the liberal theory did not go far enough, leaving almost untouched the major sources and causes of inequality. It dealt only with static forms of social inequality, the unfair outcomes, and not the deep structural processes that produce them.

A more broadly based critical theory of justice began to emerge in response to Rawls's work, shifting attention from outcomes as such to how and why these outcomes are socially produced and maintained. Literally dozens of books and articles reacting to Rawls's *A Theory of Justice* were published in the two decades after its appearance in 1971. A representative list of books with *justice* in their titles is included in Notes and References. What can be seen from this list is an elaboration and refocusing of the liberal theory of justice on particular forms and expressions of inequality and social discrimination. Increasing emphasis was placed on questions of racial justice, on the injustices of gender, on Marxist critiques of justice theory. Specific notions of environmental justice had not yet received widespread attention, but there were the beginnings of a geographical approach to justice studies, starting with David Harvey's *Social Justice and the City* (1973).

Of particular interest is the work of Iris Marion Young, a political philosopher and critical thinker who, in her influential *Justice and the Politics of Difference* (1990), argued forcefully for the need to contextualize justice in more concrete geographical, historical, and institutional terms. She urged us to move away from a fixation on distributive justice to focus more on the structural forces that generate inequalities and injustice. Young shifted the emphasis in justice studies from outcomes to processes and from assuring equality and fairness to respecting difference and pluralistic solidarity. As she notes, "social justice . . . requires not the melting away of differences, but institutions that promote reproduction of and respect for group differences without oppression" (1990, 47).

The emphasis and value given to differences and the right to be different arose from Young's powerful critique of traditional concepts of homogeneous communities of identity. Community in its traditional sense required rigid boundaries between we and they, who is inside and outside the community, and assumed a definitive homogeneity of outlook. For Young, this view of community was inherent in Rawls's "original position," his starting point for theorizing justice, and it led to similar problems. Seeing society as a collection of insular and tightly bounded communities, a widespread view in modern social science, not only tends to ignore internal differences of outlook but also draws attention away from significant forms of oppression arising from racial, gender, class, and other sources of injustice that cut across community lines. This prevailing view of homogenous community, Young argued, frequently failed to see the political potentialities of pluralism and the heterogeneous mixing of social groups, as might occur, for example, in coalition building.

In essence, Young was substituting a multisided concept of oppression for conventional emphases on distributional fairness. She elaborated her notion of oppression, and hence of injustice, into five distinct but interacting forms: exploitation, marginalization, powerlessness, cultural imperialism, and violence. Exploitation is essentially a matter of

class, where structural relations, social processes, and institutional practices allow a few to accumulate economic wealth while constraining such
accumulation by others through actions in the workplace as well as in
the home. This was the view of justice that most Marxists focused almost
exclusively on.

Marginalization as a mode of injustice involves curtailing full participation in social life and accessibility to societal resources and respect
for certain segments of the population, systematically reducing their
quality of life. Powerlessness specifically focuses on the draining away for
some of any sense of political power, participation, representation, and
capacity for self-expression, whether based on class, race, gender, or any
other human attribute. Cultural imperialism is a form of dominance
whereby one group or culture is subordinated and made almost invisible
by another, losing their distinctive differences in beliefs and behavior,
an idea akin to colonial domination. Violence relates to social and institutional practices that tolerate or even encourage violent acts as acceptable parts of daily life, raising danger levels for certain individuals and
groups. These overlapping aspects of oppression open up the concept
of justice to many more specific modes of expression, evaluation, and
social action.

Although Young rarely was explicitly spatial in her early work, her
arguments were taken up in the development of a spatial theory of justice, including liberal and radical formulations of notions of territorial
justice, environmental justice, and the right to the city. Young herself
contributed to spatializing justice concepts in her later writings, especially with respect to notions of regional democracy or democratic regionalism, an innovative outgrowth of her search for larger-scale sources
of pluralistic solidarity. Building on Young's retheorization of justice, we
turn next to the developing attempts by geographers and planners to
spatialize justice more thoroughly.

Debates on the Spatiality of Justice

The basic idea of spatial justice has been around for a long time. As
described earlier, democracy and justice for the Greeks were definitively
urban, and in this urbanity they become intrinsically spatial as well,
rooted in the politically charged formation and spatial organization of

the city-state, or, just as accurately, the state-city. Being political, with its etymological roots in the Greek word *polis,* was always to some degree a matter of being urban, being part of the "civilized" world of the city. Living in the city defined who were the politically active "citizens" or *polites,* as opposed to everyone else: slaves, most women, barbarians, and *idiotes,* those difficult to organize nonurban folk that Karl Marx described as immersed in the apolitical and supremely individualistic "idiocy" of rural life.

City, space, society, and the state were intricately interwoven and inseparable in the *polis* and have remained in active and politicized articulation up to the present, even if disjointed to some degree by the power of the nation-state. Think of the extensions we have in English for the Greek word *polis:* politics, police, policy, polite; and for its equivalent in Latin, *civitas:* civil, civic, citizen, civilization, city itself. The city, with its meeting places and public spaces, was the wellspring for thinking about democracy, equality, liberty, human rights, citizenship, cultural identity, resistance to the status quo, struggles for social and spatial justice. With the rise of the nation-state and the later spread of industrial capitalism, the power of the city-state ebbed but never disappeared. Although the specific spatial referent tended to be lost in the literature, the generative force of the city remained in what should always be described as *urban* industrial capitalism.

Recognition of the consequential geography of the city and the usefulness of a critical spatial perspective faded from view in the literature on both socialism and liberal democracy, at least until the turbulent 1960s, when the connections between geography and justice began to be systematically reexamined. What was happening in cities nearly everywhere in the 1960s was an often violent expression of dissatisfaction with the unequal distribution of the benefits of expansive economic development despite attempts by the most liberal welfare states to address issues of poverty and social inequality. While racial/ethnic and later gender discrimination received the greatest attention in the so-called advanced industrial countries, place of residence and the geographical distribution of wealth and poverty at urban, regional, national, and international scales also featured prominently in the new social movements that were arising to seek greater social and economic justice.

The spreading urban crises of the 1960s brought to the surface the injustices and unfair geographies that had become deeply embedded in urban life in the preceding era of mass suburbanization and metropolitan growth. Attempting to understand and act upon these explosive conditions stimulated the development of three interwoven streams of innovative thinking about the spatial or geographical aspects of (in)justice. One would eventually focus specifically on spatial justice as such, emphasizing a more balanced dialectic between social and spatial causality. Another begins with the notion of territorial justice and spins off in two directions, one building a liberal formulation based on geographical studies of inequality and social welfare, and the other taking a more radical path through Marxist geography to critical studies of the urbanization of injustice. Weaving in and out of the other two, a third stream emerges from Henri Lefebvre's ideas about the right to the city but just as significantly from the radically new theorization of spatiality that he and others began to develop in the late 1960s.

Starting with Territorial Justice

A rather pragmatic starting point for the conceptualization of spatial justice in English came from a Welsh social planner, Bleddyn Davies, who in 1968 published *Social Needs and Resources in Local Services,* a book in which he coined the term *territorial justice.* Davies presented this new idea as a normative goal for local and regional planners, a sought-for outcome of government actions in which the allocation of public services and related investments across different territorial units did not just reflect population size but met actual social needs. The concept of territorial justice continued to be referred to by some, mainly British, social planners and policy makers but was not theorized or elaborated much further, at least within the planning profession.

The concept of territorial justice was picked up and creatively expanded in 1973 by David Harvey in *Social Justice and the City.* Harvey defined territorial justice in a more dynamic and political way, as the search for a just distribution of social resources justly arrived at. Here the intersection of justice and geography did not focus just on outcomes but also on the processes that produce unjust geographies, linking the search for justice to its sources in various kinds of discriminatory practices, including those he saw as inherent to the normal operation of urban labor and housing markets, government, and planning.

Harvey's original view of territorial justice, which will be discussed in more detail in the next section, was a significant advance in spatial thinking about justice but was soon almost summarily abandoned by Harvey and many of those inspired by his work. In an astounding intellectual and political turnaround that reverberated throughout the fields of geography and urban studies, Harvey turned from his liberal formulations about social justice and the city to a socialist critique, a move that became a powerful inspiration for the development of a new field of Marxist geography. Deep structural forces linked to the demands of capitalist accumulation were behind the formation of unjust geographies, Harvey argued, and therefore significant structural change was necessary to address these contingent urban and regional injustices and inequalities. Even the most progressive forms of liberal planning and social action were not enough to counter the demanding and injustice-inducing social processes underlying capitalist development.

Harvey and other Marxist geographers subsequently theorized and analyzed the search for social justice from a critical spatial perspective but did not use the term *spatial justice* and only very rarely referred to territorial justice, preferring, when they addressed justice at all, to speak more tangentially about the urbanization of injustice. Somewhat less radical in their perspective but nearly always acknowledging the importance of Harvey's analysis of social justice and the city, another group of geographers advanced our thinking about the spatiality of justice in a different way. They concentrated on the empirical measurement, description, and interpretation of the geographical patterning of social injustice and inequality.

The first major text on this subject was *Geography and Inequality* (1977), written by Coates, Johnston, and Knox. The most important subsequent works on the geography of social justice from a critical liberal perspective were written by David M. Smith, a British geographer whose work later involved him in debates about inequality in apartheid South Africa. In all of Smith's major works on geography and social justice, there is little mention of the specific term *spatial justice*. In both the radical and liberal vocabulary, adding *spatial* to *justice* seemed uncomfortably to suggest an unacceptable spatial determinism or fetishism.

Radical Urbanism and the Right to the City

The urban crises of the 1960s generated another stream of thought about geography, justice, and the urban condition that would play a greater role in the evolution of the concept of spatial justice. I refer here to the notion of the right to the city as originally conceived by the heterodox Marxist philosopher Henri Lefebvre. Lefebvre's ideas about the right to the city, reflected in the introduction's lead quotation from Erik Swyngedouw, a geographer influenced by Lefebvre's writings, were a stirring call to everyone disadvantaged by the conditions of urban life under capitalism to rise up to take greater control over how the unjust urban spaces in which they live are socially produced.

The struggle over the right to the city, aimed in part at a fair and equitable distribution of urban resources but even more so at obtaining power over the processes producing unjust urban geographies, is as good an example as any of the complex geographical struggle over ideas, forms, images, and imaginings described by Edward Said. It also became a rallying cry for the dissidents in the turbulent events of May 1968 in Paris. Embedded in Lefebvre's ideas was a radically new way of conceptualizing space and the spatiality of social life, which, after several decades of relative neglect, reemerged in the 1990s to stimulate what has been described as the spatial turn and, more recently, many new initiatives that combine a sense of spatial justice with the call for taking more control over the right to the city. I will return to Lefebvre's ideas and inspiration in a later section.

Specifically Spatial Justice

The discourses on territorial justice, the right to the city, the geography of social justice, and the urbanization of injustice were major advances in the conceptualization of the spatiality of (in)justice, even if none of the contributors ever used the specific term *spatial justice*. Although conceptually intertwined with the others and difficult to separate clearly, the development of the literature using the specific term, with its stronger assertion of the social effects of spatial processes, deserves particular attention.

Searching the English language literature, I have found only three instances where the term *spatial justice* was used in the title of a scholarly work before the last few years of the twentieth century. The first, dated

1973, was a doctoral dissertation on racial and spatial discrimination against black American voters written by the political geographer John O'Laughlin. Although part of a developing stream of research on the geography of racial injustice and the manipulation or gerrymandering of electoral districting for racially exclusionary purposes, the dissertation and its use of the term *spatial justice* had very little effect on the larger spatial- or justice-related literature.

Ten years later, G. H. Pirie, a South African geographer affected by the experience of apartheid and reflecting on the concept of territorial justice as used in Marxist geography, published a short article titled "On Spatial Justice." Pirie expressed curiosity and concern over what he saw as a peculiar aversion to the term *spatial justice* in the writings of radical geographers. What is equally remarkable about this inquisitive paper, with its call for developing the specific concept of spatial justice, is that it is the only substantive academic publication using the term in the title published before the year 2000, other than a few referring to the spatial aspects of criminal law.

Indicative of an interesting shift in direction, the only other publication I have found using the term in its title is a small pamphlet written by Steven Flusty, an architectural critic and geographer. In *Building Paranoia* (1994), Flusty explored what he called the "erosion of spatial justice" in the built environment of Los Angeles. Influenced by Mike Davis's well-known *City of Quartz* (1990) and the work of local geographers and planners analyzing the social and economic restructuring of the Los Angeles urban region, Flusty in his use of the term *spatial justice* crystallized in print what was already in the air both in the local academic world and in grassroots organizing: a sense of the consequential geography of injustice and the need to mobilize social action to deal with the increasingly unjust geographies emerging in Los Angeles from the uneven effects of globalization, the formation of a New Economy, and other restructuring forces.

Flusty's work was an early marker of a new trajectory of theoretical and practical research on spatial justice that was rooted in the Los Angeles urban and regional context. *Seeking Spatial Justice* is a product of this trajectory, drawing insights and inspiration from the substantial literature that has been produced by local scholars on urban and regional restructuring, the productive synergy that developed between spatial theory and spatial practice among local planners and geographers, and the extraordinary resurgence of labor and community organizing that emerged before and after the Justice Riots of 1992. Before moving the discussion in this empirical direction, however, it is worthwhile taking a closer look at the work of Harvey and Lefebvre, for they contain some of the richest elaborations of a spatial theory of justice.

David Harvey and the Urbanization of Justice

Liberal Formulations

In what he called his "liberal formulations" in *Social Justice and the City,* Harvey critically reconfigured Rawls's theory of justice by moving beyond its emphasis on outcomes to focus on the processes that produce them, especially the production process itself, with its deep involvement in the social division of labor. Harvey defined territorial justice as a socially just distribution that is justly arrived at. Achieving justice was seen as an intrinsically geographical problem, a challenge to "design a form of spatial organization which maximizes the prospects of the least fortunate region" (110). He recognized the "pioneering work" of Bleddyn Davies (1968) in developing the concept of territorial justice and proceeded to define several "principles of social justice as they apply to geographical situations."

The first of these principles states that the organization of space and the regional or territorial allocation of resources should meet the basic needs of the population. To affirm and promote this foundational principle, Harvey called for the creation of socially just methods to determine and measure these needs and adds that "the difference between needs and actual allocations provides us with an initial evaluation of the degree of territorial injustice in an existing system" (107). Harvey, however, moved beyond this initial evaluation as introduced by Davies to develop a more elaborate and urban-focused geographical theorization, one that remains essential today to an understanding of the concept and practice of seeking spatial justice.

A territorial or regional allocation of resources can be made more just, he observed, when there are positive (socially beneficial) spillover or multiplier effects from the locational or spatial pattern of public and private investments and where special attention is given to redress unusual environmental or social problems. This approach steers the search for justice toward access to the positive effects emanating from the urban economy, akin to the right to the city idea, and toward fundamental questions of environmental justice and social democracy. These principles would significantly inform and affect the development of the concepts of territorial and spatial justice and the geographical study of distributional inequalities for the next three decades.

In many ways, Harvey pushed liberal egalitarian theories of justice to their progressive limits, and in doing so he plunged creatively and deeply into the social and spatial causes of territorial inequality and injustice. Among his most powerful and insightful arguments was the one concerning the dynamics of urban development and its impact on income distribution. Harvey boldly argued that the normal workings of an urban system, from housing, labor, and land markets to the strategies of retailers, developers, bankers, and planners, tend toward a redistribution of real income in favor of the rich and more politically powerful. In other words, normal urban functioning makes the rich richer and the poor, at least relatively, poorer.

Here was a rigorous analysis of how social and economic inequalities and injustices were built into the evolving geography of the city: into why the poor pay more for basic goods and services, why redlining and disinvestment as well as the location of noxious facilities occur most often in poor areas while attractive public and private investments bring greater spatial advantages to the rich, why expensive freeway construction absorbs more public funds than effective mass transit serving the needs of the poor, why almost every aspect of urban development and change has regressive and discriminatory socio-spatial effects. Empirically enriching his critique of Rawls, Harvey demonstrated that unjust outcomes arise from inherently unjust processes operating in an urban milieu preloaded with distributional injustices to begin with.

Massive social intervention was necessary, he observed, to turn these inegalitarian social and spatial tendencies around. But Harvey was increasingly pessimistic about the likelihood that grassroots political and social actions and institutional plans and policies could be redirected to favor the relatively poor populations and areas of the city rather than the more rich and powerful. Pushed to their limits, these ultraliberal formulations appeared to have no hope of being implemented, leading Harvey to turn elsewhere in his search for social justice in the city.

Marxist Geographical Perspectives

In his "socialist formulations," Harvey radically shifted gears to reformulate the debates on urban social justice in a Marxist framework, an intellectual move that stimulated the development of the distinctive field of Marxist geography and at the same time created in this radicalized form of geographical analysis a lasting inhibition, if not prohibition, regarding the concept of distributive justice and the use of such descriptors as territorial and spatial, especially among the radical geographers he influenced most. Writing about the geography of social justice, particularly in the city, was acceptable within certain limits. Writing about spatial, geographical, or even territorial justice as such became much less satisfactory, for reasons that can be traced back to Marx.

For Marx, distributive justice was essentially a diversion from the main problems of capitalist society. It was a "mistake to make a fuss about so-called distribution and put the principal stress on it," he argued, for all inequitable and unjust distributions are produced by capitalism itself. Justice, however defined, can only be achieved through the transformation of the social relations of production that characterize capitalist development. Although these social or class relations shape space significantly, as Marxist geographers continued to demonstrate so effectively in their writings, the social relations themselves should not be seen as being shaped by spatial processes or relations, as implied in such terms as spatial justice. This implicit or explicit presumption of spatial (versus social) causality seemed to fall into the traps Marx identified as either fetishism or reification, an obsessive or unconsciously innocent overemphasis on surface appearances or outcomes rather than deep and determinative structural forces.

Harvey's Marxist turn moved him away from his earlier liberal formulations of territorial justice, but in both halves of *Social Justice and the City* his critical geographical imagination produced many brilliant insights regarding the social and spatial causes of inequality and injustice, insights that he continued to elaborate creatively in his subsequent writings even without explicitly using the term *spatial justice*. His liberal formulations about the redistributive effects of the normal workings of an urban system—the everyday operations of housing and labor markets, patterns of financial investment, the distribution of positive and negative effects of public expenditure, the availability of doctors and medical facilities, the costs of insurance and retail shopping, the forms of social regulation and planning, and so on—have already been mentioned and need to be assertively remembered in any discussion of spatial justice in theory and in practice. Rather than extending these observations, however, Harvey moved on to a very different conceptualization of what he called the "urban process under capitalism."

That the outcomes of this urban process would be inherently inegalitarian and unjust was taken for granted. That urbanization generates injustice is no surprise when seen from a Marxist perspective. What Harvey most incisively addressed were the underlying structures and processes that shape urban life and urban geographies in capitalist societies and in so doing indirectly presented one of the most insightful explanations of the 1960s urban crises and especially the unexpected consequences of well-intentioned efforts at urban renewal. Looking at the built environment, he states:

> Capital represents itself in the form of a physical landscape created in its own image, created as use values to enhance the progressive accumulation of capital. The geographical landscape which results is the crowning glory of past capitalist development. But at the same time it expresses the power of dead labour over living labour and as such it imprisons and inhibits the accumulation process within a set of specific physical constraints. . . .

There is a stunning argument made here that cannot be ignored by those uncomfortable with Marxian terminology. The argument is also a major challenge to orthodox Marxism, which tended, like orthodox neoclassical economics, to treat the economy almost as if it existed on the head of a pin, with no significant spatial dimensions or spatiality. What is focused on here is how powerful social forces (arising from capitalism but it could just as well be racism or patriarchy) purposefully shape spatial form (geography, the built environment). These geographies, along with their inherent injustices and inequalities, are produced to meet the needs of those promoting the social processes (capitalists in Harvey's formulation), but that is not the end of the story. The geographies that are produced in a given time period, Harvey notes, can become out-of-date, no longer as useful, at some time in the future, when conditions have changed. The "old" geography, in other words, can become countervailing, counterproductive, imprisoning, constraining, no longer suitable to immediate needs.

Harvey goes on to say that because of this spatial-temporal tension,

> Capitalist development has therefore to negotiate a knife-edge path between preserving the exchange values of past capital investments in the built environment and destroying the value of these investments in order to open up fresh room for accumulation. Under capitalism, there is then a perpetual struggle in which capital builds up a physical landscape appropriate to its own condition at a particular moment in time, only to have to destroy it, usually in the course of crises, at a subsequent point in time. The temporal and geographical ebb and flow of investment in the built environment can be understood only in terms of such a process.

Here the urban built environment is not just shaped in significant ways by capitalism, producing unjust geographies in its wake, but these produced geographies also work to shape capitalist development itself, at times sustaining and stimulating growth, at other times imprisoning and inhibiting the capital accumulation process. This version of the sociospatial dialectic, whereby the social and the spatial are mutually formative, becomes even more complex here because of the relative fixity of built forms and socially constructed geographies. The built environment does not simply adapt to changing conditions. The Empire State Building, for example, may have been ideally located when it was originally built, but its location became less advantageous (profitable) with the changing economic geography of Manhattan. Unfortunately for its owners, however, it could not simply be picked up and moved to another site.

Asserted here is a theory of crisis formation and "creative destruction" built into the historical geography of urban development. Not only is the industrial capitalist city a machine for generating inequality and injustice, it is also a generator of crises. More than just implied here is an explanation of why cities exploded all over the world in the 1960s, and how different fractions of capital, complicated further by well-meaning planners and state bureaucrats, competed with one another over what needed to be done about declining downtowns, racial ghettos, increasing poverty, metropolitan political fragmentation, urban sprawl, and inadequate public services.

The outcomes were not predetermined, but it was no surprise that the interests aimed most directly at rapidly increasing profitability and restoring social order tended to prevail. In perhaps the majority of cases, the promoted intentions of urban renewal and poverty alleviation led instead to bulldozed buildings, radically altered property ownership, and the removal of the poor for "higher and better" (more profitable) land uses. Responding to crisis, capital was creating a new geography to meet its altered needs. In an acute turn of phrase, Harvey later described this drive toward reorganizing or restructuring (already unfair and unjust) geographies as capital's search for a rejuvenative "spatial fix." Perhaps more than any other idea Harvey developed, the concept of a spatial fix explicitly recognized the power of spatial forces in the development and survival of capitalism, although he did not openly acknowledge this spatial causality until very recently.

Deflecting the Debate on the Spatiality of Justice

These insightful arguments inspired generations of geographers and urban scholars to follow in Harvey's footsteps, at least in terms of a critical diagnosis of urban problems. With respect to the study of territorial justice, however, it created a peculiar refraction. For most Marxist geographers, territorial justice became a diversionary issue, more characteristic of liberal or bourgeois thought than a radical critique. Almost nothing was written on the specific subject up to the present, although a variation on the theme appeared in *The Urbanization of Injustice* (1996), edited by Andy Merrifield and Erik Swyngedouw, both geographers strongly influenced by Harvey's work.

The book developed from a conference at Oxford University, where Harvey had served earlier as the Sir Halford Mackinder Professor of Geography, to commemorate the twentieth anniversary of the publication of *Social Justice and the City*. The terms *justice* or *social justice* appear in the titles of eight of the eleven chapters, and Harvey discusses the emerging concept of environmental justice in his contribution, but it is almost impossible to find any specific mention of either spatial justice or territorial justice on its pages.

Reacting to the earlier submergence of the debate on territorial and/or spatial justice, G. H. Pirie in his 1983 article lamented the move away from debates on the specifically spatial aspects of justice and called, with some trepidation, for a closer engagement between political philosophers, radical spatial theorists, and applied researchers interested in justice and equity. Informed by an emerging understanding that space is a structure created by society, a social product and not just an environmental context or container for society, Pirie pondered "the desirability and possibility of fashioning a concept of spatial justice from notions of social justice and territorial social justice" (472):

> Conceptualizing spatial justice in terms of a view of space as process, and perhaps in terms of radical notions of justice, stands as an exacting challenge. . . . In spite of the challenge of spatial fetishism, and in spite of the radical assault on liberal distributive concerns, it would be worthwhile investigating the possibility of matching justice to notions of socially constructed space. (471-72)

Pirie's caution ("in spite of the challenge . . . the assault . . . it would be worthwhile investigating the possibility") reflected the virtual taboo that had developed in radical geography against giving too much attention to spatial versus social processes and relations, and especially daring to suggest that spatial processes or forms could actually shape class relations, a sign of allegedly diversionary spatial fetishism.

For other geographers involved in studying geography and inequality from a less radical or explicitly Marxist perspective, Harvey was also influential as a critical urban theorist, but there was little inclination to use either of the specific terms of spatial or territorial justice. Studying social justice geographically from a liberal-progressive but not explicitly Marxist standpoint was sufficient. Disciplined geographers, however, were also hesitant to suggest any strong sense of spatial causality, remembering the "burnt fingers" associated with nineteenth-century dalliances with geographical-cum-environmental determinism.

Until very recently, studying the geography of inequality and social injustice, for the most part, moved away from a more explicitly spatial conceptualization. In the work of David Smith, for example, there has been a turn toward moral philosophy, a field closely associated with John Rawls and critical legal studies. This has shifted attention toward notions of morally unjust geographies, and for the most part back into the Rawlsian version of justice theory criticized by Iris Marion Young, David Harvey, and others.

For more applied researchers in urban planning and public policy, Harvey's diagnoses of the urban condition were attractive, but his prognosis for social action seemed too narrowly constrained and ultimately propelled only by revolutionary practices. Remaining within this Marxian orthodoxy left very little for activists and even self-styled radical planners to do short of the total transformation of capitalism. Planners specifically interested in social justice and the city have moved increasingly out of Harvey's Marxian shadows and toward softer and less explicitly spatial notions such as the "just city," discussed briefly in the introduction.

In More Hopeful Spaces

Like Rawls many years earlier, Harvey has also been sensitively responding to some of his critics. Despite Marxism's weakened contemporary influence in geography and planning, or perhaps because of it, Harvey's recent work has loosened up some of the rigid closures many perceived in his earlier writings. In *Spaces of Hope* (2000), for example, he speaks favorably of normative and utopian thought and opens new possibilities in the struggle for human rights and environmental justice, after earlier dismissing much of the environmental movement as little more than "militant localisms" (Harvey 1996). Unfettered neoliberal globalization has created such a "maelstrom of contradictions on the world stage," he argues, "that it has unwittingly opened up several paths toward a progressive and universalizing politics," especially with regard to "a fundamental reconception of the universal right for everyone to be treated with dignity and respect." To reject these issues of human rights as unavoidably tainted with bourgeois reformism is "to turn our backs on all manner of prospects for progressive political action" (94).

There remained significant boundaries beyond which Harvey would not reach, and he maintained some caution in asserting explicitly spatial causality, but a new flexibility was evident. Noting Marx's deep suspicion that talk about rights and justice was little more than a bourgeois diversion, he asks, "what on earth are workers of the world supposed to unite about unless it is some sense of their fundamental rights as human beings?" He calls for a redefinition of "the terms and spaces of political struggle . . . in these extraordinary times" (18). Struggles over universal or fundamental human rights still tend to remain ineffectively spatialized, but at least Harvey locates these struggles in redefined political spaces, leaving open some recognition of the consequential effects of geography.

While continuing to squeeze all the meaning he can from the *Communist Manifesto,* Harvey recognizes the need to go beyond its ample insights on globalization and restructuring to emphasize an enriched interpretation of uneven geographical development. Not without irony but with due caution, he returns to Lefebvre and one of the most powerful assertions of spatial causality in the literature, the idea that the very survival of capitalism has depended on the production of space:

> While Lefebvre (1976) perhaps exaggerates a touch, I think it worth recalling his remark that capitalism has survived in the twentieth century by one and only one means—"by occupying space, by producing space." It would be ironic indeed if the same were to be said at the end of the twenty-first century. (31)

It was precisely this kind of assertion of how geography shapes social relations of production and class that turned Harvey, Manuel Castells, and other geographers and sociologists away from Lefebvre in the 1970s, deflecting both the radical retheorization of space Lefebvre was advancing (see below) and the debates on territorial and spatial justice. At that time, a balanced socio-spatial and geo-historical dialectic was almost inconceivable on the Marxist left, and for various other reasons, Lefebvre's ideas remained buried for more than two decades. While Lefebvre's spatial explanation of the survival of capitalism was muted in its impact, Harvey came forward with his very similar idea that capitalism seeks a spatial fix when faced with crisis. Harvey was careful not to make this spatial fix, with its intonations of urban and regional restructuring and the spatial transformation of the built environment, appear too likely to succeed, for crises, by their very nature, always had to carry the possibility of revolutionary transformation.

With the resurgence and transdisciplinary diffusion of critical spatial perspectives in the last decade of the twentieth century, a deeper and broader meaning of Lefebvre's assertive and explanatory spatial arguments has become more widely understood. Although he characteristically takes a step back before moving forward in his spatial thinking, Harvey's explorations of the spaces of hope build on the Lefebvre revival and add significantly to the development of a spatial theory of justice, democracy, and human rights. Harvey's cautious creativity and conservative openness are never more evident than in his recent renewal of interest in "the right to the city" (2003, 2006, 2008).

In his recasting of Lefebvre's original concept, Harvey presents the usual Marxist warnings about using bourgeois notions of universalized rights. If they are mainly about property and profit, then he wants none of it. But he goes on to recognize "a huge movement for global justice" that is searching for viable alternatives to the social processes that produce cities "marked and marred by inequality, alienation, and injustice." Here are some extracts from Harvey's cautious embrace of Lefebvre's ideas:

> A different right to the city must be asserted. Those that now have the rights will not surrender them willingly: "Between equal rights, force decides." This does not necessarily mean violence (though, sadly, it often comes down to that). But it does mean the mobilization of sufficient power through political organization or in the streets if necessary to change things. But by what strategies do we proceed?
>
> . . . Derivative rights (like the right to be treated with dignity) should become fundamental and fundamental rights (of private property and the profit rate) should become derivative. . . . [We can exploit the] contradictions within the capitalist package of rights. . . . But new rights can also be defined: like the right to the city which . . . is not merely a right of access to what the property speculators and state planners define, but an active right to make the city different, to shape it more in accord with our heart's desire, and to re-make ourselves thereby in a different image.
>
> The creation of a new urban commons, a public sphere of active democratic participation, requires that we roll back that huge wave of privatization that has been the mantra of a destructive neoliberalism. We must imagine a more inclusive, even if continuously fractious, city based not only upon a different ordering of rights but upon different political-economic practices. If our urban world has been imagined and made then it can be re-imagined and re-made. The inalienable right to the city is worth fighting for. "City air makes one free" it used to be said. The air is a bit polluted now. But it can always be cleaned up. (2003, 941)

In an article on "The Right to the City" published in the *New Left Review* in 2008, before the full economic meltdown took effect, Harvey reviews his arguments about capitalism's "perpetual need to find profitable terrains for capital-surplus production and absorption," updated to include the mega-urbanization of China, and traces the history of urban revolutions and the crises that "repeatedly erupt around urbanization both locally and globally." The modern metropolis, he argues, is now the focus of intensified struggles over the "developmental drive that seeks to colonize space for the affluent." His final paragraph, while maintaining a cautious stance, is a compelling call for a radical right to the city movement and a frank admission that he was wrong in rejecting, along with many other Marxists at the time, Lefebvre's idea that all social revolutions must also be urban (i.e., spatial) revolutions:

> [C]rises repeatedly erupt around urbanization both locally and globally . . . the metropolis is now the point of massive collision—dare we call it class struggle?—over the accumulation by dispossession visited upon the least well-off and the developmental drive that seeks to colonize space for the affluent.
>
> One step towards unifying these struggles is to adopt the right to the city as both working slogan and political ideal, precisely because it focuses on the question of who commands the necessary connection between urbanization and surplus production and use. The democratization of that right, and the construction of a broad social movement to enforce its will is imperative if the dispossessed are to take back the control which they have for so long been denied. *Lefebvre was right to insist that the revolution has to be urban, in the broadest sense of that term, or nothing at all.* (emphasis added)

I will return to Harvey's most recent observations on the urban causes of the current financial crisis in the concluding comments to chapter 6. To better understand what is happening today, however, and to put Harvey's recent admissions into perspective, the work of Lefebvre needs to be addressed in more detail.

Henri Lefebvre and the Right to the City

As repeatedly noted, the right to the city idea occupies a special place in *Seeking Spatial Justice.* The two concepts, spatial justice and the right to the city, have become so interwoven in their contemporary usage that it has become increasingly difficult to tell them apart. With resonances that connect back to all the previous discussions, I will use the concept of the right to the city here as a framework to summarize and synthesize the preceding debates on the spatial theory of justice, elaborate upon the new spatial consciousness that has been emerging in association with the revival of the right to the city idea, and connect this discussion to the following chapters on seeking spatial justice in Los Angeles.

The Lefebvrean Version

The concept of the right to the city as originally formulated by Lefebvre reestablishes the urban foundations of seeking justice, democracy, and citizen's rights. After centuries during which the national state defined citizenship and human rights, the city is seen again to be a special space and place of social and economic advantage, a focal point for the workings of social power and hierarchy, and therefore a potent battleground for struggles seeking greater democracy, equality, and justice.

As Harvey later elaborated in his liberal formulations, Lefebvre saw the normal workings of everyday urban life as generating unequal power relations, which in turn manifest themselves in inequitable and unjust distributions of social resources across the space of the city. Demanding greater access to social power and valued resources by those most disadvantaged by inequitable and unjust geographies defined the struggle to reclaim the manifold rights to the city. The aim, at least from a liberal egalitarian point of view, is to gain greater control over the forces shaping urban space, in other words to reclaim democracy from those who have been using it to maintain their advantaged positions.

Lefebvre's view, like Harvey's, extended well beyond these liberal egalitarian formulations. Seeking the right to the city is a continuous and more radical effort at spatial reappropriation, claiming an active presence in all that takes place in urban life under capitalism. As such, it generates a constant challenge to what Lefebvre described as a "bureaucratic society of controlled consumption" promoted by the increasing penetration of the state and the market into all aspects of everyday urban life. In Lefebvre's view, often forgotten or misunderstood by even his most ardent contemporary exponents, this bureaucratic society and its extension through planning and public policy do not just affect those living in the city proper but impose their powerful influence everywhere via the operations of the state and the market. It is in this sense that Lefebvre claimed the whole world was being urbanized. The struggle over the right to the city, despite Lefebvre's occasional remarks to the contrary, extends regionally to the countryside, to rural areas and the rain forest as well.

This broadened view of the regional right to the city, as I have been arguing persistently, can be best understood when urbanization and the organized space of the city are seen as generative forces, wellsprings of societal development, technological innovation, cultural creativity, as well as social stratification, hegemonic power, inequality, and injustice. Things do not just happen in cities, they happen to a significant extent because of cities. While Lefebvre looked at the formal city in his specific Paris-in-mind discussions of *le droit à la ville,* his other writings about the urban condition encompassed a larger, multiscalar vision of the global spread of urban industrial capitalism and the spatialization of class struggle.

This forceful appreciation of consequential geographies, the idea that space matters much more than most scholars ever imagined, drove Lefebvre's thinking about the right to the city. For most Marxists and social scientists at the time and extending up to the present for many, it was difficult to understand and accept these ideas about the generative power of urban spatiality. This resistance explains a great deal about why Lefebvre's ideas were buried under various persistent orthodoxies for decades, and why even today they remain for many scholars either incomprehensible or naively hyperbolic.

For Lefebvre, however, there was an even stronger spatial argument behind his conceptualization of the right to the city, an argument that Harvey referred to in his earlier quote saying it might be "a touch" exaggerated. Struggles over the right to the city are a vital political response to capitalism's efforts to create geographies suited to its fundamental interests, which Lefebvre described as the reproduction of the social relations of production, in other words, keeping capitalism going and growing even through times of economic crisis. Lefebvre's arguments about consequential geographies and the socio-spatial dialectic can be explained best through his own words:

> Space and the political organization of space express social relationships but also react back upon them. . . . Industrialization, once the producer of urbanism, is now being produced by it. . . . When we use the words "urban revolution" we designate the total ensemble of

transformations which run throughout contemporary society and which bring about a change from a period in which questions of economic growth and industrialization predominate to the period in which the urban problematic becomes decisive.

This quote is taken from a postscript to Harvey's *Social Justice and the City* (1973, 306) and is a focal point for Harvey's earlier discomfort and disagreement with Lefebvre, a reason for contending that Lefebvre was going too far in his claims. Lefebvre, however, goes further.

Capitalism has found itself able to attenuate (if not resolve) its internal contradictions for a century, and consequently, in the hundred years since the writing of *Capital*, it has succeeded in achieving "growth." We cannot calculate at what price, but we do know the means: *by occupying space, by producing a space.* (1976, 21)

In other words, the production of space and especially urbanized space has been crucial to the very survival of capitalism since at least the midnineteenth century, when cities all over the world exploded with unrest and frustration over existing socio-spatial injustices. At every moment in its history but especially in times of crisis, urban industrial capitalism is engaged in a pivotal struggle over geography, over maintaining its ability to shape space in ways that meet its immediate needs. As Edward Said notes, this struggle extends far beyond soldiers and cannons. For Lefebvre, it revolves centrally around struggles over urbanized space between those seeking continuing advantage and the disadvantaged fighting to take greater control over how space is socially produced in order to make major transformations to better meet their basic needs.

The idea that the survival of capitalism depends fundamentally on the production of (predominantly urban) space is one of the strongest assertions of the significance of social spatiality ever made by a prominent scholar. It is the foundational argument behind Harvey's concepts of a spatial fix and capitalism's perpetual struggle over the built environment, as well as the notion of a socio-spatial dialectic and much that has been discussed here about the search for spatial justice. It also helps to explain why I have been so insistent in asserting the importance of using the explicit adjective *spatial* rather than any other alternative. I still am amazed that other scholars have given so little attention to this provocative idea.

On a more philosophical and hopeful plane, Lefebvre adds:

> The dialectic is back on the agenda. But it is no longer Marx's dialectic, just as Marx's was no longer Hegel's. . . . The dialectic today no longer clings to historicity and historical time, or to a temporal mechanism such as "thesis-antithesis-synthesis" or "affirmation-negation-negation of the negation" . . . To recognise space, to recognise what "takes place" there and what it is used for, is to resume the dialectic; analysis will reveal the contradictions of space. (1976, 14, 17)

With this background, Lefebvre's specific conceptualization of the right to the city and the "urban problematic" can be better understood:

> The right to the city, complemented by the right to difference and the right to information, should modify, concretize and make more practical the rights of the citizen as an urban dweller (*citadin*) and user of multiple services. It would affirm, on the one hand, the right of users to make known their ideas on the space and time of their activities in the urban area; it would also cover the right to the use of the center, a privileged place, instead of being dispersed and stuck into ghettos (for workers, immigrants, the "marginal" and even for the "privileged"). (1996, 34)

As noted earlier, the word *droit* in French means both law and right. Its plural, *droits,* is used in such terms as *droits civils* (civil rights) and *droits de l'homme* (rights of man or human rights). Lefebvre combined all these meanings and references in his strategically spatialized notion of *le droit à la ville.* He also combined the right to the city with what he called the right to difference, the right to be different as a means of challenging the controlling forces of homogenization, fragmentation, and uneven development imposed by the state, the market, and the bureaucracy working together to foster mass consumerism and heightened social control.

For Lefebvre, the urban dweller, by the very fact of urban residence itself, has specifically spatial rights: to participate openly and fairly in all the processes producing urban space, to access and make use of the particular advantages of city life, especially in the highly valued city center (or centers), to avoid all forms of imposed spatial segregation and confinement, to be provided with public services that meet basic needs in health, education, and welfare. In this version of seeking spatial justice, the concrete urban geography, the full spatial specificity of the city, becomes charged with practical and political meaning.

Lefebvre's ideas about the right to the city played a major role in the Paris student and worker uprising in May 1968, an event that can be described as perhaps the first mass protest consciously seeking social justice through explicitly spatial strategies. At the time, Lefebvre's particular focus on the right to the use of the center reflected a major change in the residential geography of Paris that was rapidly taking shape in the 1960s. As discussed in chapter 2, the working class in Paris had become heavily concentrated in the central areas of Paris in the postwar era, to the point where they were becoming an electoral majority. In the French version of urban renewal, large numbers of workers were moved out of central Paris to suburban high-rise concentrations, or *banlieues*. The uprising of 1968 was not just a general protest against the prevailing form of French capitalism but also a more specific attack on the concrete new geography of inequality being created in Paris at the time, one that exploded most recently in the compacted immigrant *banlieues* in 2005.

This reminds us that the unjust geographies around which right to the city movements are organized change over time. The right to centrality in Paris in the 1960s is different today, in an age of regional urbanization and the rise of polycentric and globalized city regions. More and more, the rights to the city everywhere are becoming rights to the city region as a whole, to all the resources generated by the network of urban agglomerations forming the metropolitan regional economy and extending its reach to a global scale. This multiscalar expansion of the struggles over the right to the city could not have been easily foreseen in the 1960s, although Lefebvre's argument that the whole world was becoming urbanized carried with it the sense that the struggle was not confined to the formal boundaries of the city itself.

In so many ways, Harvey and Lefebvre are in accord in their interpretations of the right to the city and its past and present implications and potential. They differ mainly in how they explicitly treat the causal power of urban spatiality and the relation between social and spatial processes. Harvey, even in his more recent contributions, continues to privilege the determinative effects of social forces such as capital accumulation, while Lefebvre insisted on a more dialectical balance of social and spatial causality. For many, this may seem a minor difference, but for the arguments being presented in *Seeking Spatial Justice,* it is of crucial importance.

To give additional strength to these summative arguments, another remarkable development that was occurring during the same period that the concept of the right to the city was being formulated and tentatively practiced needs to be recognized and discussed. What follows elaborates upon the discussion of new ontological beginnings in this chapter and gives some historical background to the general overview of the new spatial consciousness presented in the introduction. Those who feel no need for such elaboration can skip to the next section on contemporary revivals.

Creating a New Spatial Consciousness

In a remarkable convergence of ideas about which very little has been written, Lefebvre and Michel Foucault, along with a few other Parisian scholars, initiated a call for a radical transformation in critical spatial thinking in the late 1960s and early 1970s. Deeply affected by the events of May 1968, both argued in very similar ways that prevailing approaches to thinking about and theorizing space were too confining and insufficient to understand the modern world in all its historical and social complexity. In their view, spatial thinking tended to be straitjacketed into a tight dualism that limited its critical capacity, especially in comparison with critical historiography and social theory.

Most spatial thinkers at the time, they argued, emphasized a materialist concept of space, characterized by concrete, mappable, and empirically defined geographies, or "things in space." Spatial analyses of this sort were either highly descriptive of existing conditions or else sought to explain empirical patterns through spatial covariation or association, how one empirically defined geography correlates with others. A minority of spatial thinkers put their primary emphasis not directly on material things but on "thoughts about space," how materialized space is conceptualized, imagined, or represented in various ways, from the subjective mental maps of the world we all carry with us to scientific epistemologies and philosophies of space and place. Then, and now, these two ways of thinking about space were seen by most spatial thinkers as filling the entire scope of the spatial or geographical imagination.

Lefebvre defined the first as *perceived* space, shaped by materialized and objectified spatial practices; and the second as *conceived* space, various often subjective representations of space in ideas, images, ideologies. Foucault similarly recognized this split between material and imagined spaces and, like Lefebvre, argued that this double-barreled approach, while it created important and useful knowledge and should not be neglected, had certain significant limitations and did not fill the entire field of possibilities for critical spatial thinking. Another and different way of thinking spatially was not only possible but necessary if the intellectual and epistemological privileging of time over space, and hence historical over spatial thinking, were to be reduced if not eliminated in a critical rebalancing of the historical and geographical imaginations.

For Lefebvre, a more comprehensive and theoretically richer way of thinking about space combined materialist and idealist approaches while also at the same time opening up new ways of interpreting what he would call the (social) spatiality of human life. He called this third way an understanding of *lived* space and linked it to a biographical and historical notion of lived time, as well as to that primordial lived space, the human body. What Lefebvre was saying was that we are all, individually and collectively, spatial as well as temporal and social beings. Our biographies are just as much spatial as they are temporal and social. This was a central message in his major work, *La Production de l'espace,* published in 1974 and translated in 1991 as *The Production of Space.*

Lived space like our lived time is never completely knowable, Lefebvre argued. Beneath all surface appearances, there is always something mysterious, undercover, undiscoverable. A team of the best biographers on earth will never be able to discover everything about our individual spatio-temporal lives. We can only learn about our lived times and spaces in increments, never satisfied with existing levels of knowledge but constantly moving on, almost like philosophical nomads, to search for the new, to push the frontiers of knowledge and understanding forward, and hope for the unexpected. I have tried to follow this path in seeking a spatial theory of justice.

The implications were clear: without adopting a lived space perspective, remaining confined by the materialist–idealist dualism, critical spatial thinking can never hope to reach the same levels of insight and understanding that derive from a critical historical perspective. The traditional bicameral geographical imagination, for all its valuable contributions, is not enough to allow spatial thinkers to compete with the "history boys."

Following a remarkably similar line of thought, Foucault also identified an alternative, or third, way of looking at and interpreting human spatiality. In a lecture that was published after his death in 1984 as "Of Other Spaces" ("Des espaces autres"), he described his more comprehensive, combinatorial, and critical spatial perspective as "heterotopology," and proceeded to describe a series of particular examples illustrating his distinctively different approach to understanding human spatiality. Foucault saw all geographies, from those produced by what he called the little tactics of the habitat to the global realm of geopolitical confrontation and conflict, as filled not only with injustice and oppression but also with potentially emancipatory and liberating opportunities. Foucault did not focus on the city per se, but by looking at the "heterotopias" that arise from the intersection of space, knowledge, and power, he opened up new ways of thinking spatially.

These innovative reconceptualizations of space demanded a new and different form of spatial consciousness, a way of thinking that recognized that space is filled with politics and privileges, ideologies and cultural collisions, utopian ideals and dystopian oppression, justice and injustice, oppressive power and the possibility for emancipation. To see space and geography in this more comprehensive and challenging way, several almost axiomatic principles need to be recognized, starting with the ontological assertion of the fundamental spatiality of being. At the risk of being somewhat repetitive, let me outline briefly some of the principles of a new spatial consciousness that derive from the work of Lefebvre and Foucault.

The starting point remains the same: human spatiality in all its forms and expressions is socially produced. We make our geographies, for good or bad, just or unjust, in much the same way it can be said that we make our histories, under conditions not of our own choosing but in real-world contexts already shaped by socio-spatial processes in the past and the enveloping historically and socially constituted geographies of the present. This profoundly displaces the idea of space merely as external environment or container, a naturalized or neutral stage for life's seemingly time-driven social drama.

That our geographies and histories are socially produced and not simply given to us by god or nature leads to an awareness that the geographies in which we live can have both positive and negative effects. They can provide advantage and opportunity, stimulate, emancipate, entertain, enchant, enable. They can also constrain opportunity, oppress, imprison, subjugate, disempower, close off possibilities. In our terms, geographies or spatialities can be just as well as unjust, and they are produced through processes that are simultaneously social and spatial, subjective and objective, concretely real and creatively imagined. Geographies, in other words, are consequential, not merely the background onto which our social life is projected or reflected.

For Lefebvre and Foucault, space not only mattered, it was a powerful shaping force in society and in politics at every scale and context, from the intimacies of the body and the little tactics of the habitat to the playing out of global geopolitics and the repetitive crises of capitalism. For Lefebvre in particular, a special place was given to the city as perhaps the greatest achievement of human creativity. In his vivid terms, the city is both *produit* and *oeuvre*, a material outcome of human action and a representational work of art. For Foucault, every space is a heterotopia, a realized and imagined space of resolvable oppositions, and heterotopology becomes a way of looking at and interpreting all spaces and their consequential effects.

Moving closer toward a strategic spatial consciousness and thus a spatial theory of justice, it becomes evident and challenging that these socially produced geographies, because they are created by human actions, can be changed or transformed through human agency—for better or for worse, it must be added. Human geographies are not merely external containers, given and immutable. Their changeability is crucial, for it makes our geographies the targets for social and political action seeking justice and democratic human rights by increasing their positive and/or decreasing their negative effects on our lives and livelihoods. Without adopting this expanded form of spatial consciousness promoted by Lefebvre and Foucault, the objectives of seeking spatial justice and demanding the right to the city are difficult to comprehend and even more difficult to put into practice.

These radically new ideas about critical spatial thinking were deflected in the years following the perceived failure of the 1968 Paris uprising. For many feminists, labor and community leaders, civil rights activists, and others involved in the social movements that were expanding in the 1970s and 1980s, specifically spatial targets seemed too peripheral, abstract, and confusing. Old ways of thinking about space only as physical form and background environment made the notion of socially produced spatial justice and injustice almost incomprehensible. For more orthodox Marxists, the very idea of a Marxist geography was perplexing if not politically dangerous. Neo-Marxist spatial thinkers, such as Harvey and Castells, recognized Lefebvre's urban achievements but thought he went too far in promoting them. The more politically ambiguous Foucault was almost entirely ignored.

Confusing matters further, geographers did little to encourage the spread of this new critical perspective until the mid-1990s. Most geographers either did not or could not understand the call for a new spatial perspective and the critique of traditional forms of geographical thinking that was inherent in the writings of Lefebvre and Foucault, or else they somewhat proudly acknowledged them as leading figures from outside the discipline who were supporting (rather than deeply criticizing) the geographer's traditional ways of thinking. Outside geography, in the wider realms of social theory and philosophy, there were several important contributions to the debates on space and time made between 1970 and 1990, such as the time-space structuration theory of Anthony Giddens, but they had little effect in countering the powerful force of social historicism.

Today, however, the attention given to Lefebvre and Foucault inside geography and, with the spatial turn, in many other disciplines seems to have exploded exponentially, and with this has come renewed appreciation for foregrounding space as an interpretive perspective. I conclude this chapter with a brief discussion of the expanding resurgence of interest in Lefebvre's notion of the right to the city.

Contemporary Revivals

Beginning around 2000, the idea of the right to the city took off as the subject of academic writing, meetings, and conferences and increasingly as a mobilizing concept for social and political organization and action. Today, if you enter "right to the city" in your search engine, there are nearly nine million hits. National or international conferences with right to the city in their thematic titles have multiplied, some of which are listed in Notes and References.

Spurring the globalization of the concept is the World Charter for the Right to the City, appearing in 2004 in conjunction with the Social Forum of the Americas held in Quito and the World Urban Forum in Barcelona. Attempting to draw together the global justice, environmental justice, and human rights movements, the charter begins by recognizing that the city "is a rich and diversified cultural space that belongs to all its inhabitants," and that everyone "has a Right to the City free of discrimination based on gender, age, health status, income, nationality, ethnicity, migratory condition, or political, religious, or sexual orientation, and to preserve cultural memory and identity." Citizens are defined not just as permanent inhabitants but also those "in transit." There is a list of "Principles of the Right to the City," including democratic management, full exercise of citizenship and use of economic and cultural resources, equality and nondiscrimination, special protection for vulnerable persons and groups, and economic solidarity and progressive policies. That the right to the city is not confined to the formal city is recognized:

> Urban territories and their rural surroundings are also spaces and locations of the exercise and fulfillment of collective rights as a way of assuring equitable, universal, just, democratic, and sustainable distribution and enjoyment of the resources, wealth, services, goods, and opportunities that cities offer.

Deserving special recognition in the contemporary right to the city revival are the regional movements developing in Athens, Greece, the originating polis. Coalitions of city movements demanding more open space, better housing, and various forms of environmental justice began to form after the return to democracy in 1974, initially through existing political parties but by the 1980s mainly in the autonomous organization of neighborhood groups. In 2004, a new right to the city alliance was formed to focus on struggles over public and private investments in the Olympic Games, stimulating hundreds of citizen's initiatives across the Greater Athens area. This regionalization of struggles led to the creation of the Panattic Network of City Movements in 2007 and an allied group, reminiscent of Justice for Janitors in Los Angeles, the Panattic

Union of Cleaners and Domestic Personnel. See Notes and References for more on these developments.

Most of the growing literature on the right to the city makes some reference to Lefebvre's original idea, but there is usually very little critical evaluation of the concept or explicit discussion of a critical spatial perspective. In many cases, the notion of the right to the city seems to be little more than a slightly different way of speaking about human rights in general or merely a generic reference to the need for more democratic forms of planning and public policy. For the most part, the assertively spatial approach of Lefebvre and the notion of consequential geographies are ignored, and his radical political objectives reduced to softer liberal egalitarianism or normative platitudes.

Amid this liberal co-optation, however, a more critical if still appreciative approach to Lefebvre and the right to the city idea has begun to develop, for the most part from scholars connected in some way with either the geographer-planners in Los Angeles, where the first conference on the right to the city held in the United States took place, or with the now New York–based David Harvey and his productive writings on the urban condition under capitalism. An early representative of this second stream is *The Right to the City: Social Justice and the Fight for Public Space* (2003), written by Don Mitchell, a leading figure in the People's Geography Project, a kind of clearinghouse of information and support for urban scholars and activists based in Syracuse, New York.

Mitchell, who also wrote an excellent book on migrant workers in California (1996), roots his analysis of struggles over free speech, homelessness, and the use of public space in the work of Harvey and Lefebvre, significantly advancing our understanding of the urbanization of injustice and efforts to reappropriate the right to the city in ways that avoid the limitations of both Harvey's and Lefebvre's approaches. Mitchell's Marxist perspective is open-minded and flexible, but an old taboo lingers in his relative avoidance of explicitly discussing spatial processes and their effects on social form in comparison with the more comfortable emphasis on social processes shaping spatial form. There is a concluding section on spaces of justice and ample discussion of the geography of social justice, but the term *spatial justice* is not used at all.

Inspired in part by Harvey but more open to Lefebvre's assertive spatiality and to the need to create new spaces of opportunity and hope between revolutionary radicalism and liberal egalitarianism are the writings of three geographer-planners associated with UCLA Urban Planning and Geography: Neil Brenner, Mustafa Dikec, and Mark Purcell. All three have written important critical analyses of Lefebvre's writings and have specifically addressed the right to the city idea.

Dikec's work on justice and the spatial imagination and the French *banlieues* has already been mentioned. In all his work, including critiques of French urban policies and *politique* (referring simultaneously in French to politics, policy, and police), Dikec draws creatively on Lefebvre and the right to the city concept. Brenner has become a leading figure in studies of the state and state restructuring, the social production of scale, and spatial theory more broadly, referring often to Lefebvre as well as translating several of his writings, including much of the four-volume work *De l'État*. Bringing the debates on the right to the city up-to-date and effectively connecting to the present discussion of seeking spatial justice is the work of Purcell and especially the recently published *Recapturing Democracy: Neoliberalization and the Struggle for Alternative Urban Futures* (2008).

Purcell presents an insightful reevaluation of Lefebvre's ideas, surveying the recent literature and cautioning against any reductionist interpretation of the call for a radical urban metamorphosis, including Lefebvre's own often-implied narrowing of the struggle to include only the working class as agents of change. The right to the city is seen not just as a right to appropriation, participation, and difference but even more broadly as a *right to space,* the right to inhabit space. In stretching the concept to a larger global scale, Purcell (2008) quotes Brenner:

> Urban social movements . . . do not merely occur within urban space but strive to transform the socioterritorial organization of capitalism itself on multiple geographical scales. The "right to the city" . . . thereby expands into a broader "right to space" both within and beyond the urban scale. Even as processes of global capitalist restructuring radically reorganize the supraurban scalar hierarchies in which cities are embedded, cities remain strategic arenas for sociopolitical struggles which, in turn, have major ramifications for the supraurban geographies of capitalism. (102)

That struggles over the right to the city are fundamentally struggles against the oppressive effects of capitalism and more particularly its neoliberal variants is made clear, but there are also openings to a multiplicity of agents and targets that widen the scope of political action to include what I have been describing as the production of discriminatory and unjust geographies of many different kinds, relating to gender, race, sexuality, environmental factors, and others. Here it is important to recall Iris Marion Young's more pluralistic five-sided concept of injustice as oppression, in which class struggle per se focuses primarily around economic exploitation at the workplace and place of residence while other structures of social advantage and hierarchical power define broader fields of social action related to cultural and political domination and other axes of discrimination.

Combining Purcell and Young opens up the converging movements for spatial justice and the democratic rights to urban space to many new possibilities. The more monolithic and focused forms of class struggle inherent in Lefebvre's and Harvey's approaches are not rejected but expanded to meet the multifaceted and multiscalar demands for justice in the contemporary world. Most important for the challenges of seeking specifically spatial justice is the implied necessity to build diverse coalitions and networked social movements that extend beyond the narrow and often essentialist channels of the past. In today's world, separate movements for labor, against racism, patriarchy, or cultural domination, or to achieve peace or respond to global warming or to promote local community development are less likely than ever before to be successful. Crosscutting alliances and coalitions are becoming increasingly essential.

In an insightful turn of phrase, Purcell calls the right to the city, especially in its sense as a right to occupy and inhabit space, an organizational and mobilizing "linchpin," suggesting that it forms an integrative umbrella for coalition building, a kind of connective tissue or "glue" that can help to *unite diverse and particularized struggles into larger and more powerful movements.* The new spatial consciousness and its expression in the search for spatial justice provide just such an integrative umbrella. We all experience in one way or another the negative effects of unjust geographies. This makes struggles over space and the right to the city a potentially powerful source of shared identity, determination, and effectiveness in changing the world for the better. This may be the most important political lesson learned from the development of a spatial theory of justice.

These comments and conclusions bring into a new perspective the inaugural meeting of a national alliance of labor and community-based organizations on the right to the city that took place in January 2007 in Los Angeles. In many ways, this was a breakthrough moment in the revival of Lefebvre's original concept in the United States and at the same time the starting point for new and exciting initiatives. The meeting also provides a useful bridge to a discussion of how the search for spatial justice and the right to the city has developed over the past forty years in the urban region of Los Angeles.

4 ——————————————————————————————

—————————————Seeking Spatial Justice in
Los Angeles

THE LABOR MOVEMENT IN LOS ANGELES, largely through coalition building between union locals and a wide range of community-based organizations, has been experiencing an extraordinary resurgence in recent years. Innovative organizing strategies, especially with regard to immigrant workers, and a series of successful campaigns aimed at achieving greater social and economic justice for the nearly 40 percent of the population described as the working poor, have transformed what was once considered an intensely antilabor environment into what some national observers today see as the most vigorous and effective urban labor movement in the United States.

The resurgence of labor–community coalition building has its roots in the early development of *community unionism,* inspired in large part by the United Farm Workers (UFW) campaigns to achieve justice for immigrant workers in California in the 1960s and 1970s. UFW activities tied the labor movement more closely to both the wider immigrant, mainly Latino/a, community as a whole and, more directly, with local neighborhood and community groups and their priorities. Struggles over wages and workplace conditions were extended to include demands for better housing, schools, social services, and other residential rights to justice and equality. New labor–community coalitions, often assisted by university-based activism and research, began to emerge and to take the lead in promoting a regionally based justice movement of unusual strength and persistence.

The union–community linkage worked effectively in both directions. Community support gave added strength to the labor movement and increased its sensitivity to the local and regional geographies in which work and workers' lives took place. At the same time, ties to local unions and workers' issues bolstered community development efforts and fostered new strategies for achieving what would come to be described as development with justice. As place-based knowledge and strategic action became increasingly important, civil society in Los Angeles changed significantly. What was once a relatively "placeless" urban world, where local communities rarely impinged on people's lives, has today become a hive of community-based organizations and grassroots activism.

These local and regional achievements are even more remarkable given the deteriorating national economy, huge job losses, and declining union power that have characterized most of the rest of the country over the past four decades. A graph recently produced by the UCLA Institute for Research on Labor and Employment shows union density rates for Los Angeles, California, and the United States from 1996 to 2008. A divergence is clear between the steady national decline and the relatively increasing unionization rate in Los Angeles, with the gap being greater today than ever before. Los Angeles also grew faster than California, with a large jump occurring between 1999 and 2002, reflecting the unionization of in-home caregivers and other largely minority occupations, including what was in 1999 one of the largest one-year increases in union membership in U.S. urban history.

How did this transformation take place? Why did it happen in Los Angeles, of all places? What are the distinctive features of the new labor–community coalitions that have emerged? To what extent can the new coalitions be seen as struggles for spatial justice? What has been the role of the university in these movements? What can be learned from the recent Los Angeles experience that can better inform public policy and help mobilize effective labor–community coalitions in other areas of the country? What follows is an attempt to provide at least some preliminary answers to these questions.

To set the scene for this focused discussion, the chapter begins by placing the Los Angeles experience within the larger context of economic restructuring, the globalization of capital, labor, and culture, and other forces of change that have been reshaping modern metropolises all over the world during the past four decades. Particular emphasis is given to the intensification of economic inequalities and increasing social polarization that have accompanied these changes almost everywhere, making the search for social and spatial justice increasingly urgent and demanding.

This general discussion of urban restructuring and the forces reconfiguring the modern metropolis will be familiar to many readers. This is not surprising since a large portion of the wider academic literature on the urban restructuring process and such related concepts as world city formation, post-Fordist industrialization, flexible production systems, industrial clusters, and the formation of polycentric global city regions draws heavily on studies of Los Angeles by local researchers seeking to understand larger comparative and global restructuring trends by examining their particular empirical expressions in the Los Angeles urban and regional context.

Some have claimed that this accumulation of research and writing on Los Angeles signifies the creation of a new "school" of urban and regional studies comparable to the Chicago school of urban ecology that formed in the interwar years and projected Chicago as the prototypical modern industrial metropolis. While I reject the idea of Los Angeles or, for that matter, any other place being singled out as an urban prototype and will not defend the idea of an emergent Los Angeles school, I do argue that the collection of writings focused on the urban restructuring of Los Angeles, more so than the literature on this topic for any other major urban region, has two distinctive qualities. It has been directly stimulated by unusually close contacts between urban researchers and local labor and community-based organizations, and derives its most important insights from the theoretical and practical application of a critical spatial perspective.

Following this background discussion is a comprehensive history of labor and community movements in Los Angeles from the time of the Watts Riots in 1965 through the Justice Riots of 1992 to the disruptive events of September 11, 2001. Four arguments shape the discussion:

1. The recent resurgence of labor–community coalition building in Los Angeles represents a local response to the especially intensive

and polarizing effects of globalization and economic restructuring in the Los Angeles metropolitan region.

2. The uprising and riots of 1992 marked a turning point for labor and the working poor in Los Angeles, stimulating a growing recognition that government was unlikely to respond effectively and that new methods and strategies were needed in the struggles for greater social and economic justice.

3. Distinguishing these movements from their counterparts in other metropolitan regions is their heightened awareness of the politics of space and the potential strategic importance of seeking spatial justice and democratic rights to the city.

4. The relatively higher spatial consciousness of the local movements and the emergence of specifically spatial strategies of political activism derive in large part from linkages between activist groups and university students and faculties involved in urban planning and geography.

Setting the Scene: Urban Restructuring and Metropolitan Transformation

All the world's cities have experienced an unusually intense period of economic restructuring and social change in the four decades following the so-called urban crises of the 1960s. In retrospect, the explosions of social unrest that occurred in a large number of the world's major cities in the 1960s, from Paris and Milan to Los Angeles, Detroit, and Mexico City, were a major turning point in the history of the twentieth century. They signaled the end of the long postwar economic boom in most of the advanced industrial countries and, at the same time, were the wellspring for a new era of capitalist development, one in which the need to find more effective ways to arrest decline, stimulate economic recovery, and prevent further social unrest took on a special urgency.

Using Los Angeles as an empirical laboratory, a cluster of scholars mainly in geography and urban planning made the practical and theoretical understanding of these urban restructuring processes their principal research focus. Central to the work of this Los Angeles research cluster, as I will call it, was a critical spatial perspective as well as a particular sensitivity to the synergies arising from the connections between theory and practice. Understanding the dynamics behind the restructuring of the modern metropolis became the foundation for a mutually stimulating relationship between university researchers and the grassroots labor and community organizations that were growing rapidly during this period.

An extensive bibliography for this research cluster is presented in Notes and References, and a detailed history of these university–community connections is discussed in the second half of this chapter. Here the writings are used to outline a general picture of the restructuring of the modern metropolis, followed by a more focused look at the particularities of the Los Angeles experience.

Deindustrialization and Reindustrialization

During the early years of post-1960s economic restructuring, what was most evident was a process of deindustrialization, provoking the first observers to declare the coming of what was described as postindustrial society. This characterization reflected the steep decline in the unionized manufacturing sector of the national economy through massive job losses and factory closures, and the concurrently rapid growth of services or tertiary sector employment, much of which paid low wages and provided many fewer benefits. Hardest hit by this early deindustrialization process was the vast American manufacturing belt, stretching from St. Louis and Chicago east to Detroit, Cleveland, Pittsburgh, and on to New York City, Philadelphia, and Boston. Similar "role reversals of regions," where once-leading manufacturing areas saw significant decline, occurred in northeast England, the Ruhr region of Germany, and in many other established industrial centers of Western Europe.

While many industrial blue-collar communities across North America were devastated and the power of the national labor movement was significantly weakened, many argued that these destructive effects were the inevitable growth pains of an emerging new postindustrial society in which the services sector and consumer demand, sustained by what came to be called supply-side economics, would be the driving forces for economic recovery and expansion. Here again there was talk of a temporary phase of "creative destruction," just as took place in response to the onset of the Great Depression forty years earlier.

As subsequent developments have shown, the postindustrial thesis not only oversimplified what was happening during the period from the 1960s to the mid-1980s, it also deflected attention away from understanding the core processes that were shaping what today is generally described as the New Economy. Accompanying deindustrialization and relatively unseen in these earlier years was a process of *reindustrialization* that was reshaping the very nature of industrial production and the relations between labor and corporate management.

Far from disappearing, industrialization in its new information-intensive, flexibly organized, and spatially reconfigured form, backed by a burgeoning producer services sector, continued to be the main driving force of urban, regional, and national development. From the standpoint of the present, we can say that the industrial era was not ending but was being profoundly restructured into something significantly different from what it once was.

Crisis-Generated Restructuring

The concatenation of crises that ended the long postwar boom in the United States and elsewhere in the industrialized world revolved around what has come to be called a crisis of Fordism, the general term used to describe the system of mass production, mass consumption, and highly regulated relations between labor, management, and government that led the postwar economic expansion. The Fordist economy, in the United States at least, was fueled and consolidated by a tacit social contract between big government deeply involved in economic expansion, big capital led by the manufacturers of automobiles and related products, and big labor organized around powerful national unions and collective bargaining agreements that traded control over labor militancy for rising wages and benefits for workers. In the thirty years following the end of World War II, the American middle class became larger than it ever was, and in a closely related development, the country experienced a mass suburbanization process that complemented and sustained the booming Fordist economy.

The crisis of Fordism in the 1960s and the restructuring process that followed involved both a breaking down, a kind of selective deconstruction, of the old national economy, and a significant economic reconfiguration that developed a number of descriptive names to highlight its differences from the preceding regime. Perhaps the most innocuous was post-Fordism, but at least this term was indicative of something quite different than postindustrialism. More powerful and influential as a descriptive term for the New Economy, however, was *global* or *globalized,* reflecting intensified transnational movements of capital investment, labor, and production processes.

Globalization, especially in terms of command and control over the transnational flows of money, credit, and investment, became a catchword to explain virtually everything that was happening in the last decades of the twentieth century. In terms of urban and regional change, globalization was undoubtedly a forceful process, creating the most culturally and economically heterogeneous cities the world has ever known, while at the same time spurring the formation of a new hierarchy of what were called world cities (Friedmann and Wolff 1982) or global cities (Sassen 1991).

Also driving economic restructuring and shaping the emergent New Economy was a revolution in information, communications, and manufacturing technologies. New technologies facilitated the globalization of capital, labor, and culture, the concentration of financial power in global cities, and a radical shift away from the traditional heavy industry of Fordism to the production, exchange, and consumption of information. The information technology, or IT, revolution was also interpreted by such spatially aware scholars as Manuel Castells (1996, 1997, 1998) as leading to the formation of a new informational mode of development, informational cities, and the network society.

The New Economy was also described as "flexible" to reflect the specialized production processes, corporate organizational structures, and labor–management relations that were emerging in an attempt to avoid the rigidities of Fordism. With the assistance of computers and robotics, the production of goods and services was made more responsive to changing consumer demands, as well as to changing fashions and fads, than was the case in Fordist assembly-line mass production. Flexibility also facilitated corporate restructuring both as a tool for increasing productivity and profits and for greater control over labor.

Restructuring did not happen all at once, nor was it the result of some conscious steering by corporate or government leaders. It also was not immediately successful. For almost two decades after the turning-point year of 1973, national economies were in a perplexing flux and so too were the leading theoretical and political interpretations of what was happening. By the early 1990s, however, a key time for the story of the resurgent labor movement in Los Angeles, the post-Fordist, global, flexible, and information-intensive New Economy had become sufficiently consolidated to at least create some common agreement on its key features. Rather than elaborating further on these general interpretations, I will focus on one key argument, that the *restructuring process has built into it a powerful tendency toward increasing economic inequality and social polarization.* In other words, globalization, the formation of the New Economy, and the IT revolution have been inherently conducive to the intensification of social and spatial injustices.

The Widening Divide between Rich and Poor

In 1970, the income distribution in the United States had become more equitable than at any other time since the pre-Depression years, at least when measured by the size of the middle class and the disparity between the richest and poorest segments of the populations. The so-called social contract, the American variant of the thriving welfare states of Europe, had succeeded in spreading the growing wealth to very large segments (disproportionately white) of the working class. Nowhere was this more evident than in the thriving blue-collar suburbs that surrounded most large cities. The United States had become a predominantly suburban nation with an income distribution that bulged out in the middle more than ever before, and probably also more so than in any other country.

Between 1973 and the crash of 2008, major changes took place in the income distribution and in the nature of economic inequality and injustice in the United States. The most dramatic and troubling of these changes can be seen in two kinds of statistical measures, one that compares the relative incomes of the rich and the poor and the other charting the changing median family income. Starting off slowly but accelerating over the past twenty years has been an enormous concentration of wealth in the richest 1 percent of the population and even more in the top 0.01 percent. By 2000, this tiniest one hundredth of 1 percent of the U.S. population, approximately thirteen thousand families, earned almost as much income as the twenty million poorest households and three hundred times that of the average family (as against seventy times the average in 1970) (Krugman 2002, 2008).

While the incomes of the "fortunate fifth" (the upper quintile) of the population have been growing rapidly, the incomes of the less fortunate, lowest quintile actually declined between 1970 and the economic crash of 2008. In 2001, the poorest fifth of the population controlled only 3.5 percent of the aggregate national income, the lowest share ever. At the same time, the richest fifth controlled slightly more than half the total income, and the top 5 percent held nearly a quarter on their own, both record highs. There is also abundant evidence to suggest that these statistics, if anything, worsened during the Bush-Cheney regime, as subsidizing the rich through tax breaks and other means reached unprecedented levels. The latest data I have seen, for example, show that the proportion of total national income held by the richest 1 percent reached record levels in 2005 (21.2 percent), as did in reverse the proportion held by the bottom 50 percent (12.8 percent).

Although statistics can be manipulated to reduce the apparent magnitude of these changes, there can be no doubt that since 1970 the rich have become richer at a rate that probably surpassed that of any other comparable period in the twentieth century, while the poor have become significantly poorer in both relative and absolute terms. Today, the poverty rate and income gap in the United States are the highest among the advanced industrial countries and are accompanied by persistently high rates of infant mortality and adult illiteracy, and lower life expectancy than in many less developed countries, especially for men. According to all available evidence, this pronounced income polarization in the United States reaches its peak intensity in New York City and Los Angeles, the bicoastal pillars of the New Economy.

In the midst of this polarization, the middle-class bulge of the postwar era has been significantly squeezed. Over the past thirty years, median family income has risen by not much more than 10 percent, but almost all of this gain has come from increased working hours (now reputedly the highest in the Western world) and from increasing numbers of women, especially with children, entering the labor market, at least part-time. Indeed, if it were not for the longer workday and the huge increase in women working, the average income of the middle quintile of households would probably have dropped between 1970 and today. However the relative distribution is measured, the well-off middle class, especially those with job security, substantial health and other benefits, and suburban lifestyles, has been reduced significantly in numbers, with a trickle moving up the income ladder but many more sliding down into or close to poverty levels.

The issue of rising inequality in the United States has become hotly debated and deeply politicized. Many conservative and some liberal thinkers have rationalized inequality as a positive force for—or at least an inevitable by-product of—successful capitalist development, especially during a period of rapid economic change. Others recognize rising inequalities as a problem but explain it as (1) an unavoidable by-product of globalization and the relocation of jobs to areas of cheaper labor; (2) an effect of skill-based technological change, with the benefits of innovation going to the most highly educated and appropriately skilled; or (3) an enormous increase in income for successful CEOs and entertainment and sports celebrities in what some call a new casino or tournament economy. Much of popular opinion and some academic writings simply attribute the widening gap and increasing poverty statistics to the accelerated immigration of poor and uneducated people from Third World countries, feeding the extremist ideas that the rising income inequalities would disappear if immigration were stopped or the poor returned to their original homelands.

None of these arguments presents adequate explanations for the rising economic polarization and the squeeze on the middle class. What we do know is that when globalization, economic restructuring, and the impact of new technologies are allowed to expand without significant national control and constraint—the central objective of what has come to be called neoliberalism—tendencies to increasing disparities between rich and poor are intensified. This becomes especially evident when the United States is compared to the still-robust welfare states of continental Europe (the UK is much closer to the U.S. case).

Another way of expressing the particularity of the U.S. experience is to describe the problem in terms of the breakup (or breakdown) of the social contract that was the foundation for much of U.S. postwar economic expansion. The problem of rising inequalities (and the seeds of the economic crash of 2008) can be connected here with the neoliberal ideology of deregulation, privatization, and promoting the intrinsic values of small government versus big government; the reorganization of the welfare system and efforts to dismantle the legislative framework of the New Deal; the reassertion of trickle-down notions to rationalize growing tax breaks for the rich; the increasing acceptance if not encouragement of corporate greed; and the massive decline in industrial unionism.

Associated with rising inequality and urban poverty over the past thirty years and the attack on industrial unions has been a major change in the U.S. labor movement, one that has special relevance to more recent developments in Los Angeles. Developing at different rates in different parts of the country have been two major responses to the decline in industrial unionism. One has been the rise of what some call social movement unionism, an expansion in the scope of union struggles to involve other major social forces linked to gender, race, ethnicity, and, more recently, immigrants' rights, the environment, and sexual preferences. The second has involved an increasing localization of the labor movement, with increasing ties to and coalition building with a wide variety of community-based organizations focused on the particular conditions of local urban and regional contexts. Accompanying these changes in the scope of union activities has been a shift away from narrowly defined equity-oriented and wage-related struggles at the workplace to a broader politics focused more on such concepts as local democracy, community development, and *justice* in its growing multiplicity of forms.

The key point being made here is that the new labor movement and the expanding focus on justice are closely related to urban restructuring and the changing income distribution that have been driven by unconstrained globalization and the formation of the New Economy. Also important to recognize, the income disparities between the rich and the poor, along with the squeeze on the middle class and blue-collar workers, differ in their intensity from country to country, and in the United States from one city or region to another. Putting these two arguments together, we turn next to the particular context of Los Angeles and an attempt to explain why Los Angeles rather than New York, Chicago, or San Francisco has become the most innovative center of the new labor movement and for labor–community coalition building.

Transforming Los Angeles

The changes that have taken place in Los Angeles since the Watts Riots of 1965 have been as extensive and far-reaching as in any other modern metropolis. Between 1970 and the present, the total population of the five-county Greater Los Angeles area grew from about eleven to more than seventeen million, one of very few metropolitan regions in the advanced industrial world to have experienced such substantial growth. Even more dramatic has been the changing ethnic, racial, and religious composition of the population. In 1965, the year of the Watts Riots, the population was overwhelmingly (more than 80 percent) "Anglo" or non-Hispanic white, and decidedly more Protestant than that of any other large U.S. city. African Americans were the largest minority and were highly concentrated in an area to the south and west of the downtown, what would come to be known first under the collective name of Watts and later as South Central. Today, Los Angeles is one of the most culturally heterogeneous urban regions in the world, with the Anglo population now less than 40 percent in L.A. county and Asian Pacific Islanders outnumbering African Americans. It is also reputed to contain one of the world's largest Catholic archdioceses.

The new majority population is defined as Latino, a term that developed early on in Los Angeles to represent a new form of transhemispheric cultural and political identity. Although Latinos include Portuguese and English speakers and others from Latin American and Caribbean countries, Spanish predominates and has once again become the everyday language of Los Angeles, as it was more than 150 years earlier. Mexicans and Mexican Americans (Chicana/os) are by far the largest group in this Latino metropolis, but there are also significant numbers of residents from El Salvador, Nicaragua, Guatemala, and almost every other Spanish-speaking country in the Western Hemisphere. Asian and Pacific Islanders, especially those from Korea, Vietnam, the Philippines, Thailand, Samoa, and Taiwan, as well as people from Iran, Armenia, and the Indian subcontinent, also form major population clusters.

Thirty years ago, the clear division between black and white populations made Los Angeles one of the most segregated cities in the country, according to widely used statistical measures. Today, the ethnic geography has become much more complex. New and old barrios, especially in East Los Angeles and a large wedge of municipalities southeast of downtown, are more than 90 percent Latino, and many new ethnic enclaves have formed, such as Koreatown, Little Saigon, and Thai Town. But there have also emerged large zones of extraordinary cultural heterogeneity, with some municipalities such as Carson and Gardena having nearly equal percentages of black, white, Latino, and Asian populations

(Soja 2000). This complexity has made it difficult to say whether residential segregation has been increasing or decreasing over the past three decades. What is much clearer is that the urban labor force is now among the most heterogeneous in the world.

Accompanying these demographic and cultural changes has been an equally dramatic shift in the geographical distribution of the population and in the relations between city and suburb. Once the model of the low-density sprawling suburban metropolis, not inaccurately described in the 1960s as "sixty suburbs in search of a city," Los Angeles has become the densest urbanized region in the United States, having passed metropolitan New York in 1990. This stunning reversal deserves some further comment, for it challenges nearly all public and academic images of Los Angeles and is a key feature of what can be called the region's new labor geography.

Like many other metropolitan regions in the United States, the central core, or inner city, of Los Angeles experienced a significant loss of population after the urban uprisings of the 1960s, as large numbers of Anglo and black workers moved in waves into the inner and outer suburban rings and beyond. This was not a simple process of sprawling suburban growth, for in certain metropolitan regions such as Los Angeles, Washington, D.C., and the Bay Area, it took on the features of what some have called the "urbanization of suburbia." At least three large "outer cities," with high concentrations of residents, offices, industrial parks, jobs, entertainment centers, shopping malls, as well as museums, crime, drug problems, and other activities once considered distinctively urban, have emerged in what was once seen as classical American suburbia.

The largest and perhaps also the oldest of these new kinds of cities, or urbanized suburbs, is located in Orange County, a prototype for many local studies of urban and regional restructuring. Lacking a clearly identifiable urban core or traditional downtown, but no longer simply a stretch of traditional commuting suburbs, the Orange County metropolis is comprised of a clustering of municipalities that has been described as a postsuburban county-city, with more than 2.5 million residents and no city containing more than 400,000 people. The only exception today may be Santa Ana, the county seat and largest municipality, and reputedly the largest predominantly Latino city in the United States. Indicative of the county's urban status, there are probably now more jobs than bedrooms in many municipalities, and more commuters flow from Los Angeles County across the border into Orange than in the reverse direction.

A second outer city now exists in the San Fernando Valley and nearby areas of Los Angeles and Ventura counties, and another in what is called the Inland Empire, including part of San Bernardino and Riverside counties, consistently ranked among the fastest-growing counties in the United States for the past four decades. Vast areas of traditional suburbia still remain, but even they are no longer what they used to be and cannot be understood and studied as if they were. In a sense, the entire metropolitan region is being densely urbanized as a new regional urbanization process is replacing suburbanization as the prevailing form of urban expansion.

Decentralization from the old inner city and the partial urbanization of suburbia were more than matched, however, by a recentralization of extraordinary proportions. More than five million immigrants have poured into the region over the past forty years, the vast majority concentrating in a ring around the downtown Central City. In this collar of diverse immigrant populations, densities are now at levels comparable to Manhattan. Indeed, the hundred densest census tracts in Los Angeles are now more densely populated than the hundred densest in New York, or, for that matter any other urbanized area in the United States. Also notable is that these densities have arisen without significant expansion in the housing stock, creating a degree of residential overcrowding as well as homelessness that is almost surely unmatched in any other large U.S. city.

This remarkable refilling of the Los Angeles urban core has resulted in an unusually large geographical concentration or agglomeration of the working poor, a term that has arisen to distinguish workers, many with multiple jobs, who remain at or below poverty levels, from those (domestic and immigrant) without jobs and almost entirely dependent on welfare. Some estimates show that the percentage of the total population of Los Angeles County that can be classified as working poor has hovered around 40 percent in recent years. This concentration of the working poor, a vital feature of the new labor geography, has emerged as the product of a larger-scale transformation of the urban and regional political economy.

The economic restructuring of Los Angeles can be described as a complex combination of deindustrialization and reindustrialization, terms that are similar and related to the combination of geographical decentralization and recentralization just discussed as part of the regional urbanization process. Although it was not well known, Los Angeles in 1970 was already the leading industrial metropolis in the country, measured in terms of the numbers of people employed in manufacturing. More than any other metropolis outside the American manufacturing belt in the Northeast, it typified Fordist industrialization, with concentrations of factories mass-producing automobiles, tires, glass, steel, and related transportation machinery, including aircraft, mainly located in a large industrial zone between downtown Los Angeles and the growing twin ports of Los Angeles–Long Beach.

The deindustrialization of Los Angeles took place in two main phases. The first, peaking between 1978 and 1982, resulted in the loss of 75,000 to 100,000 manufacturing jobs, emptying Los Angeles almost entirely of its automobile assembly and related tire, glass, and steel industries, where unionization rates and wages were relatively high. The job losses and factory closures were particularly devastating in residential communities such as South Gate, once a nationally well-known magnet for (white) workers seeking the American suburban dream. This triggered an unusually rapid urban residential transformation, as the primarily southern white working class abandoned most of the cluster of municipalities southeast of downtown, with Anglo populations greater than 80 percent, to be rapidly replaced in less than two decades by a new population that in some cases is today more than 95 percent Latino.

The African American population, although close by the main nucleus of Fordist manufacturing jobs, never benefited greatly from this proximity, as they were separated by one of the most formidable racial divides in any U.S. city, located along Alameda Avenue and locally described as the Cotton Curtain. This first phase of deindustrialization did have the effect of eradicating this racial divide and setting in motion a westward drift of the main African American concentrations in Los Angeles toward Los Angeles International Airport (LAX) and what was then a major area for the aerospace, missile, and electronics industry. Many African Americans settled in Inglewood, which would become the battleground for local struggles against Wal-Mart in the early 2000s (see chapter 6).

Significant numbers of African Americans also began moving out of South Central to the growing outer cities of the San Fernando Valley and the Inland Empire, as well as back to the southern states from which their families originated, mainly Texas and Louisiana. Overall, however, the economic conditions in predominantly black Los Angeles did not improve, and in many areas significantly worsened, from what they were in 1965, the time of the Watts rebellion against poverty, racism, and police brutality.

The second phase of deindustrialization occurred in the late 1980s and early 1990s, a time of national recession. The greatest job losses here were concentrated in the aerospace industry, which had been the leading sector in the continuous expansion of manufacturing employment in Los Angeles since before World War II. Aircraft manufacturing had expanded rapidly, along with related weapons and electronics production, after 1970, especially through billions of dollars worth of defense contracts from the federal government. Rather than reflecting a decline of Fordist industry, as did the first phase of deindustrialization, the second round of job losses, with some estimates as high as 300,000, signaled the beginnings of what might be described as a crisis of post-Fordism, a breakdown in the globalized New Economy of flexible capitalism in the place, Los Angeles, where it had achieved one of its most notable successes.

Here we arrive at a significant turning point in the transformations of Los Angeles in the forty-year period since 1965, the shift from a long period of crisis-generated restructuring to a time of multiplying restructuring-generated crises, marked by increasing expressions of social unrest and economic frustration arising from the problems associated with the uneven effects of globalization, the restructured post-Fordist economy, and the IT revolution. In 1992, the new Los Angeles exploded in one of the most destructive urban uprisings in U.S. history. While there were earlier stirrings, the Justice Riots of 1992, as many now call these events, became a crucial moment in redefining not just the local but the national labor movement and the connections that would develop between labor, community, and other organizations.

Before moving on to discuss these developments, a few words need to be added concerning the extraordinary agglomeration of the working poor in the inner city of Los Angeles, for it is here where the most important of the new movements were generated and empowered. The coalitions that emerged in the 1990s have focused in particular on the rights of the immigrant working poor not just in the workplace, the traditional sphere of labor organizing, but also at the place of residence and more widely in the larger urban and regional context. Not only has this focus markedly increased union membership, it has expanded the social and spatial scope of the labor movement in innovative ways.

The core agglomeration of the working poor in Los Angeles has become a generative force in linking unions to various urban social movements, ethnic and community-based organizations, and struggles that extend well beyond the place of work and the specific place of residence to the larger regional economy and geography. In this sense, it provokes comparison to Manchester, the iconic industrial capitalist city, in the second half of the nineteenth century, when its huge agglomeration of workers generated innovative developments in the British labor movement. It can be argued that something similar has been happening in the core agglomeration of workers in Los Angeles today, through the innovative struggles for worker justice and more specifically for spatial justice and the right to the city.

A History of Social Activism in Los Angeles

The labor movement and coalition building between unions, community-based organizations, and the university have developed over the past forty years through a series of phases punctuated by three violent and destructive explosions of urban unrest: the Watts Riots of 1965, the Justice Riots of 1992, and the attacks on the World Trade Center in New York City on September 11, 2001. Each of these events marks a moment of crisis, transition, and redevelopment in the history of social activism in Los Angeles.

Labor and community organizing in the postwar era in most large North American cities developed along many different pathways. Always present were traditional labor union struggles over workers' rights and conditions at the workplace. In the decades of expansive Fordism that followed World War II, workplace and wage negotiations usually involved basic agreements between powerful national unions, large corporate interests, and supportive government agencies. Alliances with political parties in the American version of the welfare state were of crucial importance in maintaining this mode of Fordist industrial unionism. As union power became increasingly challenged under the impact of economic restructuring and unsupportive federal governments, the labor movement branched out in new directions. The earliest and perhaps most widespread strategy was to make strategic connections to the workers' place of residence in what came to be called community unionism. Community-based organizations focused for the most part on local issues such as housing and basic public services. Union ties expanded their scope and to some extent modified their tactics. Links to the community had a localizing effect on unions and the labor movement, bringing about a greater awareness of the importance of location and embedding labor activism more deeply in the urban geographical context.

Labor–community coalitions expanded in many other directions, linking up with the social movement politics developing during this period, especially around struggles for civil rights. These links reduced the dependency of unions on party politics and forged greater ties to local communities and to wider networks of urban social activism. To varying degrees, labor–community coalitions linked up with the environmental justice movement, the women's movement, and efforts to fight against racial and ethnocultural discrimination.

Particularly important in Los Angeles, with its unusually large concentration of often-undocumented immigrant working poor, was the issue of immigrants' rights. There were major tensions in this connection since immigrant workers tended to be seen by many labor organizers as a tool used by employers to discipline, if not displace, unionized employees, especially when the immigrants were undocumented and more vulnerable to such abuse. Immigrants, by their very nature, were also seen as almost inherently difficult to organize. If there were to be serious alliances between unions and local communities, however, the organization of immigrant workers was essential.

Building on the innovative community-linked unionism of the United Farm Workers, organizing immigrant workers became the fulcrum around which labor–community coalition building took place in Los Angeles. It brought with it closer ties to local communities, attracted academic activists and researchers into the coalitions, and led to the development of new action strategies involving a wider range of objectives, from housing and public health to quality education and renters' rights. Workplace conditions also became central, as sweatshops multiplied in both growing industries, such as apparel, and those that were declining, such as automobile parts production.

The explosive events of spring 1992 brought these streams of activism together to produce some of the most innovative and successful grassroots urban and regional social movements in the United States. The story of these developments is presented in three time periods: 1965–79, 1979–92, and 1992–2001.

The Birth of Community Unionism, 1965–79

By 1965, the labor movement in Los Angeles was divided into three distinct and largely ethno-racial streams. By far the largest and most prominent was based on localized extensions of national industrial labor unions. This leading edge of the regional labor movement was overwhelmingly white or Anglo, and unusually content with its economic position at the crest of the postwar boom. From the 1940s to the 1970s, the metropolitan region of Los Angeles led all others in the net addition of manufacturing employment, and this industrial boom combined with national organizing efforts by industrial unions helped to create what many considered to be the most prosperous and attractive blue-collar urban and suburban communities in the country. Cities such as South Gate and Lakewood were not just western extensions of Fordist or mass-produced Levittowns, they were the epitome of the blue-collar American Dream, attracting families from all over the United States to their palm tree–lined streets, green gardens, efficient freeway system, superb climate, and expansive economy. Perhaps more than any other metropolitan area, Southern California represented the peak achievements of the postwar social contract between big government, big business, and big labor for the white working class.

A second and much smaller stream of labor activism focused on African American workers. They too shared some of the benefits of the postwar industrial boom but were much less connected to and dependent on national labor unions. The prevailing trends of industrial unionism in the United States focused on organizing at the workplace and directly around work-related issues to bargain collectively for expanding real incomes for union members. Black workers, to the extent they were accepted into the large unions, benefited somewhat from these efforts, but had little autonomous power in bargaining with corporate management. This led to a different organizing focus, still rooted in unions but aimed at federal, state, and local government, the courts, and the promotion of race-based civil rights, especially after the passing of the Civil Rights Act of 1964.

The African American population had grown rapidly just before and after the war, with the majority of migrants coming from Texas and the states of the lower Mississippi Delta, the poorest region in the United States since at least the mid-nineteenth century. Two job sectors became the major focus of the black labor movement: local government and the aerospace and related defense industries. In these sectors, continued racist practices in hiring and union recruitment (as well as in housing) were blunted both by federal government legislation and the effects of local community organizations empowered by the early civil rights movement.

In some ways, Los Angeles also epitomized the peak achievements of African American workers in the United States, with a small but growing middle class living in low-density suburban housing areas even in the heart of the so-called ghetto. But the separation and economic polarization of the white and black working class in Los Angeles also reached unusually high levels. Housing segregation and related indicators of school segregation were worse than in any other major metropolitan area. A 1963 lawsuit by the American Civil Liberties Union, for example, focused attention on two high schools located 1.5 miles from each other, one (South Gate) all white and the other (Jordan) all black. These efforts helped to generate vigorous countywide school desegregation and busing programs but also heightened interracial tensions and further divided the labor movement.

A third stream in the local labor movement as it existed in 1965 was Latino and based primarily on the organizational efforts and strategies of the United Farm Workers (UFW) throughout California. The UFW was headquartered in Southern California and helped to define a distinctive form of union activism that would significantly shape the local (and national) labor movement over the next forty years. While the

African American labor movement was absorbed into the civil rights movement and white union workers remained relatively content with their conditions, the emerging Latino/a and Chicano/a labor movement was beginning to open new and innovative strategies of labor organizing with respect to immigrants' rights, linkages with community issues such as housing and education, and the empowerment of women of color.

It was this third stream that was most responsible for the birth of what labor historians call community-based unionism. The ideas and strategies advanced by the UFW, such as the boycott, the fast, clergy–labor partnerships, and door-to-door voter outreach, strongly influenced some national unions, such as the UAW, and stimulated a rethinking of organizational strategies that recognized the need to go beyond immediate workplace issues to address wider community interests. Ever since, the ties between local unions and community-based organizations have been especially intense and productive in Los Angeles. Community-based unionism also opened up new possibilities for university-based activism, as the strict boundaries of union membership became more porous.

The Watts Riots

In 1965, Watts, the symbolic heart of black Los Angeles, exploded. In the following year, the Latino barrio in East Los Angeles became unsettled through a series of protests over school segregation and educational quality, and then in 1970, in what came to be called the Chicano Moratorium, 30,000 antiwar demonstrators took to the streets in the largest Latino protest movement in the United States up to that time. It seemed to many that the Los Angeles economy was in deep crisis. What followed, however, was not an amelioration of the problems of racism, poverty, and segregation but an even greater intensification. Significant in these developments were another event that occurred in 1965, the passage of the Immigration Reform Act, and the beginnings of rapid expansion of Asian and Latino migration to Southern California.

The Anglo labor movement continued to prosper in the post-Watts period. The Los Angeles County Federation of Labor, then as today a powerful force in local government and politics, reached its early peak membership of 300,000 in 1970, when the regional economy was still expanding at a fever pitch. In the 1970s, when much of the rest of the United States was experiencing huge job losses and the early phases of deindustrialization, the Los Angeles region added 1,315,000 new jobs, more than the net regional population growth of around 1,300,000. During the same period, while the New York regional economy lost about 300,000 manufacturing jobs, Los Angeles added nearly a quarter of a million. Economic conditions changed significantly at the end of the decade, but for most of the post-Watts period, the Anglo labor movement remained tranquil about workplace issues. For the nonwhite minorities, however, organizing around the place of residence and community issues began to occupy social activism and local politics.

For the most part, the Anglo and black working-class populations became even more polarized after Watts. This division was most visibly manifested around the issue of school busing programs, initiated as a last-ditch effort to deal with some of the highest levels of housing and school segregation in urban America. Although some achievements were made, the Los Angeles County school district remained the most segregated in the country. In 1970, long after the *Brown v. Board of Education* decision, more than 25 percent of Mississippi schoolchildren and 45 percent of those in South Carolina had integrated, while the figure for Los Angeles was 6 percent.

Part of this slow pace of desegregation was caused by white families withdrawing their children from the public school system in reaction to busing and related programs. Another factor was the physical migration of the white working class from its high concentration in southeast Los Angeles County into more predominantly white areas of the county as well as to other counties. This initiated what became, with the full impact of deindustrialization, one of the most pronounced examples in metropolitan America of what has been called racially motivated "white flight."

With some irony, these residential strategies of the white middle and working class contributed to a resurgence of interest in locality and to a much wider and more dramatic change in what might be called the geographical consciousness of the Los Angeles population. Los Angeles as a sprawling metropolis had been popularly described as sixty suburbs searching for a city. Within the more academic literature, it epitomized the "non-place urban realm," where propinquitous community or neighborhood identity was almost entirely absent (Webber 1964). What began to happen after 1965, although not necessarily caused entirely by the

Watts Riots, was a dramatic reversal of these trends, marked by a growing sensitivity to place of residence, location within the larger urban fab-
ric, and the importance of local community. With the labor movement
playing a minor role, Los Angeles began to become an important center
for what can be called the community development movement.

Community Development Corporations (CDCs)

Grassroots organizing in low-income neighborhoods, primarily black or
Latino, expanded rapidly after 1965, especially through the formation
of community development corporations (CDCs). CDCs concentrated
on localized issues of housing, education, job training, and social services provision. Although some CDCs expanded their efforts beyond their
core neighborhood, there was relatively little interorganizational connection or networking. Regional or even countywide coalition building
was virtually nonexistent, but many of the most successful community-
based organizations developed spheres of influence that extended beyond
their immediate local boundaries.

The first of the major CDCs to emerge after the riots was the Watts
Labor Community Action Center (WLCAC). The inclusion of "labor
action" in the title reflected the fact that among the founding group of
activists were fourteen union members with organizing experience in
the civil rights movement. Early ties were also established with the UCLA
Institute of Industrial Relations and later with the Urban Planning program, making the WLCAC one of the earliest major labor–community–
university coalitions in the region. Although it began operating before
the riots, the organization grew as perhaps the most important and
effective agency assisting in the redevelopment of the area most heavily impacted by the massive destruction that was caused in the heart of
black Los Angeles.

Although called Watts, the name of an area that was part of the
City of Los Angeles, the "Watts Community" also included areas closer
to downtown, parts of L.A. County such as Willowbrook, and the independent municipality of Compton. Other predominantly black areas
located elsewhere in the county were also, at least implicitly, included,
and some ties were also created with the local Latino community. Indicative of this expanding scope was the creation in 1969 of the Greater Watts
Development Corporation and the initiation of major new campaigns

for community economic development. One of the earliest of these campaigns involved the creation of a coalition of eighty organizations to promote the construction of the Martin Luther King/Drew Medical Center, what today would be called a "flagship project" for the Greater Watts area. Such efforts at local economic development were the main focus throughout this period.

As early as 1966, the WLCAC joined with the United Farm Workers to deal with the growing problems of immigrant workers and to encourage the formation of more "community unions." The best known of these community unions and today probably the largest in terms of monetary involvement is The East Los Angeles Community Union (TELACU), founded in 1968 in the heart of the Mexican American barrio of unincorporated East Los Angeles. TELACU took local economic development very seriously. It started, as others did, as a social services agency (in cooperation with a local of the UAW) but became a pioneer of public–private partnerships and the attraction of venture capital for industrial development and job generation (Chavez 1998). TELACU was never a major actor in the Chicano movement in Los Angeles, and although "Community Union" remained in the title, it was quite innovatively a community development corporation.

Another major Latino CDC, CHARO Community Development Corporation, was founded in 1967 and is today one of the largest Latino nonprofits in the country. Additional community service centers, later CDCs, were created to serve the growing Asian population. The Korean Youth Center was established in 1975, incorporated in 1982, added "Community" to its name in 1992 (KYCC) as well as created an Alliance for Neighborhood Economic Development Unit, and recently was renamed the Koreatown Youth and Community Center. Also developing later in the Korean community was KIWA, the Korean Immigrant Workers Association. KIWA became one of the most active networking community-based organizations in the region. In 1979, the last of the major community organizations that were founded in this period, the Little Tokyo Service Center, was created and became a full CDC in 1993.

Quietly in the background during these developments, at least with respect to the strategies of labor unions, were two other local social movements that would also foster greater attention to locality and geography, the renters' or tenants' rights movement and the environmental justice movement. These two movements encouraged increased sensitivity to locality and neighborhood community and played important roles in the emergence of new and expanded labor–community coalitions in the 1980s. As both had particularly close connections with UCLA Urban Planning, they are discussed in more detail in chapter 5.

The Beginnings of Justice-Based Coalitions: 1979–92

The Los Angeles economy began to feel the full brunt of the deindustrialization of America in the early 1980s, following a decade of extraordinary job and population growth. The impact of this deindustrialization, however, was very selective geographically and socially. The worst-hit area in terms of job losses and closed factories was the huge industrial zone stretching south from downtown Los Angeles to the twin ports of Los Angeles–Long Beach, although other communities in the Inland Empire to the east and in the San Fernando Valley were also badly hurt. In terms of the labor market, the most negatively affected groups were skilled unionized workers in the manufacturing sector, including many women and minorities, who together formed the core of the thriving blue-collar middle class.

The Los Angeles economy had always been shaped heavily by the federal government in one way or another, and it continued throughout this period to be fed by billions of dollars of Defense Department and related contracts, especially in the aerospace and missiles sector. Los Angeles had become the world's arsenal, capital of the warfare state, the largest concentration of the so-called military-industrial complex. This special role sustained continued expansion of the regional economy and diverted attention away from the increasing community devastation that was occurring in Fordist Los Angeles. This pathway of "creative destruction" was also paved from Washington, D.C., in this case related to the rise of Reaganomics and its associated emphasis on deregulation, privatization, and increasingly vigorous attacks on unions, welfare legislation, and nearly all major social movements.

What began to emerge in the communities of Los Angeles feeling the full force of the neoliberal package of deindustrialization, globalization, and Reaganomics was a closer and more balanced interrelationship between unions and community organizations and between the labor and community development movements. This revitalized labor–community linkage also formed the core of more expansive coalitions that cut across the boundaries of race, ethnicity, class, and gender and attracted other progressive activists from the universities, religious organizations, groups involved with tenants' rights, environmentalists, the peace movement, and even a few higher-income homeowners associations. It became clear to many that fragmentation of progressive forces into separate movements would not be effective in trying to ameliorate the devastation taking place, nor would the federal government, now dominated by conservative forces, be a reliable source for welfare-based financial assistance.

The Coalition to Stop Plant Closings

One of the best examples of these new coalitions was the very explicitly named Coalition to Stop Plant Closings (CSPC), or, as it was later called, the Los Angeles Coalition Against Plant Shutdowns (LACAPS). The primary aim of the coalition was to organize workers to fight against factory closures that were taking place throughout this period from the late 1970s to the mid-1980s in what was the largest Fordist industrial concentration west of the Mississippi. Before deindustrialization, Los Angeles was the second-largest automobile assembly center after Detroit, the largest tire producer after Akron, Ohio, one of the largest producers of glass for automobiles, and a major center for the production of steel and many different consumer durables, the lead industries of the postwar economic boom and the definitive industries of Fordism in the United States. By the end of this period, all of the automobile and tire factories and most of those producing steel and glass had closed permanently.

Seen from the vantage point of the present, the efforts of the CSPC were almost surely doomed to fail. The forces of globalization and economic restructuring were creating a New Economy all over the world, and this post-Fordist, globalized, more flexible economy and geography was literally "replacing" the old, Fordist, mass production–, mass consumption–based national economy and geography. Driving the formation of the New Economy were footloose forms of capital able to kill two birds with one stone, that is, able to find new sources of profit as well as escape from urban social unrest by seeking places with cheaper labor supplies and less well-organized (i.e., less unionized) labor and community movements. The labor–management relation in the United States was always more unequal than in most of the welfare states of Western Europe. With the deep restructuring of national economies that accelerated after the turnaround year of 1973, the relative power of capital over labor was amplified significantly.

An early expression of the intranational relocation of capital in the United States was the great Frostbelt-to-Sunbelt regional shift in economic and political power, a shift that in itself meant a decided decline in the role of industrial trade unions. At a more local scale, as in Los Angeles and throughout the American manufacturing belt, it was expressed in a rash of factory closures, huge job losses, and the destruction of once-thriving blue-collar communities. In Los Angeles, however, there was also an exceptionally vigorous reindustrialization, unusually intense job generation (although most were low paying), and a massive in-migration that further fed the regional economy with cheap and, at least initially, malleable and nonunionized labor supplies. As with the Frostbelt-Sunbelt shift, this reorganization of the labor geography of Los Angeles was also associated with a steep decline of industrial trade unionism and, for at least the mid- to late 1980s, a significant weakening of even the most powerful service sectors unions, such as the Service Employees International Union (SEIU).

Although the CSPC failed to achieve its principal objectives, the struggle against plant closures was the seedbed for many developments that would significantly shape the future revitalization of the Los Angeles labor and community movements. The most prominent example was the pioneering work of Eric Mann. After moving to Los Angeles in the early 1980s to work at the General Motors plant in Van Nuys, he faced a threatened closure in 1982 and began organizing what became the Van Nuys Labor/Community Coalition. While every other automobile assembly factory in the region closed, the Van Nuys plant stayed open until 1992, an achievement detailed in Mann's book *Taking on General Motors* (1987). A veteran of the civil rights movement and longtime activist for the Congress of Racial Equality (CORE), Mann has continued to contribute significantly to radicalizing and redefining the union movement in the United States. Particularly noteworthy was the cofounding in 1989, with his wife Lian Hurst Mann, of the Labor/Community

Strategy Center, the think tank/act tank that was the major force behind the Bus Riders Union decision in 1996.

Actively participating in the CSPC was the Reverend Richard Gillett, founder of the religion-based organization Clergy and Laity United for Economic Justice, or CLUE. His commitment was crucial in bringing the power of progressive religious organizations into labor–community coalition building, first in the efforts to stop plant closures and community decline and more recently in the development of the living wage campaign and the activities of the Los Angeles Alliance for a New Economy (LAANE), one of the most prominent of contemporary coalitions. Gillett has not just contributed significantly to local struggles for social and economic justice but has also become internationally recognized for his religion-based urban activism (Davey 2002).

Several activists affiliated with Urban Planning at UCLA participated in the CSPC. Gilda Haas, who received her MA in Urban Planning in 1977, has been a major force in connecting the labor and community movements in Los Angeles. Described as an "insurgent planner," Haas began her urban activism with a focus on housing and community development. She was an organizer for the Coalition for Economic Survival and played an important role in the rent control movement in Santa Monica, West Hollywood, and the City of Los Angeles, as well as in the formation of community development corporations specialized in providing affordable housing. After her participation in the CSPC (see Haas 1985), she was cofounder of the South Central Federal Credit Union, a pathbreaking community bank for low-income residents; founder of Communities for Accountable Reinvestment, an organization aimed at fighting redlining and promoting new forms of community economic development; a cofounder and director (1991–99) of the Community Scholars Program in Urban Planning at UCLA; and since 1994 the director of one of the most influential and effective labor–community–popular education organizations in Los Angeles, Strategic Actions for a Just Economy (SAJE). She and SAJE are today spearheading the national organization the Right to the City Alliance.

Also involved in the CSPC were Goetz Wolff, then a doctoral student in Urban Planning, and two professors, Rebecca Morales and myself. Working with the coalition stimulated a number of publications, perhaps the most relevant being Soja, Morales, and Wolff (1983), one of the earliest articles on urban restructuring and spatial change (see also Mahdesian et al. 1981). More on this connection is presented in chapter 5.

What was happening through the 1980s with the CSPC and other coalitions was not just a significant cementing together of labor–community–university linkages and solidarity but also a major shift in strategy and objectives. Whereas at first the struggles were defensive ones against the deindustrialization processes affecting local communities, the emerging new wave of efforts aimed at achieving greater justice and equality for all workers in the New Economy. This generated a more provocative activist agenda in which the concept of and struggle for justice in all its various meanings, but especially with regard to jobs, education, public services, and immigrants' rights, became central.

The failed efforts to stop plant closures clearly demonstrated that traditional forms of labor and community organizing were unlikely to be successful. It was also fairly evident that what was emerging as social movement unionism was not simply a matter of moving from workplace to place of residence as primary sites of mobilization and social action. Coalition building had to be both broadened and more specifically focused, especially with regard to the needs and demands for justice emanating from the extraordinary agglomeration in Los Angeles of five million immigrant working poor. Perhaps more than anything else, the creative synergies coming out of this agglomeration provided the driving force behind the emergence in Los Angeles of not just an innovative local and regional movement but one that would become nationally and internationally recognized.

Justice for Janitors

The leading edge of these new developments was the Justice for Janitors (J4J) movement. Founded in Denver in 1985, J4J began its organizing efforts in Los Angeles in 1988, led by Local 399 of the Service Employees International Union (SEIU) but allied with many other local activist organizations. The SEIU had successfully organized earlier janitors' strikes in Pittsburgh and Denver, but the background conditions in Los Angeles were unusually ripe for a much larger confrontation. Research had shown that janitors in downtown Los Angeles, in comparison to downtowns in other major U.S. cities, were experiencing increasingly lower wages and declining unionization rates. What this probably reflected, at least in part, was the unusually large supply of low-wage, nonunionized, and undemanding workers who were also undocumented and able to survive on subpoverty incomes.

In the early 1980s, janitorial workers in Los Angeles were predominantly African American, unionized, and earning a relatively high wage, over $7 an hour in 1981. By the end of the decade, the vast majority were nonunionized, Latino, and working for far less wages than janitors in New York, Chicago, or San Francisco. The often undocumented immigrant janitorial worker effectively symbolized the New Economy in Los Angeles. Like the expanding army of gardeners, housecleaners, day laborers, and others swelling the ranks of the working poor, the janitors served multiple purposes. They were a vital part of the massive infusion of cheap and manipulable labor into the regional economy, certainly one of the major factors behind the economic expansion and the unusually rapid growth in jobs and office space of the 1980s and 1990s. This enlarged labor pool was used as an effective tool to weaken union power not just in the service sector but in manufacturing as well. Immigrant workers provided an important lubricant for the deep restructuring of the regional economy.

Up to 1990, the prevailing wisdom in the American labor movement was that immigrant workers were almost impossible to organize. They were seen as integral parts of the "informal economy" and beyond the reach of regulatory systems as well as formal union organization. In Los Angeles, however, the immigrant working poor had several distinctive features that made them more open to effective organizing efforts. First was their sheer numbers and, especially, their extraordinary concentration in the core of the metropolitan region. The density of social interaction and the consciousness of their special position in the regional economy were unusually high for the clustered immigrant working poor in the inner city.

Another factor was labor-organizing experience. The community-based unionism of the United Farm Workers was infused throughout the large Mexican immigrant population, as well as among Chicano/a residents. Traditions of militant labor organizing were particularly intense in the Korean community and among the nearly one million immigrants from El Salvador, Nicaragua, and other Central American countries. And in comparison with New York, Chicago, and other large cities outside the southwestern United States, there was also a sense of cultural redemption among the Latino population. Los Angeles was once part of Spanish-speaking Mexican territory and was now becoming predominantly Spanish-speaking again.

Adding further to the successful drive to organize immigrant workers was what might be called media savvy, an awareness of the significant role the mass media play in obtaining public support as well as the knowledge of how best to attract useful media attention. This factor may be difficult to measure, but it can fairly surely be said that Los Angeles is one of the world's mass media centers and that media attention figures as deeply in daily life in Los Angeles as in New York, probably its closest rival. Whatever the comparative situation may be, however, there is no doubt that the Justice for Janitors movement used the media with great effectiveness throughout its existence and perhaps never more so than in the event that most triggered its initial public empowerment, the Century City demonstrations of June 15, 1990.

Century City was built on the property of the movie giant Twentieth Century Fox as one of the earliest and largest edge cities in Los Angeles. The movie lot remains reduced in size but still famously visible from its entranceway on Pico Boulevard. The largest cluster of high-rise buildings outside downtown Los Angeles, occasionally used as a Manhattan setting for films, now marks the new Century City and includes, in addition to the headquarters of the Fox Corporation, theaters, a shopping mall, L.A.'s largest cluster of law offices, and the staid and iconic Century Plaza hotel. In 1967, while President Lyndon Johnson was barricaded inside, one of the largest local antiwar demonstrations took place in front of the hotel and was forcibly and violently put down by the Los Angeles Police Department (LAPD). In 1990, Justice for Janitors brought their struggles to a head at the same site but with very different methods and results.

What occurred in 1990 represented a new mode of labor activism, more like a Situationist happening than a conventional nonviolent sit-in or strike. Four hundred or more janitors with their signature red T-shirts and strike caps danced and sang as they moved carefully along the streets and sidewalks, always aware of the LAPD presence on foot and horseback. The demonstrators also were aware of the location of the media and of the invisible lines of public/private transgression on the streets and sidewalks, at least as far as expected police reaction was concerned. Eventually, lines were crossed, the police reacted, two dozen janitors were injured, and everything was videotaped. The tape would later be used in a lawsuit that resulted in the LAPD being blamed for starting the riot as well as forced the city to pay SEIU Local 399 $3.5 million for damages. The formal victory was a new contract raising wages 25 percent and providing much-needed health benefits, but there was an even larger aftereffect.

The event galvanized community and government support, and despite some later setbacks, spread its impact regionally and to some extent nationally and internationally. The globalization of J4J began in 1990. Janitorial services in Los Angeles and major cities throughout the world were at that time, and today, dominated by a multinational corporation, Integrated Services Solutions (ISS), based in Copenhagen, Denmark. With local landlords able to pass the buck in terms of contract negotiations, the J4J organizers went to the source in Copenhagen to lobby directly against ISS, which today in its present version employs more than 400,000 janitors in fifty countries.

Commemorating the J4J movement, June 15 is now recognized around the world as International Justice Day. Further spreading the word internationally was Ken Loach's award-winning 2000 film *Bread and Roses,* named as a reminder of the 1912 textile strike in Lawrence, Massachusetts, led by women and immigrants and organized by International Workers of the World. Similar J4J strikes began to take place in other large U.S. cities, and a national workers justice movement, extending beyond janitors, gained momentum. More recently, a small movement called Justice for Cleaners, spurred on by experienced California organizers, became active in London's financial district, considered to be the richest and most wealth-generating square mile on earth. But we jump ahead of our timeline.

Coalition Building and the Search for Spatial Justice, 1992 to 9/11/2001

What many now call the Justice Riots of 1992 may have begun with the not-guilty decision of a jury in Simi Valley (with its high density of resident police officers), absolving the policemen responsible for the brutal beating of Rodney King, but the events that unfolded were much more than an expression of frustration in the African American community over police brutality and continuing racial injustices. Although the images conveyed to the rest of the world made it appear as if the implosion of violence that had characterized the Watts Riots of 1965 was simply being repeated, the uprising of 1992 was very different. It was much more multicultural in its participants, more embedded in the New Economy that had emerged in the preceding twenty years, and more global in terms of both its causes and its potential effects.

The immediate political impact of the Justice Riots was double-edged. In some ways, it had a debilitating effect on local progressive politics. For many on the liberal left, the riots were shockingly violent and exposed the incapability of all levels of government to deal with the enormous social and economic problems facing Los Angeles. Traditional urban and party politics seemed more hopeless than ever before, leading many former activists to abandon their political commitments, a choice made all the more attractive given the multitudinous diversions Southern California had to offer to those who could afford them.

For the massive agglomeration of the immigrant working poor that had grown around the core of downtown Los Angeles, there was a similar feeling that government (and public–private partnerships such as the ineffective Rebuild LA program) had not just failed them, but that government would never be able to deliver appropriate solutions to their problems. Rather than leading to hopelessness, however, the resilient working poor and their most persistent supporters increasingly realized that organizing from below, from the grassroots, was now more vitally necessary than ever before. There were similar feelings among the poor throughout urban America, but perhaps nowhere was both the abandonment of hope and confidence in local, state, and federal governments and the awareness of the critical need for grassroots organizing and coalition building as intensely felt as it was in post-1992 Los Angeles.

The failure of government and its institutional extensions through the urban and regional planning processes was made even more blatant in the early 1990s by fiscal crises and one of the deepest economic downturns in the history of what for the previous hundred years had been an almost continuously booming Los Angeles. Rather later than most major U.S. cities, Los Angeles felt the heavy pressures to get lean and mean, to restructure existing welfare systems and public benefits at a time when some would say the need for them was becoming greater than at any time since the Great Depression.

Amid all this, what was certainly a terrible localized explosion of violence and destruction was also one of the earliest major grassroots protests against the injustices associated with globalization and the New Economy. With the multiplication of antiglobalization protests in Seattle, Genoa, and other cities, there emerged a growing justice movement, which spread eventually to a global scale. In Los Angeles, however, the mobilizing metaphor of justice would take on extra meaning. To the majority of the population, there was a failure in the administration of legal justice in the Rodney King trial. Boosted by the Justice for Janitors efforts, the major demonstrations that took place in 1992 reverberated with the wider demands of "No Justice—No Peace," expanding the scope of the uprising beyond the African American community to all of the multicultural and transnational working poor who had suffered most from economic restructuring. Justice as a specific target for mobilization and action, more so than cries for freedom or equality or democracy, seemed to capture the political spirit of the times.

The governmental response, or lack of response, to the riots of 1992 provided an additional boost to the local justice movement. Perhaps more so than in other major cities, there was a realization among the most disadvantaged populations that appeals to government were not likely to be effective and that any effort to achieve social and economic justice would require a mass movement based on innovative new forms of grassroots organizing. Added to this was an acute awareness that these organizing efforts required the creation of new kinds of inclusive regional coalitions or confederations of activist groups that cut across alliances based on class, ethnicity, gender, and geographical location.

Another feature of the resurgence of coalition building in Los Angeles was its unusually productive relationship with the university. Although I focus in chapter 5 on connections with Urban Planning at UCLA, there were many other productive links made in this period with Occidental College and its Urban and Environmental Policy Institute, the University of Southern California, and several units of the California State University system. This produced expanded channels of information flow between the university and labor unions and community groups that benefited both sides, sharpening empirical and theoretical research on Los Angeles through its potential for direct application while at the same time bringing into practice some of the most advanced ideas about housing and community development, urban design, transportation planning, multiculturalism, environmental policy, geographic information systems, spatial theory, and regional political economy.

In the decade after 1992, this two-way flow of ideas was probably as intense and productive as any that had formed in other major metropolitan regions in the United States. Among its many effects was a filtering in to at least some grassroots community and labor organizations of a strategic spatial perspective and an awareness of the latest ideas about urban restructuring, regionalism, and the practical and political relevance of urban and spatial theory. The Justice for Janitors movement had already begun to be examined from a "labor geography" perspective (Savage 1998, 2006), and a strong antiracist spatial perspective derived from radical architectural theory (Dutton and Hurst Mann 1996) was quite independently part of the activities of the Labor/Community Strategy Center and the Bus Riders Union. Examined next are some of the other innovative coalitions that developed between the Justice Riots of 1992 and the explosive events of September 11, 2001.

Organizing for a Living Wage

Building on the earlier successes of the Justice for Janitors campaign and responding to the urgent problems of a riot-torn economy, a reinvigorated union movement sparked the development of new coalitions that cut across lines of class, race, gender, and ethnicity. In what had become one of the most culturally and economically heterogeneous cities in the world, coalition building was necessarily multicultural, multilingual, and powerfully shaped by the huge agglomeration of the immigrant working poor. It is noteworthy but not very surprising under these conditions that a prominent leadership role in the new coalitions was filled by radical women of color.

One of the first major manifestations of the post-1992 efforts was a vigorous campaign for both immigrant rights and more generally for a living wage, an especially vital issue in a high-cost-of-living urban area with unusually high rates of poverty and where minimum-wage laws were either ignored, especially for undocumented workers, or were entirely inadequate to meet household needs. The living wage campaign and coalition in Los Angeles, which would become one of the most successful in the country, was led by three unions: Hotel Employees and Restaurant Employees union (HERE), Service Employees International Union (SEIU), and Union of Needletrades, Industrial and Textile Employees (UNITE). Their organizing efforts, advanced by such influential figures as Maria Elena Durazo and Madeline Janis-Aparicio (now Madeline Janis), focused specifically on certain sectors with especially large numbers of low-wage immigrant workers, such as tourism, office development, home care, restaurants and hotels, and the garment industry.

Assisted by the presence on the city council of the veteran activist Jackie Goldberg, a living wage ordinance was passed for employees of the City of Los Angeles in 1997. Two years later it was extended to county employees, and in 2001 an even stronger ordinance, affecting private businesses of a certain size and location receiving grants from the city, was passed in Santa Monica after a campaign led by HERE local 11, whose director was Durazo, and Santa Monicans Allied for Responsible Tourism (SMART). Backing them were SMART's parent organization, the Los Angeles Alliance for a New Economy (LAANE), directed by Janis-Aparicio, and Clergy and Laity United for Economic Justice (CLUE), led by Richard Gillett.

There are continuing efforts to defend these living wage laws against fierce opposition, but the early victories became central to a national living wage movement that has extended similar campaigns to more than one hundred cities. The countywide success of the living wage coalition also helped sustain an expanding regional and multicultural justice movement for workers and communities that, while not explicitly aimed at spatial justice per se, was strategically informed by a new regional consciousness and awareness of the importance of location and the spatial logic of public and corporate job providers.

Footloose private corporations, for example, were not the target, as they were for the earlier Coalition to Stop Plant Closings. Targeted first was the one large source of employment that was less footloose and more unable to shift to another location than any other: local government. After achieving this anchoring foothold in local living wage ordinances, the new coalition began to pressure particular segments of private capital that depended most on both public financial support and subsidies as well as on what the economic geographers call regionally specific assets, such as the tourist, hotel and restaurant, and entertainment industries. It was almost as if local organizers had read the latest academic debates on urban restructuring and the New Economy.

Spreading the Struggle for Jobs with Justice

Joining in the struggle for jobs with justice and many other related issues were such new collective action groups as the Los Angeles Metropolitan Alliance, an organization aimed specifically at regional coalition building among diverse community and labor organizations. Its core components included Action for Grassroots Empowerment and Neighborhood Development (AGENDA), SEIU Locals 347 and 1877, West L.A. Metro Alliance, Community Coalition for Substance Abuse Prevention and Treatment, and Silverlake/Hollywood/Echo Park Metro Alliance.

In 1999, the Metropolitan Alliance succeeded in creating a jobs training and education program to help workers respond effectively to federal welfare-to-work initiatives through jobs in the public sector. In 2000, these efforts at worker training and education were extended to the entertainment industry through the alliance's Workplace Hollywood campaign and teaching agreements with the Community College District and DreamWorks film studio. The Metropolitan Alliance shifted its attention after 2000 to improvements in regional health care through a campaign for Good Jobs for Healthy Communities, urging creation of a regional comprehensive job training program for health care occupations.

The specific problems of the garment industry spawned other grassroots efforts. Los Angeles had replaced New York City as the largest center of garment production, and by the turn of the century there were around 140,000 workers in five thousand shops, the vast majority working under sweatshop conditions or worse. Almost all garment workers were non-unionized, three-quarters were women, and the total workforce, mostly undocumented, was roughly 80 percent Latino/a immigrants and 20 percent Asian immigrants. Violations of minimum wage laws and even the most basic health regulations were rampant. Even worse than the sweatshops was the growth of a new mode of quasi-slavery, where immigrants stripped of their passports and "imported" by their "owners" were forced to work and live under terrible conditions isolated from surrounding communities and services.

In 1995, more than seventy Thai workers were freed from their trapped labor in a garment sweatshop in El Monte, one of a cluster of poor Latino municipalities in eastern Los Angeles County. The freed workers joined forces with other groups to protest against those who bought and sold their labor and to raise consciousness around the country of the new slavery being created to meet the needs of the neoliberal economy of flexible capitalism. A Garment Worker Center was founded in 2001, and with the support of the Asian Pacific American Legal Center (APALC), Coalition for Humane Immigrant Rights of Los Angeles (CHIRLA), and Korean Immigrant Workers Advocates (KIWA), led the struggle against sweatshop owners and the retail outlets that depended on them. Unionization efforts were relatively successful, but the problems persist.

Adding to the strong organizational infrastructure for regional coalition building were many other grassroots groups. Focusing on the problems facing young people of color were the Student Empowerment Project, Voice of Struggle, Olin ("movement" in Nahuatl), Youth United for Community Action, Youth in Action Coalition, Community Services Organization, and Schools Not Jails. The high schools of Los Angeles became hotbeds of activism (more so than the universities) and would play an important role in nearly every public demonstration and immigrant rights campaign up to the present. In the late 1990s, CHIRLA, KIWA, the Pilipino Workers Center (PWC), and later the Garment Worker Center created a new network that in 2001 became the Multi-Ethnic Immigrant Worker Organizing Network (MIWON). Among its efforts was the Korean Restaurant Justice Campaign in 2000, involving a May Day demonstration of Latino day workers and gardeners as well as Pilipino, Korean, and other workers.

Several organizations emerged to deal with the special problem of day laborers' rights, including the immigrant rights group CHIRLA, mentioned earlier, and the Institute of Popular Education of Southern California (IDEPSCA). Almost always undocumented, without any regular employment, and often homeless new arrivals, day laborers are a common sight around DIY shops and department stores. They are also highly vulnerable to employer abuse and, like the homeless, are frequently removed from their preferred places and spaces by local authorities. CHIRLA and IDEPSCA have focused on creating free meeting centers for day workers in special job sites around the region to help them organize, present their grievances, and fight against ordinances preventing them from congregating in certain locations looking for work. They have also helped to form a National Day Laborers Organizing Network (NDLON) aimed at influencing national and local policies and advancing an economic justice agenda that has significant spatial components.

Two standout achievements of the workers' justice movement occurred around the turn of the century. In 1999, after more than a decade of struggle, SEIU Local 434B won the right to represent nearly 75,000 home care workers in Los Angeles County. This represented the largest number of new union members mobilized in a single year since 1941, when workers at that definitive symbol of assembly-line mass production, the Ford Motor Company's River Rouge Plant near Dearborn, Michigan, the largest integrated factory in the world at the time, joined the United Auto Workers. That the leadership role in the workers' movement in the United States was taken up by a service employees union, and in Los Angeles, was perhaps the ultimate symbol of the shift from Fordism to a post-Fordist national economy where the largest single employers in the country were no longer General Motors and Ford but Manpower, Inc., and Wal-Mart.

The second major achievement takes us back to the story of Justice for Janitors and the nationwide effort of more than 100,000 janitors to sign a new contract for increased wages and benefits. On April 7, 2000, the janitors of SEIU Local 1877 marched down Wilshire Boulevard from downtown Los Angeles through Beverly Hills to the memory-filled site of Century City as part of a countywide strike. It remains difficult for anyone not living in Los Angeles at the time to conceive of the positive public support the striking marchers received. In one of the most unusual and unexpected public demonstrations in the history of the American labor movement, the marching janitors started out with the Los Angeles city attorney and soon-to-be mayor in front of the parade, along with dozens of elected officials, Jesse Jackson, ministers, priests, and rabbis. As the march moved on, people came out of office buildings or leaned out windows to lend their support. People on the street started cheering. In Beverly Hills, several bystanders ran into the street to offer the janitors cash. Raised fists of support were added everywhere along the route.

Earlier rallies leading up to the march were supported by the Republican mayor Richard Riordan, who had refused to sign the living wage ordinance; Cardinal Roger Mahoney; Rabbi Steven Jacobs, who conducted a labor-oriented seder for Passover; several members of the Los Angeles City Council, who were arrested for civil disobedience in support of the janitors; Senators Edward Kennedy and Dianne Feinstein, and Vice President Al Gore. A few weeks after the march, a new contract was signed boosting wages more than 25 percent over a three-year period. At the celebration of the victory, which the *Los Angeles Times* announced had "galvanized workers across the nation," amid dancing and water spritzing stood county supervisor Zev Yaroslavsky holding a mop; Antonio Villaraigosa, currently mayor of Los Angeles but then state assembly leader, holding a broom; and Robert Maguire, a prominent developer and downtown building owner wearing a strike cap.

The Los Angeles Alliance for a New Economy (LAANE)

In any discussion of the major achievements in labor–community–university coalition building and especially with regard to the development of specifically spatial strategies of social action, the Los Angeles Alliance for a New Economy (LAANE) deserves to take center stage. It played a key role in the living wage campaign and has been a primary force in the networking of grassroots organizations throughout the 1990s and up to the present. More than any of the larger coalitions, it drew strategically on university-based research and researchers and served to bring into the public realm innovative ideas about urban restructuring, the New Economy, the dynamics of regional development, the widening divide between rich and poor, and the spatiality of injustice.

LAANE was founded in 1993 under the leadership of Madeline Janis-Aparicio, a lawyer and former executive director of CARECEN, the Central American Refugee Center. It started out as the Tourist Industry Development Council, an organization that grew directly from the first project organized by the newly established UCLA Community Scholars Program (CSP). The CSP, led by Gilda Haas, Allan Heskin, and Jacqueline Leavitt from Urban Planning and Kent Wong from the Labor Center, brought together experienced activists from various community groups and labor unions to attend classes, meet with students, and work with them in joint projects. The first of these projects, conducted in academic year 1991–92, was aimed at the local tourist industry at a time when huge investments were planned for expanding the downtown convention center and related facilities.

The CSP team sought strategies to promote greater economic benefits for low-wage workers and their communities in an industry notorious for its weak positive spillover effects and exploitative working conditions. The final report, titled *Accidental Tourism*, developed arguments that were similar to those behind the earlier Justice for Janitors campaign and reminiscent of David Harvey's analyses of the regressive effects of standard urban development practices. In addition to moral appeals to private businesses, it was argued that, without special intervention, the normal workings of public and private decision making tend to lead to results that discriminate against the poor and minorities, an outcome that was highly likely to occur again if downtown tourist development went ahead as originally planned.

Like so many of the campaigns aimed at worker and community justice, one of the primary intentions and effects of the CSP study was to raise public awareness about the location of investment and its positive and negative impacts on surrounding communities. As was the case with MTA plans for a world-class fixed-rail system and early efforts to achieve environmental justice such as the resistance to the LANCER incinerator project (see chapter 5), public officials assumed that the mere addition of jobs and improved social services would be enough to satisfy all urban residents. The particular social and spatial distribution of benefits tended to be out of sight and out of mind. While the language of *Accidental Tourism* was not overtly spatial, its underlying message and the interaction between the community scholars and the Urban Planning students were informed by a sensitivity to the spatiality of justice and injustice, especially for the mass of the working poor trying to survive in the New Economy.

Some important benefits for workers were won in the contract for the convention center, initiating what would develop into LAANE's hallmark achievement, the creation and expanded use of negotiated Community Benefits Agreements (CBAs). LAANE's offshoot, the Coalition for Growth with Justice, would succeed in promoting agreements with local governments and private developers to attach benefits to workers and minority communities to all new development plans in every sector of the local economy. In another important breakthrough, agreements were also reached to add a requirement to new developments for community impact assessments, examining the potential spillover effects of the plans on jobs, traffic, and local quality of life. Emanating from demands for development with justice, the CBA model has grown in importance in recent years and has spread both locally and to many other cities as one of the most significant contemporary innovations in community economic development planning and public policy. See chapter 6 for more on these recent developments.

Significantly, the landmark CBA was negotiated jointly in 2001 by LAANE and SAJE, Strategic Actions for a Just Economy, teaming Janis-Aparicio and Gilda Haas. The agreement was part of SAJE's Figueroa Corridor Coalition for Economic Justice campaign and was worked out in conjunction with the huge Staples Center development project in the downtown area, near the convention center. It included provisions for living wage jobs, affordable housing, local hiring, and green space. It came as the culmination of a long series of LAANE's accomplishments and struggles, summarized in the notes and references for this chapter.

After the events of September 11, 2001, LAANE won job retention for hundreds of security workers who would have lost their jobs when airport security was taken over by the federal government. LAANE also worked with HERE in a massive worker relief effort providing food and access to government services for union members who lost their jobs in the declining tourist industry after 9/11. In the same year, LAANE helped extend Community Benefits Agreements to several other areas of the county and, in recent years, throughout the state of California, connecting with the Center on Policy Initiatives in San Diego, Working Partnerships in Silicon Valley, and East Bay Alliance for a Sustainable Economy in Oakland.

LAANE and SAJE have as much as any other organizations contributed to the unusually productive interaction between the university and the wider community and to the filtering into local activism of strategic spatial and regional thinking. Justice for Janitors, the Living Wage Coalition, the LANCER project and subsequent environmental justice efforts, the Metropolitan Alliance, MIWON, and many other organizations aided in stimulating a notable sense of locational and geographical awareness in what was formerly one of the most footloose and unneighborly urban populations in the country, but hard evidence of consciously spatial strategies for all these organizations is not easy to find. Informal interviews with several leaders of the workers' justice movement outside LAANE and SAJE indicated little explicit awareness of the importance of specifically spatial strategies and actions, although nearly everyone agreed on the necessity for regional coalition building and the importance of understanding the dynamics of the regional economy and private-sector location strategies, lessons learned at least in part from the earlier Coalition to Stop Plant Closings.

LAANE's work, however, from the living wage campaign to the breakthrough Community Benefits Agreements, has shown an acute awareness of the geography of worker injustices as well as the necessity to organize on a regional scale. Avoiding the mistakes and failed strategies of the CSPC in the early 1980s, LAANE focused its attention on employers who were rooted in the region and could not easily relocate when being pressured by community or labor groups. As noted for the living wage campaign, local government was the obvious starting point, especially where past organizing experiences such as the rent control movement had created openings for progressives on city councils, such as in Santa Monica, the City of Los Angeles, and West Hollywood. Only when the white male monopoly on the board of supervisors was broken, in part a result of innovative GIS redistricting strategies, was the campaign extended to the county level.

Selecting strategic sites for protest and demonstration was vital. With the local government base assured, strategic action was extended to the major industrial clusters of Los Angeles, such as entertainment and the garment industry, and to the essential infrastructure of the regional tourist economy, another sector that almost by definition had to remain locally rooted. Little Tokyo and the major office blocks of downtown and Century City, the international airport, the Hollywood Redevelopment Project, drywall construction workers and tortilla makers, large hotel chains especially nearby the coastal beaches, the booming new developments in Playa Vista and Universal Studios, home care workers and day laborers, nannies and gardeners became major targets. At all times and places, serving the needs of the immigrant working poor was central. Probably more than anywhere else in the country, the notion that all businesses receiving any public subsidy have an obligation to the communities its activities affect entered into public awareness and public policy.

LAANE'S projects made no attempt to stop new development but rather worked to guarantee development with justice for workers and communities, with day care and local hiring, parks and worker centers, health benefits and living wages, in short, with democratic rights to the city and to the resources generated by and in the city and region. While not evident in all LAANE's projects, a critical spatial awareness informed many of its practices and was promoted and sustained by an extraordinary flow of hired student researchers and activists from Urban Planning at UCLA, at least thirty over the past fifteen years, with several entering into executive and managerial roles.

Another indication of the spread of spatial thinking into local political practice appeared in an article published in 2002 in the journal *Social Problems*. The authors, Robert D. Wilton and Cynthia Cranford, were two student activists who had participated in labor struggles between predominantly Latino service workers and the private University of Southern California. They wrote not only about the revival of the American labor movement spurred by the labor–community alliances they saw arising around them, including LAANE, but also about their sensing of a tangible spatial turn in what was happening. In "Toward an Understanding of the Spatiality of Social Movements: Labor Organizing at a Private University in Los Angeles," the authors argued that an understanding of these developments in Los Angeles and elsewhere in the world requires "recognition of their inherently spatial nature." Referring specifically to the recent spatial turn in social theory, they focused attention on "space as an active dimension of movement organizing" and on the usefulness of "spatial tactics of transgression" on the campus, in surrounding communities, and within regional movements for a living wage and job security.

With just a touch of optimistic exaggeration, it can be said that the spatiality of justice was in the urban air in Los Angeles in the 1990s. Coalitions organized "geographic target groups" for particular tasks, and geographic scales of organizing were widely discussed. Los Angeles became the center for the development of what came to be called community-based regionalism, a determined call for all coalitions, alliances, and networks to reach to the regional scale not just to create larger organizations but also because of an awareness that the regional economy and geography were powerful forces shaping local events and community economic development. Local knowledge and regional awareness also encouraged larger-scale perspectives, linking local movements not only to state and federal levels but to the global justice movement and the revival of struggles over the right to the city.

5

Translating Theory into Practice
Urban Planning at UCLA

THE RELATIONS between major urban-based research universities in the United States and the labor-related, ethnically defined, and community-based organizations in the cities where they are located have rarely been close and productive. This is especially true when compared to the services rendered to the private sector or, for the most part, to city governments. While a few individual faculty members and some specialized centers for ethnic studies, urban planning, social welfare, law, and industrial relations have worked closely with such nongovernmental organizations, fundamental and applied research relating to the university's urban-regional milieu has mainly been channeled through paid consulting activities to established government agencies and private businesses.

A different model of university–community linkages developed with a base in Urban Planning and the Institute for Industrial Relations (later the Labor Center) at UCLA. It revolved not around paid consultancy with governments and large funding agencies but on voluntary assistance to and educational emphasis on constituencies usually given little attention by university researchers and professors, such as labor unions, community-based nongovernmental organizations (NGOs), and other groups aiming to empower social movements among the poor and disadvantaged populations.

I have argued in earlier chapters that this mutually enhancing channel between university scholar-activists and local labor and community organizations played an important role in the resurgence of new and innovative coalitions in Los Angeles as well as in the development of more academic contributions to spatial theory and urban and regional studies. My intent in this chapter is not to heap praise on the Urban Planning program (UCLAUP) but rather to present a focused discussion of one particular example of how (spatial) theory can be effectively connected to (spatial) practice in a university setting.

Creating a Graduate School for Activists

In 1968, amid a period of growing urban crises across the country and three years after the Watts rebellion, the urban planning program was established as part of a new School of Architecture and Urban Planning at UCLA. From the beginning, the school focused on graduate education and research applied to urban problems, leaving responsibilities for undergraduate education in these areas primarily to the older programs at UC-Berkeley. To emphasize this specialization in graduate studies, the school was renamed the Graduate School of Architecture and Urban Planning (GSAUP) in 1981, by which time it had grown to be one of the largest combined architecture and planning schools in the country.

The first dean of the school was Harvey Perloff, a well-known urban and regional economist who had taught planning and economics at the University of Chicago. The first program head (equivalent to chair) of Urban Planning was John Friedmann, who studied under Perloff at Chicago and had extensive planning experience in Latin America and Asia. Friedmann had already established himself as a leading planning theorist and a prominent figure in urban and regional development planning. His ideas and progressive political stance significantly shaped the development of Urban Planning at UCLA over the next twenty-five years.

Several features distinguished UCLAUP from nearly all other urban planning or urban studies departments in the United States. First was its explicit openness to spatial or geographical approaches to urban and regional studies, both locally in Los Angeles and with respect to planning in Third World counties. This involved not just ties with architecture and urban design but also with geography and geographers, and to a lesser extent with urban sociology and urban economics. This approach established early on a commitment to the application of geographical knowledge and critical spatial thinking to the most pressing issues facing the city, region, nation, and developing world.

Friedmann received his doctorate from the University of Chicago through a special program in planning, economics, and geography, and his dissertation, *The Spatial Structure of Economic Development in the Tennessee Valley* (1955), a call for a more explicitly spatial approach to regional development planning, was published in the prestigious Chicago Geographical Series. I was recruited by Friedmann from the Department of Geography at Northwestern University, where I taught African development studies, and came to UCLA in 1972 as the first of several geographers appointed to Urban Planning, including Margaret FitzSimmons in 1980, Michael Storper in 1982, and Susanna Hecht in 1987. The appointment in 1979 of the feminist architectural critic and historian Dolores Hayden added significantly to this emphasis on critical spatial thinking.

Further stimulating these developments was the appointment of Allen J. Scott to the Department of Geography in 1978. An economic geographer and urban theorist, Scott also taught urban planning in his previous position at the University of Toronto and continued to work closely with geographers on the Urban Planning faculty. To this day, no other major urban planning department in the United States has such a large contingent of geographers on the faculty, and at least until 1994, when GSAUP was split into two separate departments, very few universities anywhere in the world had such close ties established between the three major spatial disciplines of architecture and design, urban and regional planning, and human geography.

Another distinguishing feature of UCLAUP was an explicit philosophical and educational commitment to social movement politics and community activism, combined with an attempt to keep up with the latest advances in social science theory and methods. Whereas most graduate programs in urban planning elsewhere in the country were aimed specifically at training students to take up traditional jobs as planners or planning consultants, responding to externally defined demand, at UCLA the widely shared objective was to prepare students to be innovative change agents wherever they might be employed. The curriculum was thus more broadly based and organized to encourage interdisciplinary studies and such skills as community organizing and critical thinking in addition to traditional training in quantitative methods, public resource economics, physical planning, and, later, geographic information systems (GIS).

Traditional specializations such as housing, transportation, and land-use planning were not ignored but were approached from several different perspectives, reflecting the need espoused by Perloff for critical and creative generalists to deal with the major problems facing contemporary society. Housing, for example, was studied by economists in terms of national and international policy, by sociologists and demographers as part of "planning for multiple publics," and by community organizers and urban designers as a means of local economic development and activism. Although students were formally required to choose among four areas of policy concentration (urban and regional development, social policy and analysis, built environment, and natural environment and resources), most also attached themselves to particular social movements based on race/ethnicity, class, gender, peace and justice, housing, and the environment.

Nearly all large planning departments saw themselves as working at the interface between theory and practice, but too often this theory–practice link split faculty into two opposing camps, with little interaction between the professionals and the academics, the practitioners and the theorists or social scientists. At UCLA, however, a stronger effort, not always successful, was made to encourage a more balanced and respectful dialogue between theory and practice. Planning was seen as a form of social praxis, the transformation of knowledge into action. Doctoral students in particular were encouraged to explore current theoretical debates in the social sciences and humanities with the intention not just of accumulating theoretical knowledge but also of exploring its practical applications in the public domain and civil society.

This created another distinctive feature, a critical and self-conscious commitment to not simply provide technical assistance (as experts) to targeted communities but to actively promote (as facilitators) autonomous grassroots development and activism. This meant trying to avoid as much as possible research that did little more than strip-mine communities and localities for empirical data and ideas that would lead only to career-boosting academic publications rather than improvements in the communities studied. This public commitment was promoted over the years by part-time practitioner faculty, many of whom were trained within UCLAUP, and several, such as Gilda Haas, Neal Richman, and Goetz Wolff, who remain in this position today as long-term lecturers and key contact persons with the world outside the university.

The commitment to participatory democracy was expressed in the administrative structure and the organization of the curriculum. Working groups rather than committees handled admissions, financial aid, curriculum changes, as well as academic personnel actions, and each had significant if not majority student membership. This often required significant pressure to relax established university regulations and to enable greater student participation and influence. In many ways, Urban Planning acted within the institutional framework of the university like a grassroots community organization seeking to maximize local development possibilities.

Once each quarter there was an Assembly of Working Groups, an open town meeting, which ratified (or rejected) all policy proposals, often after extensive open debate. Particularly influential student organizations developed specifically to promote and assure affirmative action for women and minorities not just in admissions but also in curriculum development and faculty hiring. By 1980, there were four women on the faculty, two African Americans (one a woman), and a Latino, all of whom would be tenured during their time at UCLA. Of the approximately twenty-five new faculty appointments made between 1979 and the present, the majority were women, and a third were ethnic minorities, rates of inclusion that were among the highest of any department at UCLA.

Flexibility and openness to alternative approaches to planning education helped to make the program a center for radical planning ideas and activism. Occasional courses were taught in Marxist economics, a course on the political economy of urbanization was introduced in the mid-1970s to deal with questions of social justice and the city, and utopian socialist and social anarchist ideas were seriously addressed across the curriculum, from advanced doctoral seminars in planning theory to basic workshops on professional development.

Several other curricular innovations encouraged closer university–community ties. Of particular importance was an innovative internship program. Every first-year master's student without extensive planning-related experience was required to take up a six-month (two quarters) active internship with an existing organization and to prepare and discuss, through an ongoing professional development seminar, a critical report on their experience. Each year in the fall quarter a jobs fair was held where various organizations presented internship opportunities for students, increasingly with pay and frequently with progressive labor, community, ethnic, and urban governmental organizations. Over the years, hundreds of Urban Planning interns linked the department with the wider regional community and helped to sustain a significant two-way flow of information, ideas, and experience.

A more organized and focused link with community groups and other local governmental and nongovernmental organizations developed in conjunction with comprehensive projects, six-month courses that brought together teams of second-year master's students around specific projects with actual external clients. One, two, or occasionally three of these project courses, with student groups ranging between six and fifteen, would be organized each year. The final reports of the project team were signed off by two faculty members and the official client, with the comprehensive project itself substituting for a thesis in fulfillment of the requirements for the master's degree. Notes and References contains a representative list of these project reports.

As a second alternative to writing a master's thesis, students could also choose to prepare individual client-oriented projects under the guidance of two faculty members and a specified client. In an average year, roughly 40 percent of the graduating class was involved with comprehensive projects, another 40 percent with individual client-based projects, and the rest with writing theses. These individual and group projects provided what were essentially free professional services to various external clients. They frequently also connected to individual faculty research projects and community activism, and to a variety of research centers and institutes on campus, adding to the wider impact of the department on the Los Angeles region.

From the beginning, Urban Planning defined itself as serving "third sector" and other disadvantaged (the poor, minorities, tenants, workers) constituencies, that is, all those located between the formal public and private sectors, between the institutional structures of government and the power of the market. Much of this took the form of providing technical and organizational assistance and targeted research to community organizations, unions, and government agencies involved in promoting local economic development in minority and poor communities. For the most part, the department avoided very large, externally funded research projects, determined not to become a research factory selling its services to the highest bidder.

Rent Control and the Tenants' Rights Movement

During a period when social movement politics was spreading across the country, protests against the Vietnam War were growing, and poverty and homelessness were on the increase, UCLAUP was well positioned to take part in a new progressive politics. By 1979, some ties were established with the civil rights, Chicano/a, and feminist movements in Los Angeles, although there was as yet relatively little contact with labor unions. The main pipeline between planning and the wider community up to the late 1980s was more populist and revolved around issues of housing, community development, and tenants' rights. Allan Heskin, one of only a small number of the early faculty with a PhD in urban planning, would play a key role here in many different ways.

Heskin was the author of an influential article on radical planning that promoted much stronger actions than were associated with what was traditionally described as advocacy planning (Heskin 1980). In the early 1980s, he helped to establish the Community Corporation of Santa Monica (CCSM), aimed at creating and preserving affordable housing. The CCSM has been one of the most successful community development corporations in Los Angeles, and currently owns seventy-five properties with 1,400 units. Its leadership from the start has been filled by ex–Urban Planning students. Like others in the Urban Planning program, Heskin was motivated by forms of social anarchism that connected back to Gramsci and Proudhon much more than to Marx. As a lawyer-activist, he thrived on direct participatory democracy, and in the 1970s, he focused his work on Santa Monica and renters' rights.

Activism with regard to housing has been at the core of Urban Planning involvement in urban development and change in Los Angeles from the earliest days to the present. Although not explicitly couched in these terms, housing activism aimed at achieving a form of spatial justice and the right to the city, in this case the right of all residents to adequate, stable, and affordable shelter. This search for just and fair housing involved legal and legislative struggles over the civil rights of tenants and renters especially with regard to rent control, efforts to provide improved shelter for the homeless, direct participation in the development of cooperative home ownership schemes in low-income communities, improving the quality of life in public housing projects through participatory design, planning, and construction, work with local governments and community-based organizations to improve housing policies, and direct provision of affordable housing through the formation of innovative community development corporations.

The relations between housing and law, framed in the context of a course on law and the quality of urban life, have been the educational foundation of housing activism in UCLAUP. Peter Marcuse, a housing lawyer and son of the radical philosopher Herbert Marcuse, was appointed to the faculty in 1972, the same year in which a concurrent MA/JD degree program between Urban Planning and Law was established. Marcuse left for Columbia University in 1975, where he forged an illustrious career in urban planning. In the same year, Marcuse was replaced by Heskin, who would become the primary motivating force behind a long-lasting involvement of students and faculty in issues of cooperative housing, tenants' rights, and community economic development.

Soon after his arrival, Heskin became directly involved in the transformation of the city of Santa Monica from a developer-dominated and politically conservative urban growth machine to one of the most progressive and innovative cities in the United States. As a housing lawyer, Heskin became a primary legal advisor to a burgeoning rent control and tenants' rights movement that had in part been mobilized by the formation of the Campaign for Economic Democracy, under the leadership of Tom Hayden, who, with his then wife, Jane Fonda, was a resident of the Ocean Park section of Santa Monica. The CED was an important unifying and energizing force for progressives in Los Angeles during the 1970s and early 1980s.

Affordable housing and rent control were obvious issues for political mobilization in Santa Monica. While the northern half of this incorporated municipality of around 80,000 was part of the wealthiest residential zone of Los Angeles, stretching along the southern slopes of the Santa Monica Mountains from the Hollywood Hills through Beverly Hills, Bel Air, and Brentwood to Pacific Palisades and Malibu, the southern half was much poorer and more densely occupied, although far from being characterized as a slum. Southern Santa Monica was adjacent to and shared many characteristics with Venice, part of the City of Los Angeles and a center of progressive activism for many decades. In the long stretch of coastline and beach communities in Los Angeles County, Venice and parts of nearby Santa Monica stood out as having the largest concentration of poor and minority residents so close to the Pacific.

Almost 70 percent of the residents of Santa Monica were renters, and many were being tightly squeezed by rising rents and increasing numbers of condominium conversions, reducing the number of available apartments. Proposition 13, controlling increases in property taxes, was passed in 1978 but offered little help to tenants, despite promises that tax savings would be passed on to them by landlords. While similar pressures were being felt throughout the greater Los Angeles region, Santa Monica emerged as the most fertile ground for progressive community organizing and social movement politics. A new organization, Santa Monicans for Renters' Rights (SMRR), was formed in 1978 and became the leading edge of the local movement for rent control and for what one observer (Boggs 1989) described as "freeing social space for democratic forces."

The emergence of Santa Monica as a municipal stronghold for progressive urban governance was built on a populist rent control movement that began in the late 1970s and grew to have significant regional and national repercussions. Dennis Zane, a master's student in Urban Planning, would take leave to become a key participant in the movement and eventually mayor of Santa Monica. Heskin and his law and planning students helped pass statewide warranty of habitability legislation regulating condominium conversions and played an important role in the preparation of the Santa Monica rent control charter amendment, the strongest rent control law in the country at the time, adopted on April 10, 1979. A rent stabilization ordinance took effect in the City of Los Angeles on May 1, 1979, and one of Heskin's doctoral students, Ken Baar, also a practicing lawyer, led the way in extending rent control (with relocation benefits) to the municipality of West Hollywood through a rent stabilization ordinance approved in 1985.

As more conservative forces took hold at the national, state, and local levels, the rent control movement waned. Heskin and his close colleague Jackie Leavitt turned to promoting cooperative housing in Los Angeles and elsewhere. Heskin personally took the lead in helping to form an innovative limited-equity housing cooperative enabling low-income and predominantly minority residents the opportunity to own their own homes. Both, along with Gilda Haas, later played a key role in creating the Community Scholars Program, which shaped and was shaped by the resurgence of labor–community–university coalitions beginning in the late 1980s.

Spatial Feminism and Environmental Justice

Theoretical and practical attention, often with a spatial twist, was also being given to other growing social movements. With the appointments of Dolores Hayden (1979), Margaret FitzSimmons (1980), Rebecca Morales (1981), Jacqueline Leavitt (1984), Gilda Haas (1984), Leonie Sandercock (1985), Susanna Hecht (1987), Carol Goldstein (1987), Julie Roque (1991), and Anastasia Loukaitou-Sideris (1991), a strong feminist perspective, especially with regard to women and the built environment, grew during the early years and shaped many of the program's activities.

Hayden's work as a feminist historian of the built environment was creatively spatial and would inspire a generation of spatial feminist scholars. Reflecting her interests in the writings of Henri Lefebvre on space and everyday life in the modern world, Hayden joined me in organizing a visit by Lefebvre to UCLAUP in 1978. In her writings, she raised questions about daily life in the city and how the built environment would need to change to reduce the controlling forces of patriarchy. She asked, for example, what would a nonsexist city look like? In other words, how would gender justice change the built environment, or, reversing the question, how can changing the built environment promote gender justice? Her research took her back to the ideas of nineteenth-century material feminists and the experimental utopian new towns created in the United States with conceptual ties to European socialist thinkers such as Fourier and Proudhon. She also embarked on a major project on what she called the power of place, rethinking the foundations of historical preservation efforts to recognize important people and places in the ethnic and labor movements in Los Angeles.

Crossing the boundary between the built and natural environments, Margaret FitzSimmons, a geographer and critical spatial scholar, and Robert Gottlieb, a widely published journalist and critic, created an innovative specialization within UCLAUP on the political economy of the environment. Gottlieb, FitzSimmons, and their students, including such leading environmental scholars of today as Laura Pulido and Stephanie Pincetl, added a strong spatial and locational emphasis to the evolving environmental justice movement, linking issues such as air and water pollution, the reduction and disposal of toxic wastes, and the misuse of toxic chemicals to ongoing research on urban restructuring, regional and community development, and new industrial technologies (FitzSimmons and Gottlieb 1996).

More so than in the larger environmental justice movement, environmental problems were directly tied to their geographical source, whether it was the factory producing pollution and toxic waste, the dry cleaning establishment using poisonous chemicals, or the government agency promoting misguided policies. Water policy and politics received particular attention. As former director of the Metropolitan Water District of Southern California, Gottlieb used his practical experience to coauthor a book on water agencies with FitzSimmons (1991), following up on an earlier, more general book on water politics (Gottlieb 1989).

Building on one of many comprehensive project courses that would be turned into published articles and books, Gottlieb and his student Louis Blumberg produced an influential treatise on solid waste disposal in 1989, *War on Waste: Can America Win Its Battle with Garbage?* In another project, Gottlieb contributed significantly to the early development of what today is called the food justice movement, advocating for food cooperatives, helping to stimulate the growth and diffusion of farmers markets in Los Angeles, and raising regional awareness of the injustices associated with geographically uneven access to fresh, nutritious, and affordable food (Gottlieb et al. 1995). Following up on his work on hazardous waste disposal issues, he and his students were also instrumental in changing the laws regulating the use of toxic chemicals in the dry cleaning industry.

Gottlieb, who studied briefly with Henri Lefebvre in Strasbourg in 1963, summarized what was happening in Los Angeles and at the national scale in *Forcing the Spring* (1993). Of particular note here was the LANCER project, one of the earliest examples of coalition building around an issue of environmental justice and locational discrimination. When in the mid-1980s an incinerator project was proposed for a predominantly African American neighborhood in South Central Los Angeles, resistance led by Concerned Citizens of South Central and supported by diverse organizations outside the area (including some Westside predominantly white and wealthy homeowners associations) and at the university (another project course guided by Gottlieb) succeeded in stopping construction.

In the LANCER case, as in other grassroots movements, public authorities failed to see the racial and spatial injustices that were associated as side effects of what seemed to be progressive and equity-oriented policy decisions. Thought by government officials to be a regenerative investment for the community, providing some much needed jobs, the unseen trade-offs relating to environmental health and unintentional racial discrimination (despite the African American mayor and local councilman backing the plan) were considered to be unacceptable by local residents. The perceived racial and spatial injustice was aggravated by a suspicion that the LANCER project was being used to force white suburban areas to accept incinerators in their neighborhoods lest they be accused of racial bias given the location of LANCER in an African American community. In any case, a new consciousness was raised about the negative spatial spillover effects of public projects and the need for coalition building to advance the goals of the environmental justice movement.

Innovative Research on Urban and Regional Restructuring

Up to around 1980, the academic literature on Los Angeles was extremely meager, especially in comparison to writings about other large cities such as Chicago and New York. Hollywood dominated the urban imagery of what was considered a bizarre exception to conventional forms of American urbanism. After 1980, however, Los Angeles became the focus for an extraordinary expansion of rigorous empirical and thoughtful theoretical work that would raise it to a central position in contemporary urban studies. Many scholars contributed to these developments, but attention is focused here on the contributions coming from the faculty and students in Urban Planning at UCLA.

Linking theory and practice, knowledge and action, has been one of the defining features of the body of research and writing on Los Angeles that has accumulated over the past thirty years. Whether one calls it a school or a research cluster or simply a collection of diverse publications is not of great consequence. What matters more for the present discussion is how this accumulation of theoretical and empirical work on urban and regional studies both shaped and was shaped by the historical development of social activism in Los Angeles. To illustrate these connections, I turn first to my own experience.

Stimulating the early development of my research and writing on Los Angeles was "The Socio-Spatial Dialectic," published in 1980 after several years of "retooling" related to my shift from geography to urban planning and a basic rethinking of my earlier career as an African development specialist and political geographer. The notion that urban society is inherently spatial and that spatial forms actively shape social processes just as much as social processes shape spatial form grew out of a sympathetic critique of Marxist geography for its seeming neglect of spatial explanation and unqualified privileging of the social. It also reflected my attempt at the time, as I was adjusting to the move to urban planning, to develop the idea of "spatial praxis," defined as I saw it as the useful application of spatial ideas and theories to social and political problems.

In a department of geography I could be as theoretical and abstract as I wanted, as long as I published in reputable journals. It was always helpful in teaching geography to give some practical applications to the theoretical debates, whether they concerned Christaller's central place theory or Marx's materialist dialectics, but it was easy to wriggle out of too much responsibility for practical applications as a scholar and social scientist doing supposedly "basic" research. Avoiding a discussion of practical applications was not so easy in an urban planning department, especially one filled with social activists, practitioners, and professionals.

In retrospect, I am convinced that I could not have developed my theoretical writings, empirical projects, and critical spatial perspective—and could not have written this book and its predecessors—as easily and effectively in a geography or sociology department as in Urban Planning at UCLA. At first, when pressed by my students to translate the conceptual and theoretical ideas they were patiently listening to in class into something they might use as practicing planners and activists in the field, I would retreat to the convenient excuses of academic freedom and pure scholarship. "You are responsible for putting the ideas to use, not I." The hollowness of such a stance became clear quite quickly, and everything I have done since as a geographer-planner reflects this realization, even when not particularly successful in affecting actual planning practice.

My empirical work on Los Angeles began soon after the publication on the socio-spatial dialectic with a collective project initiated by a request from the Coalition to Stop Plant Closings (CSPC). The Electricians Union was involved at that time in organizing workers in a General Electric plant making flatirons in Ontario, just over the border in San Bernardino County. They faced a major dilemma, however, not just because of the normal reticence of workers to risk losing their jobs by participating in union actions but also because of the then booming economy of Los Angeles. Workers would tell the union organizers, "Why bother about the plant closing? There seem to be dozens of jobs opening up all the time." This contrasted greatly with what unions were facing in the rest of deindustrializing America. Help us, they asked, to understand what is happening to the Los Angeles economy so that we can organize more effectively on the shop floor.

This request from the CSPC not only initiated my own research on urban restructuring in Los Angeles, it stimulated a larger commitment within Urban Planning to a new constituency, labor and the labor movement, outside the formal private and public sectors and virtually ignored in nearly all planning departments in the country. A planning research project was begun, led by myself and a recently hired former Urban Planning graduate Rebecca Morales, whose work focused on undocumented workers and their use in union busting and the growing number of sweatshops in the textile, automobile, and other industries in Los Angeles. Joining us among a larger group of students was Goetz Wolff, who would later become cochair of the renamed Los Angeles Coalition Against Plant Shutdowns. A brief profile of Wolff is included in Notes and References.

The project culminated in two products. One was a small pamphlet outlining the early warning signs of a plant closing, ranging from inventory meltdowns to management absenteeism. A brief text and cartoons drawn by an electrician union artist accompanied each warning sign. The tone was immediate and contemporary, but the information was based on a growing understanding of the trends emanating from the breakdown of the Fordist industrial economy of assembly-line mass production, mass consumption, and mass suburbanization, and, of particular importance in Los Angeles, the beginnings of a new industrial era based in high-technology manufacturing and new information and communications technologies.

Scholars in most of the rest of the United States tended to focus on the devastating effects of deindustrialization and the emergence of a service-based postindustrial economy and society. But while hundreds of thousands of manufacturing jobs were being lost in eastern cities such as New York, Detroit, Cleveland, and Chicago, Los Angeles in the 1970s experienced an extraordinary expansion of industrial employment. The Los Angeles urban region added more than a million new nonagricultural jobs in the decade, a figure greater than its net population growth. Against its prevailing image, Los Angeles in 1980 contained the largest concentration of manufacturing workers in North America. Even more startling was the discovery that Los Angeles had led all other cities in the net addition of manufacturing employment in every decade since the 1930s and that regional employment in the high-technology electronics and aerospace sectors by 1980 had reached a level matched only by Silicon Valley.

This did not mean that there was no deindustrialization in Los Angeles. Our research indicated that at least 75,000 manufacturing jobs were lost in the early 1980s, mainly in the comfortable blue-collar suburbs south of downtown and primarily in highly unionized sectors linked with the automobile industry. As parts of the regional economy grew rapidly, other areas were suffering devastating decline, as almost all vestiges of classical Fordist industries disappeared in the symbolic heartland of American car culture. More intensely than in most other urban regions at the time, Los Angeles was experiencing both deindustrialization and reindustrialization, economic decline in some sectors and areas and rapid expansion of employment in others.

These findings gave us some answers to the questions raised by the CSPC. There was a deep and rapid restructuring taking place in the Los Angeles economy, marked by the draining away of unionized "Fordist" manufacturing jobs and the simultaneous growth of a post-Fordist New Economy that was significantly bifurcated, with high-end jobs in science, engineering, and IT locating mainly outside the old manufacturing areas and an exploding workforce of low-wage and nonorganized immigrant labor in the services as well as manufacturing sectors concentrated around the downtown area.

Large-scale immigration was drawing into Los Angeles a huge reservoir of cheap labor that served multiple uses. Many thousands were employed, often in sweatshops reminiscent of Dickensian London, not just in the burgeoning apparel industry but also in small manufacturing workshops producing machine parts and other products and able to compete not just with nonunionized new factories in North Carolina but also with Brazil and Southeast Asia, where many of the closed factories in Los Angeles, including the flatiron plant in Ontario, were being relocated.

The pamphlet on early warning signs of plant closures appeared in print the same day that it was announced the flatiron plant would be permanently closed. It was true that many new jobs were available to displaced workers from this and other closed factories, but these were dead-end and low-paying service sector jobs, mostly without union representation and often only part-time. Workers would have to have two or three jobs to maintain their household economy at the same level, a pattern of response that would spread throughout deindustrializing America. We called what was happening to these workers K-Marting after the popular department store at the time, but it would have been even better had we called it Wal-Marting, given the malignant role this company has played over the past thirty years in the restructuring of American labor markets.

Wolff, Haas, Morales, and others channeled our findings directly into the Coalition to Stop Plant Closings, making it clear that community-based unionism was not enough to check the loss of traditional manufacturing jobs, that new coalitions with different objectives and tactics had to be built to deal more specifically with the problems of laid-off workers and the growing agglomeration of the immigrant working poor. Emerging from the immediate failures was a new agenda for grassroots social activism that would from the start be theoretically informed and actively promoted through a two-way flow of people and ideas between the university and the public arena.

Authored by Soja, Morales, and Wolff, with thanks to many others, was a summary article published in 1983 titled "Urban Restructuring: An Analysis of Social and Spatial Change in Los Angeles." As far as I can tell, this was the first analysis of the interrelated social and spatial aspects of urban restructuring in the literature. It established the term and concept of urban restructuring and stimulated its use and application to studies of urban change all over the world. It also helped to anchor the growing research cluster at UCLA.

During the 1980s, experienced labor and community organizers around the country entered the Urban Planning master's and PhD programs as the department became more widely known for its specialized activist focus. One particular UCLA alumnus stands out. After graduating with a joint master's degree in management and planning, Peter Olney became one of the founders (with Goetz Wolff) and later director of the Los Angeles Manufacturing Action Project (LAMAP—the cartographic allusion was intentional), an alliance of ten local unions aimed at organizing immigrant workers in the manufacturing sector.

Building coalitions with local immigrant ethnic organizations, church groups, and both Urban Planning and the Labor Center, LAMAP had some significant initial successes but was eventually de-funded because of internal divisions within the AFL-CIO and the difficulty national unions were having with the idea of organizing immigrants. In recent years, Olney has been associate director of the Institute for Labor and Employment at the University of California–Berkeley and organizing director of the International Longshoremen and Warehousing Union (ILWU). At the national conference of Jobs with Justice in May 2008, Olney told the cheering audience about the ILWU closure of all West Coast ports on May 1 in protest of the Iraq war. He continues to be a key figure in the California labor movement and returns occasionally to lecture in Urban Planning.

The UCLA research cluster in spatial theory, urban restructuring, and regional development continued to grow in the 1990s, although the earlier synergies between theory and practice were significantly weakened and other universities and contributors entered the picture. Two publications illustrate these trends. In 1996, there appeared the most comprehensive statement of the research cluster's work, *The City: Los Angeles and Urban Theory at the End of the Twentieth Century*. It contained essays by the coeditors Scott and Soja, Urban Planning faculty members (Ong,

Blumenberg, FitzSimmons, Gottlieb, Wachs), Mike Davis (who taught several seminars in Urban Planning during this period), the recently unseated dean of GSAUP Richard Weinstein and his architecture colleague Charles Jencks, UCLA political scientist Raymond Rocco, the sociologist Harvey Molotch (then at UC–Santa Barbara), African American journalist Susan Anderson, and, extending out to the University of Southern California, the geographers Michael Dear and Jennifer Wolch.

The title, *The City*, was an intentional reference to the major collective work of the Chicago school of urban ecology, edited by Robert Park, Ernest Burgess, and Roderick Mackenzie: *The City: Suggestions for Investigation of Human Behavior in an Urban Environment* (1932, 1967). Many of the new book's contributors plus several others had met for a weekend at Lake Arrowhead in the late 1980s to consider whether it was a useful idea to speak of a distinctive Los Angeles school comparable in scope and impact to the influential Chicago school. Cautiously, philosophical and political linkages to the Frankfurt school of critical theory were also discussed.

Nearly everyone left the meeting convinced that such labeling was premature, presumed too much homogeneity of perspectives, and was of little use in encouraging further research by its putative members. Publication of *The City*, however, rekindled the idea, especially for the postmodern geographer and trained urban planner Michael Dear, who over the next decade became a kind of impresario promoting the idea of an L.A. school and its alleged superseding of its Chicago-based predecessor. The L.A. school promotion led by Dear took off in directions that had little relation to the continuing work of the research cluster but nevertheless tended to shape how the so-called school was perceived by the outside world.

But be that as it may, there is another significant aspect of *The City*. Its subtitle specified urban theory, and although there was some reference to urban policies, there was almost no mention of the extraordinary resurgence of grassroots labor and community organizing that was occurring in Los Angeles at the time. It is difficult to find any mention of Jobs for Janitors, the Living Wage Coalition, LAANE, or the early efforts of the Bus Riders Union. It was almost a declaration that the two-way flow between social and spatial theory and practice that was vividly present in the 1980s had been disrupted in the 1990s.

The same break was evident in the next major collective work of the L.A. research cluster, *Global City-Regions: Trends, Theory, Policy,* edited by Allen Scott with an introductory chapter jointly written by Scott, Soja, Storper, and the geographer John Agnew. Based on an international conference held at UCLA in 1999 and published in 2001, the book was a landmark in the study of city-regions and globalization, building on but taking new directions from earlier work on world cities by Peter Hall and John Friedmann and global cities by Saskia Sassen, all three of whom attended the conference and have chapters in the book. Except for the geographers Soja and Storper and the retired former chair of Urban Planning John Friedmann, there were no direct connections to the Urban Planning faculty and, perhaps not surprisingly, few reflections on the resurgence of labor–community coalition building in Los Angeles. The book, however, crystallized a decade of important accomplishment in what some now call the New Regionalism and led to further international academic recognition of the L.A. research cluster in regional development studies.

The continued advancement of urban and regional development studies, while rarely addressing local and community development issues, had some indirect and unexpected influence on urban planning education and activism through its fostering of a critical regional perspective. As discussed earlier, this gave rise to a new field of planning theory and practice described as community-based regionalism. Whereas in the past, faculty involved with community organizing and local economic development had relatively little contact with the regional planning faculty, new connections between the two groups and their literatures were created around the notion of organizing local economic and community development efforts at a regional scale. Significantly, a regional perspective filtered through to affect the strategies and collective identity of many of the resurgent labor–community coalitions, carrying with it at least some of the ongoing developments in spatial theory and the fundamental ideas associated with spatial justice and the right to the city.

Urban Planning Restructured

In its first twenty-five years, UCLAUP was an unusually stimulating and productive place to study the theory and practice of progressive politics and, in particular, what has been described here as the spatiality of (in)justice and the (in)justice of spatiality. However it may eventually be described, the geographers and planners at UCLA generated many creative and cogent contributions to the academic literature in urban and regional studies, while at the same time university-based scholarship and research reached out into the wider community, helping to transform Los Angeles from a moribund political backwater into one of the leading centers of the American labor and community development movements and of the struggle for environmental and spatial justice.

Major changes in direction and emphasis, however, occurred after 1994 when a recessionary budget squeeze at the University of California led to a restructuring of the professional schools. The relatively small Graduate School of Architecture and Urban Planning was closed down, resulting in a shift of Architecture and Urban Design to the School of the Arts, and Urban Planning to a new School of Public Policy and Social Research, later to be called SPA, the School of Public Affairs. Urban Planning fought hard against this reorganization, not because its strengths depended on connections with Architecture so much as from a feeling that a small school offered a degree of autonomy and a sense of community that would be destroyed by breaking up GSAUP after twenty-five years of unusual achievement.

There were some who, against all administrative assurances otherwise, sensed a political bias behind the restructuring, especially when it became clear that closure or incorporation into another department might be the only alternative offered. For whatever reason, however, the Urban Planning program became a formal department, one of three in the new policy school, along with Social Welfare, which had also seen its independent school eliminated, and an entirely new Department of Policy Studies, relatively undefined and without any full-time faculty at first. While its professorial positions were maintained, Urban Planning lost its more flexible lines that were in the past used to hire practitioner faculty and other visiting scholars. The immediate effect of this loss of resources was to intensify competition for resources within the department, leading to infighting and friction, especially between the more theoretically oriented doctoral program and the professional master's degree faculty and students.

To cut this disturbing story short, the creative Urban Planning experiment at UCLA came to an end, ironically enough given the emphasis of the local research cluster, through a process of institutional restructuring aimed at getting lean and mean in the face of an economic crisis at the university. Since 1994, many of the academic strengths, internal organizational innovations, and community commitments have been significantly weakened. The critical urban and regional research cluster continued to expand, but global events and reactions to what some perceived as excessive Los Angeles boosterism reduced attention given the Southern California metropolis, especially in comparison to Chicago, Miami, Atlanta, and New York City, where a major new cluster of spatially minded urban theorists and analysts has formed in recent years.

The most important continuity with the past in Urban Planning today is the Community Scholars Program (CSP). The program was started in 1991 and soon became jointly organized with the Center for Labor Research and Education, under the leadership of labor activist Kent Wong. At first, most of the scholars were involved primarily with community development and housing issues, building on the housing and rent control movements of the 1980s. However, with the very first project on "accidental tourism," mentioned earlier, it was clear that the program would become an increasingly important vehicle for bringing the labor and community movements together.

Each year, ten or twelve experienced community activists were chosen to participate. Free of any tuition, they could attend regular classes, meet in special seminars often off-campus, and work with master's students on special projects. At graduation ceremonies, they would receive certificates of completion. As noted, the project reports started off with a boom in 1991-92 with an analysis of the tourist industry that led to policy changes as well as the Tourist Industry Development Council, led by Madeline Janis-Aparicio and forerunner of LAANE. The projects up to 2001 are listed in Notes and References.

Two of the CSP's ongoing series of project reports stand out as indicators of the new initiatives being taken in the local justice movement. *Wal-Mart and Wal-Martization: Challenges for Labor and Urban Planning* (2004–5) was one of the early spurs to what would become a worldwide movement against the labor policies and often destructive economic impact of this giant corporation. Most recently, *Fighting for a Right to the City: Collaborative Research to Support Community Organizing in L.A.* (2006–7) tapped into parallel developments at the international and national scales to mobilize new movements revolving around community-based regionalism and the concept of the right to the city. These and other CSP efforts, mainly under the leadership of Jackie Leavitt and Gilda Haas, helped to maintain close ties between UCLAUP and the expanding regional network of labor and community organizations.

UCLAUP today has recovered enough to be ranked first among the country's planning departments in scholarly citations and academic publications and continues to draw outstanding students, especially those with experience in labor and community organizations. The commitment to progressive activism remains high, if not quite as high as it was in the past, but this commitment becomes increasingly difficult to maintain given the financial crisis, university budget cuts, and Governor Schwartzeneggar's persistent attacks on the University of California Labor Center. Amid these changes, however, the strength of labor–community coalition building in Los Angeles continues to grow.

6

Seeking Spatial Justice after 9/11
Continuities and Conclusions

THE EVENTS OF SEPTEMBER 11, 2001, had significant immediate effects on the justice movement in Los Angeles, slowing its momentum and diverting its primary attention, at least temporarily. For example, the decision to replace contracted airport security workers with federal civil service employees had an especially hard effect on HERE, the Hotel Employees and Restaurant Employees union, one of the most active participants in regional coalition building. Large numbers of its members, mostly immigrant working poor, were suddenly unemployed and addressing their urgent needs absorbed most of the union's energies and expenditures. Over four thousand jobs in the tourist industry and as many as seventy thousand overall were lost in the aftermath of 9/11. Job loss, however, was not the only problem.

Locally and nationally, the shockwaves unleashed by 9/11 were quickly used to implement regressive economic policies that would have otherwise been publicly unacceptable, especially with regard to seeking social justice and preserving civil liberties. National policy initiatives associated with security issues and the formation of the federal conglomerate around the Office of Homeland Security had side effects that directly hit against labor and antipoverty movements across the country. Federal cuts were proposed for jobs training, health centers, child care, higher education, and many other welfare provisions at a time when in just the previous year the national population living below the poverty line had increased by more than a million and social polarization, measured by the income gap between the superwealthy and the working poor, reached levels unparalleled in American history.

In addition, anti-immigrant hysteria was intensified as not only federal police but also voluntary vigilantes gathered to protect the borders against any perceived alien incursion. The "ecology of fear" that was once confined to the cities became a national and increasingly global obsession. Having avoided the destruction that hit New York and Washington, D.C., on 9/11, Los Angeles, with its millions of immigrant working poor and national leadership in vigorous grassroots activism, was expected to suffer more than most urban regions from the regressive geopolitical aftermath. As it turned out, however, the local networks and coalitions responded quickly and capably, suggesting that a threshold of permanence and resilience had been reached.

Working together to fight against corporations using 9/11 as an excuse to hire cheaper workers, as was happening all over the country, LAANE, CLUE, and HERE Local 11 successfully promoted the passage of a displaced worker ordinance in December 2001, requiring employers to give preference in rehiring to workers laid off by the events three months earlier. L.A. labor unions also played a major role in the radical restructuring of the national labor movement. In 2004, HERE merged with UNITE, the Union of Needletrades, Industrial and Textile Employees (itself formed in 1995 by a merger of the ILGWU and ACTWU) to form UNITE-HERE. In 2005, it joined with several other unions, including SEIU and the International Brotherhood of Teamsters, to break with the AFL-CIO and create the Change to Win Coalition, now with seven unions and more than five million workers. More than at any other time in the past, Los Angeles leadership was directly represented in the core of the national labor movement.

It is also worthwhile recalling the "Great American Boycott" of May 1, 2006. More than a million people marched peacefully for immigrants' rights and against the rising national tide of anti-immigrant feeling. Some wore white shirts to protest the Iraq war, but there were very few side issues to detract from more general expressions of immigrant worker solidarity on a hitherto unprecedented scale and scope. Simultaneous marches took place throughout California, and at the busiest border crossing in the world, between San Diego and Tijuana, everything was closed for two hours. Nothing signified more vividly the continuing power of the regional coalitions and alliances of Southern California.

The broader justice movement in Los Angeles as well as its particular focus on seeking spatial justice thus seems not only to have survived the regressive siege that followed 9/11, it has emerged reinvigorated and renewed. Three of its most noteworthy new initiatives, each extending its effects from the local and regional scales to help stimulate national and to some extent global justice movements, are discussed here in more detail: (1) the growing importance of Community Benefits Agreements (CBAs), (2) the struggles against Wal-Mart, and (3) the formation of a national Right to the City Alliance. Also discussed is the less successful but nonetheless remarkable story of the South Central Community Garden, bulldozed in 2006 despite massive protests by grassroots groups.

Development with Justice: The Expanding Impact of Community Benefits Agreements

LAANE and its leading figure, Madeline Janis-Aparicio, would be particularly energized after 9/11, pushing forward the organization's major achievements to a national scale as well as linking its work more directly into the local governmental structure. At the heart of these extended developments has been the promotion of more effective Community Benefits Agreements (CBAs), the hallmark of LAANE's persistent campaign for development with justice or, as it proclaims in its current Web page, "Building a City of Justice." Drawing on the successful living wage campaign and other victories relating to jobs with justice, LAANE pioneered the CBA strategy in the late 1990s with an innovative agreement associated with the redevelopment of Hollywood Boulevard. Ever since, CBAs have multiplied throughout the city and county of Los Angeles and have been spreading to many cities across the country, including Denver, Milwaukee, Seattle, Pittsburgh, New Haven, Phoenix, and Atlanta.

Although the basic idea of a CBA is relatively straightforward, its spreading implementation can be said to represent a radical innovation in local economic development planning, participatory governance, the labor movement, and the struggle over residential rights to the city. A CBA is a legally binding document negotiated by a defined labor–community

coalition and a developer, usually but not necessarily supported finan-
cially by the local government or redevelopment agency. In return for
public subsidies, greater ease in meeting land-use and other local regulations, and the added advantage of dealing with a formally defined and
government-recognized community coalition, the developer negotiates
an agreement to provide a series of benefits that typically include quality
jobs, local hiring, affordable housing, environmental mitigations, and
various community services.

The list of benefits varies with the nature of the projects and the
needs of the community and has been growing with each successful CBA
contract. In the North Hollywood Mixed-Use Redevelopment Project,
for example, a child care center, a health insurance trust fund for local
workers, rent-free space for a worker training center, and some financial support for the North Hollywood Day Laborer Site operated by
CHIRLA, the Coalition for Humane Immigrant Rights of Los Angeles,
were part of the agreement. In another project, for an industrial park in
a poor Latino community, there were promises for traffic management,
community design review, a public art program, and improved arts education in local schools. In essence, new development projects are held
accountable for improving the quality of life and avoiding negative spillover effects in the communities within which they are located.

While this national movement was growing, something else was
happening to deepen the impact of CBAs on planning in Los Angeles.
Madeline Janis, as she now prefers to be called, was appointed in 2002 as
a volunteer commissioner to the board of the Los Angeles City Redevelopment Authority, reputedly the largest such agency in the country and
for the past four decades an enormously influential public planning organization. In 2006, the current mayor and former labor activist Antonio
Villaraigosa reappointed Janis against some opposition due to her assertive politics.

In the same year, another leading local activist, Cecilia Estolano, was
appointed chief executive officer of City Redevelopment Authority and
began a significant reorientation program for the agency, long reputed
to favor corporate interests and large-scale projects such as the Bunker
Hill redevelopment project in downtown Los Angeles. Estolano is an
environmental lawyer who served on the California Coastal Commission and as a senior policy advisor to the U.S. Environmental Protection

Agency. She also has an MA in Urban Planning from UCLA and remains in close contact with the department, occasionally teaching the required course Law and the Quality of Urban Life.

There may be a softening of its more radical edges as it expands its local power and influence, but not only has LAANE maintained its leadership in local labor–community–university coalition building, it has been a primary spark in spreading the ideas and strategic programs of these coalitions to the state, national, and global scales. This national and global reach of LAANE is exemplified further in the struggles against the world's largest retail corporation and renowned fountainhead of workers' injustices, Wal-Mart.

Wal-Mart and the Battle for Inglewood

As is now widely known, the retail giant Wal-Mart has become a prominent target for justice struggles of many different kinds locally, nationally, and around the world. An organization called the Wal-Mart Litigation Project, for example, has estimated that the corporation is sued from two to five times every day just in U.S. federal courts for more than a hundred different alleged legal violations. *Dukes v. Wal-Mart Inc.* was the largest class-action lawsuit in U.S. history, fought on behalf of 1.6 million women employees claiming various sorts of gender discrimination. Bookshelves are now filled with titles such as *How Wal-Mart Is Destroying America (and the World)*. My focus here, however, is on the role that has been played in these larger struggles against Wal-Mart by activist groups based in the Los Angeles urban region.

Perhaps not surprisingly, this L.A. story is effectively illustrated in a film (on DVD), *Wal-Mart: The High Cost of Low Price,* produced and directed by Robert Greenwald (2005). Telling the stories of people and communities across the country affected by the insidious labor policies and union-busting tactics of the world's largest retail corporation, with five thousand stores and 1.5 million employees around the world, the film reaches its crescendo of optimistic deliverance with the story of the battle for Inglewood, a successful effort to fight against Wal-Mart's "invasion of urban America" that would stimulate many dozens of similar victories. After telling the Inglewood story, a long list of small-town and big-city victories against Wal-Mart is scrolled across the screen at the film's ending.

In addition to being a vital part of the larger anti–Wal-Mart struggle, the battle for Inglewood illustrates the continued expansion of labor–community–university coalition building in Los Angeles. Inglewood is an independent municipality located near Los Angeles International Airport (LAX) and reputedly one of the largest majority African American cities in the country. Its population is a little more than 115,000, with just about as many Latino residents today as African American and with more than 20 percent of the population living below the poverty level. Within its boundaries are Hollywood Park Race Track and the Forum, formerly the main arena for the Los Angeles Lakers professional basketball team before its move to the Staples Center in the heart of downtown Los Angeles.

In the early 2000s, Wal-Mart, with its traditional base in small-town America, was developing an urban strategy aimed at relatively poor but densely populated urban communities with a special emphasis on California, where other big-box retail chains such as Costco had captured a lion's share of the market. Inglewood, for many reasons, was an especially attractive target for entering the second largest urban market in the country.

In March 2002, LAANE, through its development monitoring program and association with the United Food and Commercial Workers union (UFCW), discovered that Wal-Mart through an intermediary developer had purchased an option on a site near the Forum located in a sixty-acre area thought to be one of the largest pieces of undeveloped land in the entire county. Almost immediately, LAANE began organizing to resist this "invasion," spurred further a month later when Wal-Mart announced its plans to build forty big-box supercenters in California, including a flagship store in Inglewood. Early organizing efforts contributed to the successful passage in the city council of an ordinance banning big-box stores. In reaction, Wal-Mart brought out its biggest guns to threaten legal action against the city, while at the same time gathering signatures for a referendum to, in their view, let the people decide. In December, the city council rescinded the ordinance, and the battle for Inglewood began in full force.

The first major offensive in the battle came in August 2003, when a very unusual ballot initiative was submitted backed by the (submissive) Citizen's Committee to Welcome Wal-Mart to Inglewood. The initiative, if passed, would not just allow Wal-Mart to build a superstore on the sixty-acre lot, it would give them the equivalent of extraterritorial rights to their own virtual fiefdom on the land. Wal-Mart was allowed, indeed invited, to do whatever they wanted with the site, without government, judicial, or community oversight. Stunned by this presumptive strike, LAANE with assistance from Clergy and Laity United for Economic Justice (CLUE), local religious leaders, and grocery workers, began their strategic coalition-building efforts in earnest, leading to the creation of a new organization, the Coalition for a Better Inglewood (CBI).

In addition to organizing help, LAANE contributed in two other vital areas, promoting extensive analytical research as well as effective public relations and media linkages. A series of courses, ranging from undergraduate honors seminars to Community Scholars Program projects, was held in UCLAUP, leading to a variety of reports such as *Researching Wal-Mart: A Guide to an Annotated Bibliography, Wal-Mart and Wal-Martization: Challenges for Labor and Urban Planning,* both mentored by Jackie Leavitt, and *The Price We Pay for Wal-Mart,* published by the ILWU Educational Committee with the assistance of Goetz Wolff and three Urban Planning graduate students. The latter report included some detailed comparisons between Wal-Mart and Costco, a more progressive as well as efficient big-box retailer.

The ballot initiative was scheduled to be voted on in April 2004. Early polls showed roughly 60 to 40 percent in favor as Wal-Mart waged its own media blitz on the people of Inglewood. CBI's efforts were weakened by what would turn out to be a lengthy countywide strike against the two leading retail grocery giants in the Los Angeles region, propelled in part by efforts to control, if not lower, wages in the face of potential Wal-Mart superstore competition. Wal-Mart's campaign emphasized its traditional arguments that its low prices were serving the urgent needs of the relatively poor, that it achieved these low prices by keeping labor and other costs low, and that its stores created vitally needed jobs and raised local tax revenues. Was it not the democratic way to let the people decide whether or not they wanted a store to be built?

Wal-Mart clearly underestimated the power of the resurgent coalitions of Los Angeles. Counterarguments were developed to show that wages at Wal-Mart were so low that its workers had to rely on state welfare benefits to survive. In a report chaired by Congressman George

Miller (D-Cal), it was estimated that these low wages were subsidized by California taxpayers to the amount of nearly $50 million. How Wal-Mart estimated its net effect on jobs and tax revenues was challenged as giving insufficient attention to wider spillover effects on surrounding areas in terms of lost jobs and revenues, especially with respect to smaller retail stores forced to close because of the insurmountable competition. The long list of labor grievances and lawsuits was also marshaled against the corporation, as were stories of Wal-Mart closing its stores soon after subsidies ran out and its creation of a specialized executive cadre of union busters.

On April 6, 2004, a month after the grocery strike ended, the people of Inglewood rejected the initiative by 61 to 39 percent, but this was not the end of the battle. Wal-Mart, after spending $1.5 million to promote the initiative, proceeded to purchase the land anyway. This triggered a vigorous response from CBI and LAANE. New campaigns were initiated, first to require Community Benefits Agreements for any large development project in Inglewood and second to create legislation that would give residents detailed information about the community impact of superstores. A year after the election, CBI sent a delegation of community leaders to Bentonville, Arkansas, Wal-Mart's global headquarters, for the company's first ever "Media Day" conference. There the CBI challenged Wal-Mart to accept Community Benefits Agreements for all its projects and urged the company to stop spending millions of dollars on its public relations efforts and instead invest the money in improving the lives of their workers. In July 2006, a superstore ordinance similar to one enacted in the City of Los Angeles two years earlier was passed by the Inglewood City Council requiring the completion of a full economic impact report before approval could be considered.

Wal-Mart was not stopped entirely in its plans to expand in California, but there is little doubt that its ambitions were significantly thwarted by the power of local grassroots coalitions. The battle for Inglewood played an important role in globalizing what has been happening in Los Angeles and, at the local scale, in bringing together many different streams and strategies of coalition building. There was no overt mention of spatial or territorial justice, nor were there any explicit claims about the right to the city, but I think it would not be stretching things too far to say that these concepts and their related strategies were involved in a significant way.

The Failed Struggle to Save the South Central Community Garden

Amid these success stories is a more complex tale of a failed effort at coalition building, one that reflects the continued power of corporate interests to shape urban space, the weakness of the local state even when supporting the efforts of activists, and the persistence of ethnoracial divisions that can work to fracture collective struggles for social and spatial justice. I refer to the July 2006 bulldozing of the South Central Community Garden, at the time one of the largest urban farms anywhere in the United States. Painful though it may be for those involved, the story of the garden also symbolizes many of the strengths of coalition building in Los Angeles and needs to be remembered.

The story begins, interestingly enough, in 1986 when the City of Los Angeles, using its powers of eminent domain, acquired a parcel of land in then predominantly African American South Central Los Angeles for the purpose of building a waste-to-energy incinerator known as LANCER, the Los Angeles City Energy Recovery Project. As discussed in chapter 5, the proposed LANCER project became one of the earliest successes of the environmental justice movement. Led by Concerned Citizens of South Central Los Angeles and supported by many other organizations and activists in the region, vigorous protests arose against the project and its promotional promises of job generation and positive environmental impact.

Due to community opposition, the project was abandoned, and the land, around fourteen acres located near the corner of East Forty-first and South Alameda Streets, was left open. Eminent domain procedures gave the right to repurchase the land to the original owners should the city be unable to sell it for nonpublic or nonhousing purposes within ten years. The idea was that eminent domain required "developmental" use of the land. The parcel remained empty, like so much of deindustrialized South Central L.A., until 1994, when it was sold to the L.A. Harbor Department, which turned it over to the L.A. Regional Food Bank, a private nonprofit food distribution network located across the street from the incinerator site, to use as a community garden. The Regional Food Bank was then part of a vigorous "food justice" movement aimed at providing fresh produce at reasonable prices, especially to low-income communities.

The South Central Farm or, as it came to be known, the South Central Community Garden (SCCG) began cultivation even earlier, soon after the Justice Riots of 1992. It became one of the largest community gardens in the United States and a leading edge of the national urban agriculture movement. At its peak, the SCCG involved nearly four hundred families, predominantly Latino immigrants reflecting a major shift in neighborhood demography. Everything began to change, however, in 2001, when Ralph Horowitz, a partner in the real estate firm that formerly owned the property, sued the city for breach of contract.

The legal argument raised claimed that the land was not being used for appropriate developmental purposes and therefore the original owners had been denied the right to repurchase after ten years. The city denied the claim but entered into secret negotiations that led to a settlement in 2003 that astounded the community gardeners and their supporters. In return for little more than a promise to donate some of the land to build a soccer field, Horowitz was able to buy back the land for almost the same roughly $5 million paid for it in the eminent domain seizure ten years earlier, despite the enormous increase in value that occurred in this time period. Complicating matters were indications that some African American community leaders in the earlier protests against the LANCER project were supportive of the decision, thinking perhaps that the community garden had not had sufficient developmental benefits for African Americans living nearby.

Buoyed by expectations that the new mayor, Antonio Villaraigosa, would strongly back their claims, the farmers in response formed a new organization, South Central Farmers Feeding Families, and attracted widespread support from environmental groups, Hollywood celebrities, and others throughout the region. Despite lawsuits aimed at invalidating the sale of the property, attempts to purchase the property to restore the garden, passionate appeals to the mayor and city council, and almost daily protests at the site, on the morning of June 13, 2006, the farmers began to be evicted. At least forty protesters were arrested, including the actress Daryl Hannah. On the following day, a private security firm occupied the property to prevent farmers returning, and a few weeks later bulldozers leveled the property.

Horowitz later claimed that he would not sell the land even for $100 million, because of alleged anti-Semitic remarks and picketing of his home. His current plans are to build a warehouse and distribution center on the bulldozed site. The city, while still refusing to release documents on the 2003 negotiations, offered some publicly owned land at an alternate site located underneath high-voltage power lines. Five months after the eviction, more than sixty South Central Farmers relocated to the site near Avalon Boulevard in Watts and have made it a symbolic and organizational spearhead for the Los Angeles Community Garden Council, one of the largest such organizations in the country.

The South Central Garden experience has entered into the national and to some degree international community activist and environmental justice traditions today as an example of organizational strength and commitment to a variant of what I have been describing as residential rights to inhabit the city and shape the production of urban and regional geographies. This spirit of resistance and renewal has been captured in an outstanding documentary film, *The Garden*, produced and directed by Scott Hamilton Kennedy and nominated for an Academy Award in 2009. *The Garden* adds to the growing list of films about the surge of coalition building in Los Angeles, along with Ken Loach's *Bread and Roses* on Justice for Janitors, Haskell Wexler's *Bus Riders Union,* and Robert Greenwald's *Wal-Mart: The High Cost of Low Price.*

Building a National Coalition on the Right to the City

The revival of the idea of the right to the city as an organizing principle and focus for strategic activism reached a significant political threshold in January 2007 with the inaugural meeting of a new national coalition that would be called the Right to the City Alliance. In the story of the search for spatial justice and the rise of labor–community–university coalition building in Los Angeles, the creation of an expanding organization of "regional networks" inspired and mobilized around an explicit idea of urban-based human rights and regional political democracy is a momentous achievement. The Alliance is still in its early stages, and its ambitious objectives are just beginning to be actively implemented, but its formation has already helped to crystallize and consolidate contemporary struggles for social and spatial justice at many different operational scales, from the local to the global.

The inaugural meeting of the Alliance took place January 11–14, 2007, at the Japanese American Cultural Center in Little Tokyo, Los Angeles. The coalition-building event was called by three organizations, the Miami Workers Center, Strategic Actions for a Just Economy (SAJE), and Tenants and Workers United, a group from Northern Virginia. Also participating were more than thirty community-based organizations from eight metropolitan areas (Boston, Washington, D.C., Los Angeles, Miami, New Orleans, New York City, Oakland, Providence, and San Francisco) and seven academics, including Jackie Leavitt (UCLA), Manuel Pastor (UCSC, now USC), Nik Theodore (Chicago), and Dick Walker (UCB). The volunteers and note-takers were all graduate students in Urban Planning at UCLA. More detail on the participating organizations is given in Notes and References.

Three objectives were made clear: (1) to begin the process of building collective capacity for local urban struggles to become a national movement around the right to the city; (2) to provide a frame and structure to set the stage for regional organizing and for connecting intellectuals to the work being done; (3) to build a national network/alliance that will allow organizations to learn from one another, create national debate on issues affecting urban communities, and help coordinate an expanding national program. Framing the discussion was a broader ambition aimed at asserting a new vision of democracy that would build on a contemporary understanding of the dynamics of urban and regional development and change.

At the core of the action programs discussed were the problems of gentrification and displacement. This focus on gentrification reflected the interests of the key participating organizations, all of which, except for the special case of New Orleans, were centered in expanding urban regions with rising house prices and growing income polarities. A discussion led by a representative from the Miami Workers Center identified a series of restructuring processes that had intensified the problems associated with gentrification over the past thirty years, including the decline in federal support for urban programs, privatization and massive outsourcing of public services, deindustrialization, inflated real estate and housing markets, the increasing gap between rich and poor, and the criminalization of poverty. This "New Gentrification" was seen as the strategic mobilizing focus for the right to the city movement, at least in its early stages.

New theoretical approaches were also discussed, particularly with regard to the rise of neoliberalism and the uneven effects of globalization and the New Economy. Particular attention was given to the need for regional organizing, especially for the creation of regional networks that would extend beyond the core urban areas into the larger metropolitan regions. Also introduced were the original ideas of Henri Lefebvre about the colonization of urban space by capital and the culture of consumption. In the words of René Poitevin from NYU, "Right to the city is the response of oppressed communities to the attempt by market forces to reshape the city as if these communities don't matter, as if they don't have every right to be here, and to shape the city in ways that meet their needs and their visions."

Although there was little or no discussion of a critical spatial perspective (except for the emphasis on regional networking and indirect associations with environmental justice) and only some mention of the more empowered notion of justice, there were many links to the ideas and arguments discussed in *Seeking Spatial Justice*. The "new theoretical approaches" reflected many of the findings of the Los Angeles research cluster on urban and regional restructuring, the polarizing effects of globalization, and the widening income gap associated with the New Economy. At the core of the approach outlined was the strategic objective of creating more lasting and effective ties between separate social movements and activist struggles based on a shared experience of the injustice and oppression inherent in the social production of urban space. Activists tended to be isolated in their own separate fields of action, it was argued, making the formation of collective alliances difficult. The formation of regional networks around the right to the city concept provided a new and potentially more effective mobilizing and unifying force in fighting all forms of discrimination.

The Right to the City Alliance has become a vital part of what is expanding rapidly into a global movement of unusual proportions. Googling "right to the city" today, for example, brings up nearly nine million entries. In many ways, this expanding global movement is a fitting concluding example of many of the ideas and arguments discussed in the previous chapters, from the cross-disciplinary diffusion of a critical spatial perspective and the formation of a new spatial consciousness, to the debates on the spatiality of injustice and the injustice of spatiality, to the translation of urban spatial theory into practice through the remarkable resurgence of grassroots activism and coalition building in Los Angeles.

At the same time, it is also just the beginning of a new stage in the struggle for spatial justice and regional democracy that is being made more urgent and necessary by the deepening world economic crisis. I conclude with a brief commentary on how the crash of 2008 affects and might be affected by the theory and practice of seeking spatial justice.

Concluding Remarks: Seeking Spatial Justice after the Crash of 2008

I began writing this book with a sense of strategic optimism. Looking back at what I have written, I remain strategically optimistic even as the world plunges further into the worst economic crisis since the Great Depression. I use the word *strategic* to describe my optimism because it expresses a hopefulness that may not be justified by the hard evidence I see around me: the persistent geopolitical conflicts raging around the world; the stubborn resistance arising in the United States against the innovative health, environmental, and other social policies of the new presidential regime; the signs of weakness growing at the local level at the universities, in civil society, and in bankrupted state and local governments. Avoiding despair, I could retreat into normative idealizations, calling for little more than conventional progressive or radical democratic politics and practices, but the critical spatial perspective that I have spent so many pages explaining and promoting demands more than this.

A critical theoretical perspective of any kind aims at producing knowledge and understanding that have the potential to change the world for the better. Critical thinking is driven by strategic optimism and expectation, by the goal of making theoretical and practical-political sense of the world so that we can act more appropriately and effectively. I am optimistic today for many reasons that relate in large part to our accumulated practical and theoretical understanding of the contemporary condition and the crisis-generated restructuring processes that have been reshaping our consequential geographies over the past forty years. There is little doubt that the crash of 2008 marked a crucial turning point in these restructuring processes and that new directions of change are likely to be set in motion, but what we have learned from the application of a critical spatial perspective has the potential for stimulating continuing innovation and perhaps unexpected breakthroughs in the search for greater social and spatial justice.

What we have learned tells us that though there are many significant continuities with the past, the present is a time for innovative departures, for political actions that can take effective advantage of the new and different opportunities and challenges arising from the current period of what can be called restructuring-generated crises. The contemporary moment is so different from what existed twenty or thirty years ago—some would say even one or two years past—that to react as if the conditions were the same, just another in a long stream of economic crises, almost surely will not lead to very positive results for the disadvantaged populations of the world. What then might guide these new departures?

Not surprising to the reader, I start with the need for an even more assertive spatial perspective, one that recognizes the consequential spatiality of our lives and understands how social and spatial processes intertwine to produce oppressive as well as enabling geographies. This recognition of a new spatial consciousness is likely to continue spreading into many more fields of theory building, empirical analysis, and social activism. Most optimistically, I foresee a sea change in intellectual and political thought in the twenty-first century, as the deep distortions of the late-nineteenth century are recognized and reconsidered, and the consequential spatiality of human life is given critical attention equal to that traditionally assigned to our historically defined sociality. Whether or not this sea change develops, a critical spatial perspective will be almost surely more central and essential than ever before in meeting the challenges of the future.

Driving the spatial turn still further will be currently emerging ideas about the importance of urbanization, regionalism, and the interconnectivity of geographical scales from the global to the local. Studies of the generative effects of urban agglomeration and cohesive regional economies are still in their infancy, but they have attained an extraordinary threshold, leading a growing number of scholars to recognize these generative effects as the primary causes of economic development, technological innovation, and cultural creativity. That they are also generative of unjust geographies, deepening inequalities of social and political power, and the explosive crises of capitalism such as the economic meltdown of 2008 needs also to be addressed with equal diligence and emphasis.

What we have learned from the debates on and struggles for spatial justice and the right to the city is leading to a more spatial interpretation of what happened in 2008, especially with regard to its rootedness in the deep restructuring processes that occurred in the decades after 1970. During this period, capitalism experienced a profound reconfiguration, a significant part of which was a spatial fix. The geography of cities, regions, national states, and the global economy was reshaped in an effort to recover from the multiple crises of the 1960s and reduce the possibility of disruptive social unrest. Let us look at some of these spatial changes, for they provide insight into the crash of 2008.

After the early 1970s, the relatively simple spatial structure of metropolitan urbanization, with its clear and typically monocentric division between the urban and suburban ways of life, became more heterogeneous and intermixed, blurring old boundaries and creating increasingly polycentric networks of expansive city regions or regional cities of unprecedented size and complexity. The modern metropolis, shaped in the postwar era by some blend of Fordist mass production and Keynesian welfare statism, morphed into a post-Fordist, postmodern postmetropolis, with a qualitatively different form of urbanism. Among many changes, the density contrast between inner and outer cities declined as suburbia became increasingly urbanized and regional urbanization began to replace metropolitan urbanization and purely suburban expansion and sprawl.

As these more amorphous city regions formed into a new global hierarchy, the old international geographical division of labor between First, Second, and Third Worlds experienced a similar spatial reconfiguration. The Second World of socialist states led by the Soviet Union disintegrated, newly industrialized countries (NICs) entered the First World, and the Third World became increasingly differentiated and redefined. Accelerated globalization cut across old boundaries and fostered worldwide networking among the major city regions, homogenizing as well as differentiating the global cultural economy.

Bursting through this global restructuring on its own terms was China. Its distinctive blend of communism and capitalism brought to one-sixth of the world's population the most rapid urban-based industrialization in history. Some consider the one-sixth of the world that is India to be catching up. New supranational organizations and trading blocs multiplied over the past thirty years, hoping to form larger and more competitive markets based on the model of the European Union. Amid this restructuring of the capitalist world order, exceptional China has come to occupy an increasingly powerful if somewhat ambiguous position, whether alone or in such combinations as Chindia (China and India, representing one out of every three people on earth) and BRIC (Brazil, Russia, India, and China).

Another spatial fix was occurring at the state and regional scale to adapt to the reorganization of global and metropolitan economies. While urban agglomerations and city regions became increasingly important and new influences emerged at the supranational and global scales to challenge state sovereignty, many states and the national economies they controlled were restructured. The leading edge of this state restructuring process was the rise of what has come to be called neoliberalism, a system of governance and its associated ideology that encouraged economic growth based on unregulated markets, privatization, and the creation of new sources of superprofitability based on various kinds of financial manipulation. As I will come back to shortly, it was this neoliberal profit bubble that burst in 2008.

As state sovereignty changed, at times extending state control supra- and subnationally, at other times giving rise to signs of declining state power, regionalisms experienced a notable resurgence. States such as Yugoslavia, Czechoslovakia, and the Soviet Union disintegrated, Belgium and Italy faced similar threats, and greater devolution of state powers occurred in the United Kingdom, Canada, Spain, and other countries in response to regional pressures. Regionalism exposed the gap between stubbornly resistant governance structures and more flexibly adaptive transnational and global economic relations and flows. It also stimulated the development of critical regional studies and the emergence of what some have called a New Regionalism. Unlike the regional thinking of the past, the New Regionalism reaches above the scale of the nation-state to focus on multinational organizations and trading blocs, and to the metropolitan and local scale to regionalize the urban discourse and debates on local democracy and the right to the city.

Simplifying somewhat, the crisis-generated restructuring processes and the attempted spatial fixes that occurred through the 1970s and 1980s, encouraged by the highly but very selectively profitable neoliberalism associated with the regimes of Reagan and Thatcher, consolidated enough in the 1990s to be understood as a new mode of capitalist development. Popularly known as the New Economy, it is more flexible in its organization of production and management, infused with new information and communications technologies, globalized in its reach, and built around such growth sectors as business services, investment banking, and the umbrella term FIRE for finance, insurance, and real estate.

Beginning as early as the stock market crash of 1987, the many events of 1989 (Tiananmen Square, the Berlin wall, Soviet *perestroika*), the Los Angeles Justice Riots of 1992 and subsequent antiglobalization uprisings, the Asian financial crises of the 1990s, and somewhat less directly the events of 9/11, crisis-generated restructuring has begun to shift into an era of restructuring-generated crises, episodes of unrest and economic decline that are caused more by the new forms and structures that were created after 1970 than by older contradictions and conflicts. It is in this sense that the crash of 2008 can be attributed to the particular features of neoliberal capitalism and its most propulsive FIRE sector, especially as they had grown in the United States and to a lesser extent in Western Europe.

The FIRE sector's contribution to the gross national product and to overall employment in the United States grew at extraordinary rates over the past thirty years, but what developed outside the normal limits of the real economy was even more amazing. A ballooning and computerized credit economy became bloated with trillions of dollars' worth of semifictitious exchange value in the form of hedge funds, credit default swaps, private equity funds, and other electronically recycled forms of capitalization that did not exist before 1970. Absorbed into this weakly regulated FIRE-fed financial bubble and its often Ponzi-like investment streams were worker pension funds, household savings, first and second mortgages, bank reserves, any source of capital not yet involved in high-risk investments.

For around thirty years, the payoffs for those participating were impressive, at least on paper. They helped to generate a pronounced polarization of incomes in the United States, with an enormous concentration of real and putative wealth in the upper 1 percent of the income ladder, while the bottom 40 percent experienced what all signs suggest was an absolute decline in wages and a growing gap in household income when compared to the superrich. However measured, the income distribution became more regressive and unjust than at almost any other time in U.S. history. The geography of economic inequality was affected but not nearly as much. There was the Frostbelt-to-Sunbelt shift, a relative concentration of wealth along the Atlantic and Pacific coasts versus the interior, and a growing urbanization of poverty, the concentration of the poor in major urban agglomerations (where there was also a concentration of the rich).

I am sure that there are other and perhaps very different explanations for what happened in 2008, but for present purposes and future prospects for seeking spatial justice, it can be said that this neoliberal bubble exploded, marking at least the beginning of the end of an era of economic restructuring. It is certainly not the end of capitalism or even the end of its neoliberal variant, for the future may bring about its reconstitution. What I will say is that what is happening today is both a growing awareness of the injustices and inequities embedded in the New Economy and an increasing need to find better ways of achieving greater justice however defined.

This brings the concluding discussion back to David Harvey, Henri Lefebvre, and the debates on the right to the city. In a keynote address to the World Social Forum held in Belém, Brazil, on February 13, 2009, Harvey extended his thinking about the right to the city to an interpretation of the current financial crisis, describing it as essentially a crisis of urbanization. After apologizing to the audience for speaking in English, the language of international imperialism, he proceeded to present a characteristically insightful analysis of capitalism's perpetual and crisis-filled struggle to construct a built environment and specific geography to sustain its imperative drive to accumulate, to find profitable outlets for its surplus product.

Drawing on unnamed sources, he claimed that there have been 378 financial crises around the world since around 1970, nearly seven times the number estimated for the period between 1945 and 1970. In his view, at least half of the post-1970 crises were fundamentally urban crises. They "have a basis in urbanization," caused in large part by housing and property speculation and shifts in investment from productive and employment-generating activities to consumption-driven urban redevelopment and financed by a swelling credit bubble that grew in estimated value to ten times the gross national product of the world.

Emphasizing continuities with the past rather than the new and different conditions of the present, Harvey presents a vivid interpretation of the economic crash of 2008 as specifically a crisis of urbanization, in other words a fundamentally spatial crisis. He develops his earlier arguments about accumulation by dispossession and links them to rising property values, the explosion of subprime mortgages, the record growth of household debt, spreading foreclosures especially for minority populations but also in once booming, predominantly white suburbs, and what he argues has been the greatest loss of asset value for the poor (and I would add the middle class as well) in history. In reaction to today's "big crisis that keeps going and going and going" like the battery-driven bunny, he turns to the need for a renewed struggle over the right to the city:

> My argument is that if this crisis is basically a crisis of urbanization then the solution should be urbanization of a different sort and this is where the struggle for the right to the city becomes crucial because we have the opportunity to do something different. . . . We need a national movement of Urban Reform like you have here [in Brazil]. . . . We need in fact to begin to exercise our right to the city . . . to reverse this whole way in which the financial institutions are given priority over us . . . to ask the question what is more important, the value of the banks or the value of humanity . . . to take command of the capitalist surplus absorption problem. We have to socialize the capital surplus. We have to use it to meet social needs.

These remarks take the current debates on the right to the city—and the search for spatial justice that I have connected to it—to new levels of practical and political understanding, as Harvey has done so often in the past. I do not hesitate to agree with him that the current financial crisis is fundamentally an urban-generated crisis and that an appropriate response to it must also be fundamentally urban-based. However, there are some significant qualifications that need to be made about these broad conclusions.

First of all, the struggles over the right to the city must not be reduced only to struggles against capitalism. There is no doubt that unjust geographies are created to a significant extent by the exploitative effects of capitalist accumulation backed by a conciliatory state and powerful market forces. But there are many other forces shaping these unjust geographies, such as racism, religious fundamentalism, and gender discrimination, as well as spatial practices that are not necessarily designed only or always to reinforce class differences, such as the drawing of electoral district and other boundaries, the siting of toxic facilities, the building of mass transit systems, the location of schools and hospitals, the formation of neighborhood associations, community gardening and food production, zoning laws, the residential clustering of particular occupations such as artists or engineers.

Recognizing the multiple forces that shape the social production of urban space leads away from the creation of monolithic and narrowly channeled social movements and toward more crosscutting coalition building. Mobilizing community- and labor-based regional coalitions and alliances around the right to the city must be kept radically open to multiple constituencies and to what in the past might have been considered strange bedfellows, such as labor leaders and yuppies or union locals and homeowners associations or, for that matter, black and white, man and woman, straight and gay. Forming such crosscutting alliances is not easy, but as I have been arguing repeatedly in previous chapters, the new spatial consciousness that has been developing over the past decades provides new opportunities to mobilize, sustain, and strategically advance the objectives of recombinative coalitions. Hence the argument that the right to the city needs to be seen much more explicitly than it has been in recent years as overarchingly spatial, as a struggle for spatial justice.

As I have also argued, such coalition building to achieve spatial justice and the right to the city should not be confined to city dwellers, whether implicitly or explicitly. These coalitions must seek to mobilize and organize across geographical scales and to learn from comparable experiences in other countries, regions, cities, neighborhoods, and households. The search for spatial justice must connect more closely with the environmental justice movement and help to redefine and redirect existing movements against globalization, neoliberalism, global warming, species extinction, nuclear weapons, religious intolerance, and torture of any kind. In much the same way that coalitions need to be built within urban regions, they need to reach out to other regional networks and across scales from the global and transnational to the local and the intimacies of the household and home.

The world changed dramatically in 2008, raising to new heights both the dangers and the opportunities associated intrinsically with crisis. Seeing the present almost entirely as a continuity with the past, another in an unending parade of almost unavoidable problems associated with capitalism or racism or patriarchy, may help us learn from history but is not enough to deal effectively with the challenges of today and tomorrow. We must approach the future with strategic optimism, with a radical openness to new ideas, and, if there is one lesson to be learned from all that I have been saying, with the theoretical and practical insight that comes from a critical spatial perspective.

────────Acknowledgments

I BEGAN WRITING THIS BOOK MORE THAN TEN YEARS AGO and published some initial ideas about spatial justice in *Postmetropolis: Critical Studies of Cities and Regions* (2000), especially in the concluding chapter. A year after this publication I received a small grant from the Institute for Labor Education at UCLA (now IRLE, Institute for Research on Labor and Employment) for a project on spatial justice and the resurgence of labor–community–university coalition building in Los Angeles. In many ways, *Seeking Spatial Justice* is an expanded final report for this project, and I thank the Miguel Contreras Labor Program and the IRLE for their support and patience. In this book the objective to reach and perhaps helpfully inform an audience of labor and community activists remains central.

I would like to take the opportunity here to thank the outstanding group of students who provided research assistance on this project and continue to help in developing the theory and practice of seeking spatial justice. They include Mustafa Dikec, Joe Boski, Tom Kemeny, Walter Nichols, Alfonso Hernandez-Marquez, Stefano Bloch, Ava Bromberg, and Konstantina Soureli. Konstantina has been particularly valuable in making editorial comments and keeping me up-to-date with recent developments. Thanks are also due the dozens of doctoral students who took the Colloquium in Planning Theory I taught for more than ten years, the last five of which focused on the theme of spatial justice. The lively discussions that arose around this topic contributed significantly to *Seeking Spatial Justice*.

At UCLA, I have been fortunate to be part of an extraordinary group of research scholars and planning activists who have made the Los Angeles urban region an unusually creative laboratory for the development of new ideas about urban and regional planning and development theory, geopolitical economy, and grassroots coalition building. I have not tried to resolve the edgy controversies that have emerged over whether these developments define a new "school" of urban and regional studies, but argue instead that the core of whatever has been achieved through the work of this cluster of geographers and planners derives primarily from a widely shared commitment to the practical and political application of a critical spatial perspective.

One final point: while writing these acknowledgments, the Institute for Research on Labor and Employment at UCLA and at the University of California–Berkeley and its umbrella organization, the Miguel Contreras Labor Program, were under siege from California governor Arnold Schwarzenegger. After failures to do so in earlier years, the Terminator Governor announced in late 2008 the defunding of the IRLE and the entire Labor Center in his proposed 2009 budget, a specific targeting that can be seen only as a politically motivated violation of academic freedom and an attack on social and spatial justice not just for university workers but for everyone everywhere. No other unit in the University of California system was stripped of its budget in this way. One can only hope that strategic optimism prevails here as well, as the center continues its invaluable work with special support from the budget-strained university administration.

Notes and References

Prologue

I want to make clear from the start that my interpretation of the Bus Riders Union (BRU) case as an example of how spatial strategies have entered political practice is not necessarily related to how the relevant organizations and their leaders view their efforts and campaigns. The best way to understand these objectives, strategies, and accomplishments is through the writings of Eric Mann, director and cofounder of the Labor/Community Strategy Center, and from the Web pages for the Strategy Center and its affiliated organizations, including the Bus Riders Union, Transit Riders for Public Transportation, National School for Strategic Organizing, and Community Rights Campaign (www.thestrategycenter.org). My thanks to Eric and Lian Hurst Mann, Manuel Criollo (currently Lead Organizer of the BRU), and Barbara Lott-Holland (BRU cochair) for making their views on racial and spatial injustice clear to me and for their critical review of an earlier draft discussing the BRU case.

For an indication of the spatial approach to racism and the injustices of capitalism taken by the leading figures behind the court decision, see Hurst Mann (1996, 1991) and Dutton and Hurst Mann (2003, 2000, 1996), listed in the prologue bibliography, which also includes other references relevant to the BRU decision. Lian Hurst Mann is an architectural critic and theorist, cofounder of the Strategy Center, editor of its bilingual political quarterly *Ahora/Now,* and currently cocoordinator of the National School for Strategic Organizing. Recently, she and several colleagues have organized an expansion in the publications and multimedia activities of the Strategy Center, producing books, pamphlets, and films. The latest book by the in-house "movement publisher" Frontlines Press is Eric Mann, *Katrina's Legacy: White Racism and Black Reconstruction in New Orleans and the Gulf Coast* (2009).

As noted in the text, there were several civil rights cases arguing for transit equity and racial justice before the 1996 decision in the BRU class action lawsuit. Planners unsuccessfully challenged the Cleveland Transit Authority in the 1970s over rail versus bus investments, and similar challenges took place in Philadelphia in 1991 (*Better North Philadelphia v. Southeastern Pennsylvania Transportation Authority [SEPTA]*) and New York in 1995 (*New York Urban League Inc. v. the State of New York Metropolitan Transit Authority et al.*). Why these cases failed and the BRU case was successful is a complex question. There is no doubt that the powerful political commitment, experience, and strategic organizing effort of the coalition mobilized by the Strategy Center was a major factor. There is also ample evidence that specifically spatial strategies played a key role in the BRU court case and in the actions of the Strategy Center before and after the 1996 decision. For examples of their critical spatial approach, see Mann et al. (1996, 1991) and, more recently, the map-rich *BRU Five-Year Plan for Countywide New Bus Services* (2005), available for purchase from the L/CSC, Wiltern Center, 3780 Wilshire Blvd., Los Angeles, CA 90010.

The major source I have used in analyzing the court case and the implications of the consent decree is the unpublished doctoral dissertation of Mark Evans Garrett. Garrett, a trained lawyer, obtained his PhD in urban planning in 2006, after serving more than ten years as a research associate on numerous urban planning research projects. Mark deserves my thanks for his comprehensive and spatially aware analysis of the history of transit politics in Los Angeles and for numerous discussions on varied topics over the years.

The BRU case is also briefly discussed and set into the context of the history of transit development in Los Angeles in the essay "Waiting for the Bus" by Sikivu Hutchinson (2000) and in her book *Imagining Transit* (2003). In the latter, she argues that "the cultural geography of transportation has had a compelling influence upon the construction of race, gender, and urban subjectivity in the postmodern city." Hutchinson is a member of the Los Angeles County Commission on Human Relations and editor of *blackfemlens.org, A Journal of Progressive Commentary and Literature.* For more on the history of transit development in Los Angeles, see Wachs (1996).

The reference to Los Angeles passing New York as the densest urbanized area in the United States in 1990 remains both startling and easily misunderstood. The statistic is based on a relatively new census category of "urbanized area," defined by the extent of census tracts having a population of 500 per square mile, somewhat like what in the past was called the "built-up area." A major factor behind the densification of Los Angeles since 1950, when it was probably the least dense major metropolis in the country, to 1990 was the net addition of 7.4 million people in this forty-year period. At least 4 to 5 million of this net increase was concentrated around the downtown core of Los Angeles, raising densities to Manhattan-like levels and creating an unusually large agglomeration of the immigrant, largely transit-dependent working poor, an important factor in the BRU court case and in the wider resurgence of labor–community coalitions in the region. For data on this topic, see *Demographia*, 1990 US Urbanized Area Density Profile, http://www.demographia.com/db-porta.htm.

Haskell Wexler's *Bus Riders Union* appeared first as a video and was shown in several parts on television. Theatrical release is listed both as 1999 and 2000. Wexler has had a long career as one of Hollywood's leading radical film directors and cinematographers. Starting with his first documentary, *The Bus* (1965), his films have creatively addressed labor and human rights issues, especially in Latin America. As a cinematographer, Wexler has had connections with other films on labor–community movements in Los Angeles, including Ken Loach's *Bread and Roses* (see chapter 4) on the Justice for Janitors Movement, and more recently with documentary films about the South Central Farm (see chapter 6). A DVD of Wexler's *Bus Riders Union* is also available from the Labor/Community Strategy Center.

Brown, Jeffrey. 1998. "Race, Class, Gender and Public Transportation: Lessons from the Bus Riders Union Lawsuit." *Critical Planning* 5: 3–20.

Burgos, Rita, and Laura Pulido. 1998. "The Politics of Gender in the Los Angeles Bus Riders Union/Sindicato de Pasajeros." *Capitalism, Nature, Socialism* 9: 75–82.

Dutton, Thomas A., and Lian Hurst Mann. 2003. "Affiliated Practices and Aesthetic Interventions: Remaking Public Spaces in Cincinnati and Los Angeles." *Review of Education/Pedagogy/Cultural Studies* 25, 3: 201–29.

———. 2000. "Problems in Theorizing 'The Political' in Architectural Discourse." *Rethinking Marxism* 12, 4: 117–29.

———, eds. 1996. *Reconstructing Architecture: Critical Discourses and Social Practices*. Minneapolis: University of Minnesota Press.

Garrett, Mark. 2006. "The Struggles for Transit Justice: Race, Space, and Social Equity." PhD diss., Department of Urban Planning, UCLA.

Grengs, Joe. 2002. "Community-Based Planning as a Source of Political Change: The Transit Equity Movement of Los Angeles' Bus Riders Union." *Journal of the American Planning Association* 2: 165–78.

Hurst Mann, Lian. 1996. "Subverting the Avant-Garde: Critical Theory's Real Strategy." In *Reconstructing Architecture*, ed. Dutton and Hurst Mann, 259–318.

————. 1991. "Crossover Dream: A Parti(r), Structures for Knowledge of Difference." In *Voices in Architectural Education: Cultural Politics and Pedagogy,* ed. Thomas Dutton, 29–64. New York: Bergin and Garvey.

Hutchinson, Sikivu. 2003. *Imagining Transit: Race, Gender, and Transportation Politics in Los Angeles.* New York: Peter Lang Publishing Group.

————. 2000. "Waiting for the Bus." *Social Text* 63, 18: 107–20.

Mann, Eric. 2002. *Dispatches from Durban: Firsthand Commentaries on the World Conference against Racism and Post–September 11 Movement Strategies.* Los Angeles: Frontlines Press.

————. 2001. "A Race Struggle, A Class Struggle, A Women's Struggle All at Once: Organizing on the Buses of L.A." In *Working Classes, Global Realities: Socialist Register 2001,* ed. Leo Panitch and Colin Leys. New York: Monthly Review Press.

————. 1987. *Taking On General Motors: A Case Study of the UAW Campaign to Keep GM Van Nuys Open.* Los Angeles: UCLA Institute for Industrial Relations, Center for Labor Research and Education.

Mann, Eric. 1996. *A New Vision for Urban Transportation: The Bus Riders Union Makes History at the Intersection of Mass Transit, Civil Rights, and the Environment.* With the Planning Committee of the Bus Riders Union. Los Angeles: Labor/Community Strategy Center.

————. 1991. *L.A.'s Lethal Air: New Strategies for Policy, Organizing, and Action/ El Aero Muerto.* With the WATCHDOG Organizing Committee. Los Angeles: Labor/Community Strategy Center.

Mann, Eric, and Manning Marable. 1992. "The Future of the U.S. Left and Socialism." Working Paper Series. Los Angeles: Strategy Center Publications.

Occena, Bruce. 2005. *Labor/Community Strategy Center Organizational Profile.* Report prepared for Margaret Casey Foundation by BTW Consultants, Berkeley, Calif.

Pastor, Manuel, Jr. 2002. "Common Ground or Ground Zero? The New Economy and the New Organizing in Los Angeles." *Antipode* 33, 2: 260–89.

Wachs, Martin. 1996. "The Evolution of Transportation Policy in Los Angeles: Images of Past Policies and Future Prospects." In *The City: Los Angeles and Urban Theory at the End of the Twentieth Century,* ed. Allen J. Scott and Edward W. Soja. Berkeley: University of California Press.

Introduction

My advocacy of a critical spatial perspective and the idea that a new mode of spatial thinking has been developing in recent years are elaborated in three interrelated books, *Postmodern Geographies* (1989), *Thirdspace* (1996a), and *Postmetropolis* (2000). The present book is both an extension of the previous three and a departure, at least in the sense of its writing style and intended audience. I continue to make theoretical demands of the reader but try much harder to avoid incomprehensible abstractions and narrowly academic jargon. Anticipating a critique from some geographers and others uneasy with such an intense spatial emphasis, I have in several chapters given extra attention to explaining my more assertive spatial perspective and to the argument that the spatial consciousness emerging in recent years is significantly different in substance and scope from that traditionally held by many geographers and most social scientists. I want to stress that I am not saying other spatial perspectives or approaches are wrong or misdirected but rather that there is a need to take them further, to expand their scope and interpretive power, as many scholars and activists are now doing.

I first discussed the *socio-spatial dialectic* in 1980 in an article critiquing Marxist geography for not being sufficiently spatial and for overprivileging historical and social relations. A modified version of this paper appears in *Postmodern Geographies* (1989). Here and in later discussions of how radical and liberal geographers have addressed issues related to justice and democracy, I suggest that a similar bias toward social and historical rather than spatial explanation paradoxically pervades much of the geographical literature today. The socio-spatial dialectic helps to explain why spatial justice should not be reduced to being merely one part or aspect of social justice. Social justice is always and inherently spatial just as spatial justice is always and inherently social. They are mutually formative, with neither privileged over the other, although most scholars are probably more comfortable seeing social justice as a higher-order concept.

References to Henri Lefebvre and the *right to the city* are listed in the notes for chapter 3. For a discussion of the idea that the entire world is being urbanized, see Soja and Kanai (2007). For another take on "struggles over geography" inspired by Edward Said's words, see Watts (2000).

Pirie, G. H. 1983. "On Spatial Justice." *Environment and Planning A* 15: 465–73.
Soja, Edward. 2008. "Taking Space Personally." In *The Spatial Turn: Interdisciplinary Perspectives*, ed. Barney Warf and Santa Arias, 11–35. New York and London: Routledge.
———. 2003. "Writing the City Spatially." *City* 7, 3: 269–80.
———. 2000. *Postmetropolis: Critical Studies of Cities and Regions.* Oxford: Blackwell Publishers.
———. 1999. "Lessons in Spatial Justice." *hunch* 1 (inaugural issue): 98–107. Rotterdam: Berlage Institute.
———. 1996a. *Thirdspace: Journeys to Los Angeles and Other Real-and-Imagined Places.* Oxford: Blackwell Publishers.
———. 1996b. "Margin/Alia: Social Justice and the New Cultural Politics." In *The Urbanization of Injustice,* ed. Andrew Merrifield and Erik Swyngedouw, 180–99. London: Lawrence and Wishart.

————. 1989. *Postmodern Geographies: The Reassertion of Space in Critical Social Theory*. London: Verso Press.

————. 1980. "The Socio-Spatial Dialectic." *Annals of the Association of American Geographers* 70: 207–25.

Soja, Edward, and J. Miguel Kanai. 2007. "The Urbanization of the World." In *The Endless City*, ed. Ricky Burdett and Dayan Sudjic, 54–69. New York: Phaidon.

Watts, Michael. 2000. *Struggles over Geography: Violence, Freedom and Development at the Millennium*. Heidelberg: Department of Geography, University of Heidelberg (Hettner Lecture 1999).

1. Why Spatial? Why Justice? Why L.A.? Why Now?

Putting Space First

The first two comprehensive texts on the spatial turn appeared in 2008. One, in German with the English title *Spatial Turn,* developed from an international conference organized by the Media Department of the University of Siegen, Germany, in October 2006. The other, *The Spatial Turn: Interdisciplinary Perspectives,* was edited by the geographer Barney Warf and Santa Arias, a professor of English and Spanish literature, and was published in 2008. One can find discussions of the spatial turn in a wide variety of disciplines, from theology and organization science to sociology, literary criticism, and history.

The reference to new developments in urban archaeology and development economics interestingly enough arises in large part from a common source, *The Economy of Cities* (1969), written by the renowned urbanist Jane Jacobs. Speaking about the "spark" of urban economic life, Jacobs was one of the first to argue that the stimulus of urban agglomeration is the primary source of societal development and technological innovation. She also said that this has been the case for the past twelve thousand years, since the origins of the first urban settlements, which she argued preceded and stimulated the agricultural revolution. Without the generative force of urbanization, we would all be poor, she argued. We would have remained hunters, gatherers, and fisherfolk. The Nobel Prize–winning economist Robert Lucas (1988) referred to her work and implied that she was deserving of a Nobel Prize for her discovery of what some economists (Henderson 1994) now call "Jane Jacobs externalities." Jacobs's ideas now appear in economics textbooks as well (McDonald 1997). I discuss her arguments about synekism, my term for the stimulus of urban agglomeration, in Soja (2000). For more extensive discussions of Jacobs, see Allen (1997).

The resurgence of interest in the generative effects of socialized space has had to contend not only with entrenched perspectives that dismiss the importance of urban spatial causality but also with an emerging argument that globalization and new information technologies such as the Internet are eroding the impact of space and geography on our lives. This counterforce to the spatial turn is built on claims that we are experiencing the "death of distance," the "end of geography," and the emergence of a "borderless world." Given instantaneous communications, everyone can work anywhere they please, leading some to say that downtowns are becoming obsolete and that cities and employment clusters may soon disintegrate and disperse. For the most part, this point of view adopts a very narrow definition of space and geography as physical form only, takes certain new trends, such as home working, and projects them to exaggerated proportions, and ignores the pioneering new work, especially in geographical economics, on the generative effects of urban agglomerations on economic development, technological innovation, and cultural creativity. Foregrounding a critical spatial perspective, as I do here, not only challenges this counterargument but suggests that, with the new discoveries and the new technologies, urban spatial causality in the form of the stimulus of urban agglomeration has been making space and geography more important than ever before in academic thought and current events.

Seeking Justice Now

As approached here, justice obtains a special contemporary meaning and relevance very much like its spatial modifier, giving the combination spatial + justice a redoubled significance. Especially important is the point made in the last paragraph of this section, on how the terms *spatial* and *justice* can be used to promote greater interconnections and more effective coalition building between various, formerly very difficult to combine social movements, based on the shared experience of being negatively affected by unjust geographies.

The justice literature tends to have two wings, one more oriented to criminology and the law, and the other aimed more broadly at social justice and human rights. *Spatial justice* was probably first used as a descriptive term with regard to criminal law.

An indicative list of organizations with *justice* in their names includes United for Peace and Justice, Interfaith Community for Economic Justice, Mobilization for Global Justice, Jobs with Justice, Environmental Justice Foundation, Community Coalition for Environmental Justice, Jews United for Justice, Clergy and Laity United for Economic Justice, Justice for Janitors, and, in response to Hurricane Katrina, Louisiana Justice Institute, New Orleans Worker's Center for Racial Justice, and Deep South Center for Environmental Justice.

Particularly noteworthy here is Jobs with Justice, a growing national movement for workers' rights that is aimed at the most difficult-to-organize workers, including independent taxi drivers, domestics, day laborers, security guards, mobile home owners, tenants, and construction workers from foreign countries. Founded in 1987, Jobs with Justice today has affiliated local coalitions in forty cities in twenty-five states campaigning for national health care, fair trade laws, rights to organize, and global peace and justice. Such justice-based organizations are filling the vacuum caused by the weakening of industrial unions, the elimination of many welfare programs, and the failures of party politics to deal with increasing poverty, unemployment, and homelessness. They also participate in what can be called the globalization of the justice movement.

Foregrounding Los Angeles

I welcome any suggestions and evidence that city regions other than Los Angeles developed equally influential flows between university-based scholarship in geography and planning and grassroots mobilization and coalition building, what I have been describing as the translation of spatial theory into spatial politics and practice. A list of representative references for the so-called Los Angeles school is presented in the notes for chapter 4.

Also emphasizing the unusual and unexpected resurgence of innovative coalition building in Los Angeles are Milkman (2006), specifically on immigrant workers and the labor movement, and Pastor, Benner, and Matsuoka (2009), a spatially informed look at movements for regional equity and community-based regionalism with a particular emphasis on what has been happening in Los Angeles.

Contemporary Applications

Worth noting here is the global organization of scholars and activists called The Space of Democracy and the Democracy of Space Network, headed by Jonathan Pugh and based at Newcastle University, UK. The network has organized a series of conferences in several different countries, including one in Long Beach, California, "Ontology, Space, and Radical Politics," with contributions by Laura Pulido, Gilda Haas, Goetz Wolff, Nigel Thrift, and Edward Soja. See also Pugh (2009). While the term *justice* is not focused on by the network, the approach to democracy is assertively spatial and builds explicitly on the spatial turn.

Geographers in England, often based in northern cities and universities, have been actively promoting such notions as participatory geographies, spaces of democracy, and struggles over displacement due to gentrification, privatization, and the impact of megaprojects such as the Olympic Games. A group called Autonomous Geographies organized a conference in Manchester in 2009 on "The Right to Stay Put," drawing on the phrase used by the American planner Chester Hartman for the fight against displacement due to gentrification (Pickerill and Chatterton 2006). See also Barnett and Low (2004). With few exceptions, such as the Newcastle-based network mentioned above, space tends to be used almost metaphorically, with very weak causal or explanatory power.

Two articles in *Critical Planning: Spatial Justice* 14 (2007) are noteworthy for their general discussion of the concept of spatial justice: Ava Bromberg, Gregory D. Morrow, and Deirdre Pfeiffer, "Editorial Note: Why Spatial Justice?" and Nicholas Brown, Ryan Griffis, Kevin Hamilton, Sharon Irish, and Sarah Kanouse, "What Makes Justice Spatial? What Makes Spaces Just? Three Interviews on the Concept of Spatial Justice." There are case studies of spatial justice in Lagos, New Orleans, post-tsunami Aceh, and the Palestinian village of Ayn Hawd.

The most promising output from the "just city" discourse can be found in *Searching for the Just City: Debates on Urban Theory and Practice* (2009), edited by professor emeritus of urban planning at Columbia University Peter Marcuse and five urban planning doctoral students. Mustafa Dikec's chapter on "Justice and the Spatial Imagination" is reprinted, and there are chapters by Fainstein and Marcuse, and one by David Harvey (with Cuz Potter) on "The Right to a Just City." Further connections between the "just city" and right to the city debates were made in the conference "The Right to the City: Prospects for Critical Urban Theory and Practice," held in Berlin in November 2008, coinciding with a celebration of Peter Marcuse's eightieth birthday. Marcuse was one of the organizers, along with Neil Brenner of NYU and Margit Mayer of the Center for Metropolitan Studies in Berlin. Although the conference, like the Marcuse-edited book, was primarily rooted in East Coast planning and geography networks, there were several links to UCLA urban planning and geography departments. Jacqueline Leavitt (formerly in planning at Columbia, now at UCLA) spoke of "Activist Intellectuals and the Right to the City in Los Angeles." The co-organizer Neil Brenner and speakers Julie-Anne Boudreau from Montreal and Roger Keil from York University have had close connections to Urban Planning at UCLA, and Marcuse himself was one of the original faculty members more than thirty years ago.

Also using the specific term *spatial justice* are several unpublished writings related to spatial planning in the European Union. See, for example, Connelly and Bradley (2004) and Dabinett and Richardson (2005) in the following list of references for chapter 1.

Allen, Max, ed. 1997. *Ideas That Matter: The Worlds of Jane Jacobs*. Owen Sound, Ontario: The Ginger Press.

Barnett, Clive, and Murray Low, eds. 2004. *Spaces of Democracy: Geographical Perspectives on Citizenship, Participation and Representation*. London: Sage.

Bromberg, Ava, Gregory Morrow, and Deirdre Pfeiffer. 2007. "Editorial Note: Why Spatial Justice?" *Critical Planning* 14: 1–6.

Brown, Nicholas, Ryan Griffis, Kevin Hamilton, Sharon Irish, and Sarah Kanouse.

2007. "What Makes Justice Spatial? What Makes Spaces Just? Three Interviews on the Concept of Spatial Justice." *Critical Planning* 14: 7–30.

Connelly, Stephen, and Karin Bradley. 2004. "Spatial Justice, European Spatial Policy, and the Case for Polycentric Development." Paper presented at ECPR workshop on European Spatial Politics, Uppsala, Sweden.

Dabinett, G., and T. Richardson. 2005. "The Europeanization of Spatial Strategy: Shaping Regions and Spatial Justice through Government Subsidies." *International Planning Studies* 103: 201–18.

Dikec, M. 2001. "Justice and the Spatial Imagination." *Environment and Planning A* 33: 1785–1805.

Döring, Jorg, and Tristan Thielmann, eds. 2008. *Spatial Turn: Das Raumparadigma in den Kultur- und Sozial-wissenschaften*. Bielefeld: Transcript.

Fainstein, Susan. 2008. "Spatial Justice and Planning." Unpublished paper presented at a joint meeting of the American Collegiate Schools of Planning (ACSP) and the Association of European Schools of Planning (AESOP), Chicago.

———. 2005. "Planning Theory and the City." *Journal of Planning Education and Research* 25: 121–30.

Flusty, Steven. 1994. *Building Paranoia: The Proliferation of Interdictory Space and the Erosion of Spatial Justice*. West Hollywood, Calif.: L.A. Forum for Architecture and Urban Design.

Fraser, Nancy. 2008. *Scales of Justice: Reimagining Political Space in a Globalizing World*. New York: Columbia University Press.

Henderson, Vernon. 1994. "Externalities and Industrial Development." *Cityscape: A Journal of Policy Development and Research* 1: 75–93.

Jacobs, Jane. 1969. *The Economy of Cities*. New York: Random House.

Knox, Paul, and Sallie Marston. 2009. *Places and Regions in Global Context: Human Geography*. 5th ed. Upper Saddle River, N.J.: Pearson Prentice Hall.

Lucas, Robert E., Jr. 1988. "On the Mechanics of Economic Development." *Journal of Monetary Economics* 22: 3–42.

MacLeod, Gavin. 2002. "From Urban Entrepreneurialism to a Revanchist City? On the Spatial Injustices of Glasgow's Renaissance." *Antipode* 34: 602–24.

Marcuse, Peter, et al. 2009. *Searching for a Just City: Debates on Urban Theory and Practice*. London and New York: Routledge.

McDonald, John F. 1997. *Fundamentals of Urban Economics*. New York: Prentice Hall.

Milkman, Ruth. 2006. *L.A. Story: Immigrant Workers and the Future of the U.S. Labor Movement*. New York: Russell Sage Foundation.

Mitchell, Don. 2003. *The Right to the City: Social Justice and the Fight for Public Space*. New York: Guilford Press.

Pastor, Manuel, Jr., Chris Benner, and Martha Matsuoka. 2009. *This Could Be the*

Start of Something Big: How Social Movements for Regional Equity Are Reshaping Metropolitan America. Ithaca, N.Y.: Cornell University Press.

Pickerill, Jenny, and Paul Chatterton. 2006. "Notes towards Autonomous Geographies: Creation, Resistance and Self-Management as Survival Tactics." *Progress in Human Geography* 30: 730–46.

Pirie, G. H. 1983. "On Spatial Justice." *Environment and Planning A* 15: 465–73.

Pugh, Jonathan, ed. 2009. *What Is Radical Politics Today?* London: Palgrave Macmillan.

Warf, Barney, and Santa Arias, eds. 2008. *The Spatial Turn: Interdisciplinary Perspectives*. New York and London: Routledge.

2. On the Production of Unjust Geographies

A distinction is made in this chapter between macro-, micro-, and mesogeographical (regional) scales, but these scales or levels of geographical resolution should not be seen as discrete layers detached from one another and somehow "natural" in their origin. They are interconnected and, like spatiality itself, are both socially produced and open to being purposefully restructured and reorganized. For those who may wish to explore the current debates on the geographical theory of scale, I present a thematic bibliography.

Bibliography on Scale

Agnew, John. 1994. "The Territorial Trap: The Geographical Assumptions of International Relations Theory." *Review of International Political Economy* 1: 53–80.

Brenner, Neil. 2005. *New State Spaces: Urban Governance and the Rescaling of Statehood*. New York: Oxford University Press.

———. 2001. "The Limits to Scale? Methodological Reflections on Scalar Structuration." *Progress in Human Geography* 25: 591–614.

———. 2000. "The Urban Question as a Scale Question: Reflections on Henri Lefebvre, Urban Theory and the Politics of Scale." *International Journal of Urban and Regional Research* 24: 361–78.

———. 1999. "Globalisation as Reterritorialization: The Re-Scaling of Urban Governance in the European Union." *Urban Studies* 36: 432–51.

———. 1998. "Between Fixity and Motion: Accumulation, Territorial Organization and the Historical Geography of Spatial Scales." *Environment and Planning D: Society and Space* 16, 5: 459–81.

———. 1997. "State Territorial Restructuring and the Production of Spatial Scale." *Political Geography* 16: 273–306.

Brenner, Neil, J. C. Brown, and Mark Purcell. 2005. "There's Nothing Inherent about Scale: Political Ecology, the Local Trap, and the Politics of Development in the Brazilian Amazon." *Geoforum* 36: 607–24.

Castree, Noel. 2000. "Geographical Scale and Grassroots Internationalism: The Liverpool Dock Dispute, 1995–1998." *Economic Geography* 76: 272–92.

———. 1999. "Self-Organization of Society by Scale: A Spatial Reworking of Regulation Theory." *Environment and Planning D: Society and Space* 17: 557–74.

Collinge, Chris. 2006. "Flat Ontology and the Deconstruction of Scale: A Response to Marston." *Transactions of the Institute of British Geographers* 31: 244–51.

Jonas, Andrew. 2006. "Pro Scale: Further Reflections on the 'Scale Debate' in Human Geography." *Transactions of the Institute of British Geographers* 31: 399–406.

Marston, Sallie. 2000. "The Social Construction of Scale." *Progress in Human Geography* 24: 219–42.

Marston, Sallie, John Paul Jones III, and Keith Woodward. 2005. "Human Geography without Scale." *Transactions of the Institute of British Geographers* 30: 416–32.

Marston, Sallie, and Neil Smith. 2001. "States, Scales and Households: Limits to Scale Thinking? A Response to Brenner." *Progress in Human Geography* 25: 615–19.

McDowell, Linda. 2001. "Linking Scales: Or How Research about Gender and Organizations Raises New Issues for Economic Geography." *Journal of Economic Geography* 1: 227–50.

Purcell, Mark. 2003. "Islands of Practice and the Marston/Brenner Debate: Toward a More Synthetic Critical Human Geography." *Progress in Human Geography* 27: 317–32.

Sheppard, Eric. 2002. "The Spaces and Times of Globalization: Place, Scale, Networks, and Positionality." *Economic Geography* 78: 307–30.

Sheppard, Eric, and Robert McMaster, eds. 2004. *Scale and Geographic Inquiry: Nature, Society and Method*. Malden, Mass.: Blackwell.

Smith, Neil. 1995. "Remaking Scale: Competition and Cooperation in Prenational and Postnational Europe." In *Competitive European Peripheries*, ed. H. Eskelinen and F. Snickars, 59–74. Berlin: Springer Verlag.

Swyngedouw, Erik. 1997. "Neither Global nor Local: 'Glocalization' and the Politics of Scale." In *Spaces of Globalization*, ed. Kevin Cox, 137–66. New York: Guilford Press.

———. 1996. "Reconstructing Citizenship, the Rescaling of the State and the New Authoritarianism: Closing the Belgian Mines." *Urban Studies* 33: 1499–521.

Exogenous Geographies

The quotation heading the introduction as well as the statement in the text about imperialism and geography are from Edward Said (1993), pages 7 and 93. The statement on the struggle over geography was also used as a lead-in to Derek Gregory (1995a). Gregory develops further his insightful interpretation of Said in subsequent writings, listed below. The Said quote at the start of chapter 1 is from Robbins et al. (1994), page 21. Said began his discussion of imaginative geographies in *Orientalism* in a section on imaginative geography and its representation (1978, 49–63). For more on his thoughts about the importance of geography and space, see Said (2000).

The political geographer John O'Laughlin has written extensively on gerrymandering (1982a, 1982b, 1982c). Drawing on his 1973 doctoral dissertation, which was the first title reference to spatial justice that I have found, he produced a series of articles on racial politics, geography, and the manipulation of electoral districts. Although I generally do not find it to be very reliable, Wikipedia has a very interesting and comprehensive entry on gerrymandering.

On apartheid in South Africa and what has been happening since its transformation, see the work of Alan Mabin, professor of architecture and planning at the University of Witwatersrand in Johannesburg. Mabin has written extensively and explicitly on issues relating to social and spatial injustice in South Africa. He presented a paper (and was a co-organizer) at the 2007 Paris conference on spatial justice and injustice titled "Suburbs, Sprawl, Planning and Spatial Justice as Viewed through Developments in Gauteng City Region, South Africa," and presented a similar paper at the joint meeting of the American Collegiate Schools of Planning (ACSP) and the Association of European Schools of Planning (AESOP) in Beijing, China, in 2008. In the abstract of his paper he notes: "In South Africa the legacy of apartheid makes the search for spatial justice the focus of any planning activity." See also his chapter in Varady (2005). Mabin's writings are particularly effective in exploring the lasting legacy of apartheid in the now multiracial but still heavily fortressed suburbs of Johannesburg. Also worthy of note on spatial justice in South Africa is the work of Philippe Gervais-Lambony (2008), a geographer at University of Paris X–Nanterre and organizer of the first international conference on spatial justice held in Paris in 2007. He writes frequently with Mabin, who also participated in organizing the conference.

The link between the imposition of colonial and postcolonial geographies and processes of underdevelopment and dependency is not well developed in the literature. Colonization and underdevelopment processes, as they are seen here, are both fundamentally forms of social control imposed in large part through spatial strategies. Apartheid, translated as "separate development," stands at the extreme end of totalizing, if not totalitarian, racial territoriality. Underdevelopment creates more subtly configured economic and political geographies to maintain distinctively different processes of development in core and peripheral countries and regions. One of the more obvious expressions of the exploitative geographies of underdevelopment are the "dendritic" transportation systems found in many colonized areas, facilitating drainage of natural and human resources from the periphery to the core. Said's imaginative geographies expand our understanding of the spatial impact of colonialism and underdevelopment in many additional directions.

I define *postcolonial* in a different way from many others, referring not simply to the persistence of colonialism after independence is achieved. In my view, the postcolonial condition and what has been called the postcolonial critique hinge on a creative reinterpretation of the relation between colonizer and colonized, core and periphery, a reinterpretation that seeks to combine the liberal narrative of capitalist development and modernization with more radical socialist conceptions of justice and equality, rather than seeing these as in complete opposition. See *Thirdspace* (1996a), pages 125–44.

Eyal Weizman (2007; Segal et al. 2003) has led the way in demonstrating very concretely the role of architects and architecture in the construction of unjust geographies. See also the writings on the unjust geographies of Israel by geographer-planner Oren Yiftachel (2006; Yiftachel and Yacobi 2005) and the comprehensive discussion of law and space in Rosen-Zvi (2004). The Israel–Palestine borderlands have been an unusually rich focus for research and writing specifically on spatial justice.

The multiplication of privatopias and the increasing "secession of the rich" from urban life and responsibility open up a need to think differently about the relative perils of gentrification, perhaps the central target of the emerging right to the city movement in the United States. Gentrification as a force behind the displacement of preexisting poor populations and a vehicle to introduce exclusive yuppie amenities to impacted urban neighborhoods must continue to be fought against, but the commitment to improving urban life carried by the gentrifiers stands in marked contrast to the more evasive flow of those moving into gated and guarded communities. Although both need to be resisted in their usual forms, gentrification processes may be easier to steer to beneficial purposes.

I thank Ava Bromberg for making me aware of how the concept of the commons might relate to the search for spatial justice.

Davis, Mike. 2007. *Planet of Slums*. New York and London: Verso Books.

———. 1990. *City of Quartz: Excavating the Future in Los Angeles*. New York and London: Verso Books.

Dikec, Mustafa. 2007a. *Badlands of the Republic: Space, Politics, and Urban Policy*. Oxford: Blackwell Publishers.

———. 2007b. "Revolting Geographies: Urban Unrest in France." *Geography Compass* 1, 5: 1190–206.

Foucault, Michel. 1986. "Of Other Spaces." *Diacritics* 16: 22–27.

———. 1980. "Questions on Geography." In *Power/Knowledge,* trans. C. Gordon, 63–77. New York: Pantheon.

Gervais-Lambony, Philippe. 2008. "Space Matters: Identity, Justice and Democracy at the Ward Level in South African Cities." *Transformation: Critical Perspectives on Southern Africa* 66/67: 83– 97.

Gregory, Derek. 2005. "Space, Politics, and the Political." *Environment and Planning D: Society and Space* 23: 171–88.

———. 2004. *The Colonial Present.* Oxford: Blackwell Publishers.

———. 1995a. "Imaginative Geographies." *Progress in Human Geography* 19: 447–85.

———. 1995b. "Between the Book and the Lamp: Imaginative Geographies of Egypt, 1849–50." *Transactions of the Institute of British Geographers* New Series 20: 29–57.

———. 1994. *Geographical Imaginations.* Oxford: Blackwell Publishers.

Mabin, Alan. 2005. "Suburbs and Segregation in South African Cities." In *Desegregating the City: Ghettoes, Enclaves, and Inequality,* ed. David P. Varady. Albany: State University of New York Press.

Mackenzie, Evan. 1964. *Privatopia: Homeowner Associations and the Rise of Residential Private Government.* New Haven, Conn.: Yale University Press.

O'Laughlin, John. 1982a. "The Identification and Evaluation of Racial Gerrymandering." *Annals, Association of American Geographers* 72: 165–84.

———. 1982b. "The Art and Science of Gerrymandering." In *Redistricting: An Exercise in Prophecy,* ed. A. Merritt, 88–105. Urbana: University of Illinois, Institute of Governmental Affairs.

———. 1982c. "Racial Gerrymandering." In *The New Black Politics,* ed. M. B. Preston, L. Henderson, and P. Puryear, 241–63. New York: Longman.

Robbins, Bruce, Mary Louise Pratt, Jonathan Arac, R. Radhakrishnan, and Edward Said. 1994. *Edward Said's Culture and Imperialism: A Symposium. Social Text* 40: 1–24.

Rosen-Zvi, Issacher. 2004. *Taking Space Seriously: Law, Space, and Society in Contemporary Israel.* Aldershot, UK: Ashgate.

Said, Edward. 2000. "Invention, Memory, and Place." *Critical Inquiry* 26: 175–92.

———. 1994. *The Politics of Dispossession.* New York: Pantheon, 1994.

———. 1993. *Culture and Imperialism.* New York: Knopf/Random House.

———. 1978. *Orientalism.* New York: Pantheon.

Segal, Rafi, Eyal Weizman, and David Tartakover. 2003. *A Civilian Occupation: The Politics of Israeli Architecture.* London and New York: Verso Books.

Weizman, Eyal. 2007. *Hollow Land: Israel's Architecture of Occupation.* New York and London: Verso Books.

Yiftachel, O. 2006. "Ethnocratic Politics in Israel: The Shrinking Space of Citizenship." In *The Struggle for Sovereignty: Palestine and Israel 1993–2005*, ed. J. Beinin and R. Stein, 162–75. Stanford, Calif.: Stanford University Press.

Yiftachel, O., and H. Yacobi. 2005. "Walls, Fences and 'Creeping Apartheid' in Israel/Palestine." In *Against the Wall*, ed. M. Sorkin, 138–58. New York: Greenwood Press.

Endogenous Geographies

Especially infused with a critical spatial perspective have been some very recent writings by legal scholars about gender, domestic violence, and rurality, challenging a perceived overemphasis on the city and urbanity in the law and justice literature. See Pruitt (2008a, 2008b). Rosen-Zvi's *Taking Space Seriously* (2004), although focused on Israel, presents a remarkably comprehensive look at the intersections of space, law, and society. Nick Blomley, professor of geography at Simon Fraser University and formerly at UCLA, has been more responsible than anyone else in bringing a critical spatial perspective and the ideas of Henri Lefebvre into critical legal studies. His work, listed below, is particularly pertinent to studies of private property and public space.

A leading specialist on race, space, and the law is Richard Thompson Ford. In two recent books (2008, 2005), he criticizes exaggerated and excessive claims of racial bias for diverting attention away from the most serious issues of racial discrimination as well as other discriminatory practices including unjust geographies. He is also coeditor, with Delaney and Blomley, of the *Legal Geographies Reader* (2001) and several articles on political geography and the law.

There are many online bibliographies available on environmental inequalities, environmental racism, and the environmental justice movement. The focus on race is so strong, however, that very few references explicitly adopt a critical spatial perspective on the environment. One major exception is David Harvey (1996), *Justice, Nature and the Geography of Difference*.

Noteworthy in presenting a critical spatial view of racism and issues relating to racial and spatial justice and identity formation is the work of the African American feminist critic bell hooks, especially "Choosing the Margin as a Space of Radical Openness" (1990), included in the reference list below on law and space. Informed in part by the writings of Henri Lefebvre, hooks calls for a consciously spatial strategy of using the margins and marginality—the condition of being peripheralized by forces of domination—as a home base for nourishing and building growing coalitions among all those seeking justice in the widest sense. What she points out so effectively is the importance of a strategic spatial consciousness and how a shared awareness of the multiple ways geographies can oppress, control, exploit, and subjugate can be used to bring together what too often have been separate and exclusive social movements organized around race, class, gender, and other axes of discrimination and subordination. The potential for providing a means of connecting social movements and building new coalitions is among the most important aspects of adding a spatial dimension to justice. A bibliography on spatial approaches to the law is presented below instead of a section reference list. For a discussion of the Mount Laurel decisions and their impact, see Haar (1996) and Kirp, Dwyer, and Rosenthal (1996).

Bibliography on Law and Space

Aoki, Keith. 2000. "Space Invaders: Critical Geography, the 'Third World' in International Law and Critical Race Theory." *Villanova Law Review* 45.

Blomley, Nicholas. 2007. "Making Private Property: Enclosure, Common Right and the Work of Hedges." *Rural History* 18, 1: 1–21.

———. 2005. "The Borrowed View: Privacy, Propriety, and the Entanglements of Property." *Law and Social Inquiry* 30, 4: 617–61.

———. 2004. "Un-Real Estate: Proprietary Space and Public Gardening." *Antipode* 36, 4: 614–41.

———. 2003. "Law, Property, and the Spaces of Violence." *Annals of the Association of American Geographers* 93, 1: 121–41.

———. 2001. "Law and Geography." In *International Encyclopedia of the Social and Behavioral Sciences*, ed. N. J. Smelser and P. B. Bates, 8461–65. Oxford: Pergamon.

———. 1998. "Landscapes of Property." *Law and Society Review* 32, 3: 567–612.

———. 1994. *Law, Space, and the Geography of Power*. New York: Guilford Press.

Blomley, Nicholas, David Delaney, and Richard T. Ford, eds. 2001. *The Legal Geographies Reader: Law, Power, and Space*. Oxford: Blackwell.

Cooper, Davina. 1998. *Governing out of Order: Space, Law and the Politics of Belonging*. New York: New York University Press.

———. 1996. "Talmudic Territory? Space, Law and Modernist Discourse." *Journal of Law and Society* 23: 529–48.

Delaney, David. 1998. *Race, Place and the Law*. Austin: University of Texas Press.

Ford, Richard Thompson. 2008. *The Race Card: How Bluffing about Bias Makes Race Relations Worse*. New York: Farrar, Straus and Giroux.

———. 2005. *Racial Culture: A Critique*. Princeton, N.J.: Princeton University Press.

———. 1999. "Law's Territory: A History of Jurisdiction." *Michigan Law Review* 97.

———. 1994. "The Boundaries of Race: Political Geography in Legal Analysis." *Harvard Law Review* 107: 1843–1921.

———. 1992. "Urban Space and the Color Line: The Consequences of Demarcation and Disorientation in the Postmodern Metropolis." *Harvard Blackletter Journal* 9: 117–47.

Frug, Gerald. 1993. "Decentering Decentralization." *University of Chicago Law Review* 60: 253–338.

Haar, Charles M. 1996. *Suburbs under Siege.* New Brunswick, N.J.: Rutgers University Press. (Mount Laurel decisions)

Holder, Jane, and Carolyn Harrison, eds. 2003. *Law and Geography.* Current Legal Issues, vol. 5. Oxford: Oxford University Press.

hooks, bell. 1990. "Choosing the Margin as a Space of Radical Openness." In *Yearning: Race, Gender, and Cultural Politics.* Boston: South End Press.

Kirp, David L., John P. Dwyer, and Larry Rosenthal. 1996. *Our Town: Race, Housing, and the Soul of Suburbia.* Princeton N.J.: Princeton University Press. (Mount Laurel decisions)

Oh, Reginald. 2008. "Taking Geography Seriously: Asserting Space into Critical Legal Theories." Paper presented at the annual meeting of The Law and Society Association, May 27, 2008.

———. 2004. "Re-Mapping Equal Protection Jurisprudence: A Legal Geography of Race and Affirmative Action." *American University Law Review* 53.

Osofsky, Hari. 2007. "A Law and Geography Perspective on the New Haven School." *Yale Journal of International Law* 32.

Pruitt, Lisa R. 2008a. "Gender, Geography and Rural Justice." *Berkeley Journal of Gender, Law & Justice* 23: 338–91.

———. 2008b. "Place Matters: Domestic Violence and Rural Difference." *Wisconsin Journal of Law, Gender & Society* 23, 2: 347–416.

Raustiala, Kal. 2005. "The Geography of Justice." *Fordham Law Review* 73.

Rosen-Zvi, Issacher. 2004. *Taking Space Seriously: Law, Space, and Society in Contemporary Israel.* Aldershot, UK, and Burlington, Vt.: Ashgate.

Silbaugh, Katharine B. 2007a. "Women's Place: Urban Planning, Housing Design, and Work-Family Balance." *Fordham Law Review* 76.

———. 2007b. "Wal-Mart's Other Woman Problem: Sprawl and Work-Family Balance." *Connecticut Law Review* 39.

Taylor, William, ed. 2006. *The Geography of Law: Landscape, Identity and Regulation.* Oxford and Portland: Hart Publishing.

Verchick, Robert R. M. 1999. "Critical Space Theory: Keeping Local Geography in American and European Environmental Law. *Tulane Law Review* 73.

Mesogeographies

I consider myself as much a regionalist as an urbanist, and have given particular attention to meso-analytical or regional approaches throughout *Seeking Spatial Justice.* In addition to earlier references to my work (1989, 1996, 2000), several more recent writings have tried to capture the significance of a regional perspective and the emergence of the New Regionalism. They are listed below, along with other references on regional development theory and the New Regionalism, as part of the bibliography on mesogeographies.

I want to make it clear to the reader that many of the arguments I present on the links between the globalization and urbanization of (in)justice and on the theory of geographically uneven development are not widely agreed upon, and there are few references that make similar arguments. My intent is not to vigorously defend my point of view, however, but rather to demonstrate how regional approaches can stimulate new ways of thinking about fundamental issues in development studies at and across all geographical scales.

The writings of Gunnar Myrdal (1957) and François Perroux (1950, 1955, 1988), while not recognized as such at the time, were among the earliest forerunners not only of the concept of underdevelopment but also of current thinking about the stimulus of urban agglomeration as a powerful force for economic development, technological innovation, and cultural creativity. The closely related idea of growth centers or development poles has been an integral part of regional development theory (and practice) for the past fifty years. For a critical look at Myrdal, Perroux, and the so-called New Economic Geography, see Meardon (2001).

Brenner, Neil. 2005. *New State Spaces: Urban Governance and the Rescaling of State-hood*. New York: Oxford University Press.

Dabinett, G., and T. Richardson. 2005. "The Europeanization of Spatial Strategy: Shaping Regions and Spatial Justice through Government Subsidies." *International Planning Studies* 103: 201–18.

Faludi, Andreas, and Bas Waterhout. 2002. *The Making of the European Spatial Development Perspective*. London: Routledge.

Harvey, David. 1989. "From Managerialism to Entrepreneurialism: The Transformation of Urban Governance in Late Capitalism." *Geografiska Annaler* 71B: 3–17.

Healey, Patsy. 2006a. *Urban Complexity and Spatial Strategies: A Relational Planning for Our Times*. London: Routledge.

———. 2006b. "Transforming Governance: Challenges of Institutional Adaptation and a New Politics of Space." *European Planning Studies* 14, 3: 299–319.

———. 2004. "The Treatment of Space and Place in the New Strategic Spatial Planning in Europe." *International Journal of Urban and Regional Research* 28, 1: 45–67.

Hirschmann, Albert O. 1958. *The Strategy of Economic Development*. New Haven, Conn.: Yale University Press.

MacLeod, Gavin. 2002. "From Urban Entrepreneurialism to a Revanchist City? On the Spatial Injustices of Glasgow's Renaissance." *Antipode* 34: 602–24.

Meardon, Stephen J. 2001. "Modelling Agglomeration and Dispersion in City and Country: Gunnar Myrdal, François Perroux, and the New Economic Geography – Critical Essay." *American Journal of Economics and Sociology* 60, 1: 25–57.

Myrdal, Gunnar. 1957. *Economic Theory and Underdeveloped Regions.* London: Duckworth; also published as *Rich Lands and Poor.*

Ohmae, Kenichi. 1995. *The End of the Nation State: The Rise of Regional Economies.* New York: Free Press.

Orfield, Myron. 1997. *Metropolitics: A Regional Agenda for Community and Stability.* Washington, D.C.: Brookings Institution Press/Lincoln Institute for Land Policy.

Pastor, Manuel, Jr., Chris Benner, and Martha Matsuoka. 2009. *This Could Be the Start of Something Big: How Social Movements for Regional Equity are Reshaping Metropolitan America.* Ithaca, N.Y.: Cornell University Press.

Perroux, François. 1988. "The Pole of Development's New Place in a General Theory of Economic Activity." In *Regional Economic Development: Essays in Honor of François Perroux,* ed. B. Higgins and D. J. Savoie, 48–76. Boston: Unwin Hyman.

———. 1955. "Note sur la Notion de 'Pole de Croissance.'" *Economie Appliquee* 7: 307–20.

———. 1950. "Economic Space: Theory and Applications." *Quarterly Journal of Economics* 64: 89–104.

Scott, Allen J. 2001. *Global City-Regions: Trends, Theory, Policy.* New York: Guilford Press.

———. 1998. *Regions and the World Economy.* Oxford: Oxford University Press.

Soja, Edward. Forthcoming. "Regional Urbanization." In *Urban Design: Roots, Influences and Trends,* ed. A. Loukaitou-Sideris and T. Banerjee. New York and London: Routledge.

———. 2009. "Regional Planning and Development Theories." In *The International Encyclopedia of Human Geography,* ed. N. Thrift and R. Kitchin, 259–70. Amsterdam: Elsevier.

———. 2002. "The New Regionalism: A Conversation with Edward Soja." An interview by R. Ehrenfurt. *Critical Planning* 9: 5–12.

Storper, Michael. 1997. *The Regional World: Territorial Development in a Global Economy.* New York: Guilford Press.

3. Building a Spatial Theory of Justice

This chapter builds on a Colloquium on Planning Theory I taught for nearly ten years to doctoral students in the Urban Planning Department at UCLA. For several years, "seeking spatial justice" was the theme of the colloquium. Students were asked to write an introductory essay theorizing spatial justice, and a substantive paper empirically illustrating its application to planning and policy issues. At the end of the course, students presented their papers at a forum open to all students and faculty. Much of what is contained in this chapter combines material from my own lectures and from the papers produced by the fifty or more students who have participated in the colloquium over the years. I want to thank them here for all that I have learned from their hard work.

New Ontological Beginnings

My approach to ontology is influenced by the early work of the critical realist philosopher Roy Bhaskar, who in *Reclaiming Reality* (1989) argues that all existing epistemologies—positivist, Marxist, empiricist, idealist, normative, hermeneutic, postmodern—are faulty to some degree and in need of a critical rethinking. In his view, epistemological debate under these conditions is not likely to be productive until and unless our ontological understanding is radically revised, for the faulty epistemologies derive primarily from faulty ontological assumptions. We must first, he says, engage in an "ontological struggle" to restructure these assumptions. In a subsequent book (1993) he accepts that this ontological restructuring involves at least in part in erasing the intrinsic privileging of time over space, history over geography, the premise of my persistent critique of social historicism and the call for a rebalanced ontology in which all aspects of human sociality are seen as spatio-temporally constituted. A similar ontology of what he calls the time-space structuration of social life was developed by the social theorist Anthony Giddens. Neither Bhaskar nor Giddens developed these ideas about the "triple dialectic" of spatiality, historicality, and sociality much further after the mid-1990s. A different version of critical realism, one that seemed to consolidate around a confident epistemology and a more formal distinction between the necessary and the contingent, entered into philosophical debates in geography largely through the work of Andrew Sayer (1984, 2000). Because of a more conventional view of space as resultant physical form, Sayer's approach diverted attention away from ontological arguments about human spatiality.

Bhaskar, Roy A. 1993. *Dialectic: The Pulse of Freedom.* London: Verso.

———. 1989. *Reclaiming Reality: A Critical Introduction to Contemporary Philosophy.* London: Verso.

Giddens, Anthony. 1984. *The Constitution of Society: An Outline of the Theory of Structuration.* Berkeley and Los Angeles: University of California Press.

———. 1981. *A Contemporary Critique of Historical Materialism.* Berkeley and Los Angeles: University of California Press.

————. 1979. *Central Problems in Social Theory.* Berkeley and Los Angeles: University of California Press.

Sayer, Andrew. 2000. *Realism and Social Science.* London: Sage.

————. 1984. *Method in Social Science: A Realist Approach.* London: Routledge.

Soja, Edward. 1989. "Reassertions: Toward a Spatialized Ontology," and "Spatializations: A Critique of the Giddensian Version." Chapters 5 and 6 in *Postmodern Geographies,* 118–56.

Theorizing Justice

Isin (2002) not only presents the best critical history of the concept of citizenship, he develops several powerful arguments about urban spatial causality. A geographer-planner, Isin draws upon Foucault, Lefebvre, Weber, and Aristotle to argue that being political is essentially a matter of being urban, that politics as well as the concepts of citizenship and justice arise from the urban habitat and contentious efforts to obtain the right to the city. Turning citizenship studies upside down, he also argues that the creation of citizens' rights was more of a power play to establish and maintain domination and control over noncitizen "others" than an expression of an idealized process of participatory democracy. There are also many other interesting echoes of Iris Marion Young in *Being Political.*

Some of the more indicative book titles published after the appearance of John Rawls's *A Theory of Justice* in 1971 include *Social Justice and the City* (D. Harvey 1973), *Social Justice* (D. Miller 1976), *Understanding Rawls* (R. P. Wolff 1977), *Justice and the Human Good* (W. Galston 1980), *Justice: Alternative Political Perspectives* (J. Sterba 1980), *Marx and Justice* (A. Buchanan 1982), *Spheres of Justice* (M. Walzer 1983), *Blacks and Social Justice* (B. Boxhill 1984), *Beyond Justice* (A. Heller 1987), *Justice and Gender* (D. Rhode 1989), *Theories of Justice* (B. Barry 1989), *Justice and Modern Moral Philosophy* (J. Reiman 1990), and *Justice and the Politics of Difference* (I. M. Young 1990).

Isin, Engin. 2002. *Being Political: Genealogies of Citizenship.* Minneapolis: University of Minneapolis Press.

Rawls, John. 1993. *Political Liberalism.* New York: Columbia University Press.

————. 1971. *A Theory of Justice.* Cambridge, Mass.: Harvard University Press.

Young, Iris Marion. 2005. "Structural Injustice and the Politics of Difference." AHRC Centre for Law, Gender, and Sexuality Intersectionality Workshop, May 21–22, Keele University, UK.

————. 2000. "Democratic Regionalism." In *Inclusion and Democracy.* New York: Oxford University Press.

————. 1999. "Residential Segregation and Differentiated Citizenship." *Citizenship Studies* 3, 2: 237–52.

———. 1990. *Justice and the Politics of Difference.* Princeton, N.J.: Princeton University Press.

Debates on the Spatiality of Justice

On alternatives to the term *spatial justice*: The adjective *territorial,* as in territorial justice, emphasizes a kind of neutral background with little causal influence in itself. In the case of another absorptive substitution, the concept of environmental justice, the influential force is displaced from the spatial to the environmental. As noted in the introduction, these alternatives enrich the concept of spatial justice but at the same time deflect the search for a deeper understanding of the consequential spatiality of justice and limit its potential for generating new ideas and innovative strategies of application. The more complex overlapping of spatial justice with concepts such as the urbanization of injustice and the right to the city will be discussed in the sections dealing with Harvey and Lefebvre.

Bleddyn Davies is Emeritus Professor of Social Policy at the London School of Economics, director of the Oxford Institute of Ageing, and founding editor of the journal *Policy and Politics.* His theory of territorial justice (Davies 1968) was popular with the Labour government of Harold Wilson but was virtually forgotten in later conservative administrations.

Boyne, George A., and Martin A. Powell. 1993. "Territorial Justice and Thatcherism." *Environment and Planning C: Government and Policy* 11: 35–53.

———. 1991. "Territorial Justice: A Review of Theory and Evidence." *Political Geography Quarterly* 10: 263–81.

Coates, Bryan E., R. J. Johnston, and Paul C. Knox. 1977. *Geography and Inequality.* Oxford: Oxford University Press.

Davies, Bleddyn. 1968. *Social Needs and Resources in Local Services: A Study of Variations in Provision of Social Services between Local Authority Areas.* London: Joseph Rowntree.

Flusty, Steven. 1994. *Building Paranoia: The Proliferation of Interdictory Space and the Erosion of Spatial Justice.* West Hollywood, Calif.: Los Angeles Forum for Architecture and Urban Design.

Merrifield, Andrew, and Erik Swyngedouw, eds. 1996. *The Urbanization of Injustice.* London: Lawrence and Wishart.

O'Laughlin, John. 1973. *Spatial Justice for the Black American Voter: The Territorial Dimension of Urban Politics.* PhD diss., Department of Geography, Pennsylvania State University.

Pirie, G. H. 1983. "On Spatial Justice." *Environment and Planning A* 15: 465–73.

Smith, David. 2000. *Moral Geographies: Ethics in a World of Difference.* Edinburgh: Edinburgh University Press.

———. 1994. *Geography and Social Justice*. Oxford: Blackwell.

———. 1988. *Geography, Inequality, and Society*. Cambridge: Cambridge University Press.

Smith, David, and Roger Lee. 2004. *Geographies and Moralities: International Perspectives on Development, Justice, and Place*. Oxford: Wiley-Blackwell.

David Harvey and the Urbanization of Injustice

Although David Harvey never, as far as I can tell, used the specific term, many today think that the spatial justice discourse began with *Social Justice and the City* (1973). Harvey may have initiated a spatial approach to justice, but he also created, even if unintentionally, a long-lasting prohibition among geographers to using the words *spatial* and *justice* together. Also avoided for many of the same reasons is the term *geographical justice*, which I have not used, only because it would confuse the debate further. Harvey's writings on the right to the city are included in the bibliography for Lefebvre and the right to the city.

Harvey, D. 2006. *Spaces of Global Capitalism: A Theory of Uneven Geographical Development*. London and New York: Verso.

———. 2005. *A Brief History of Neoliberalism*. Oxford: Oxford University Press.

———. 2003. *The New Imperialism*. Oxford: Oxford University Press.

———. 2000. *Spaces of Hope*. Berkeley: University of California Press.

———. 1996. *Justice, Nature, and the Geography of Difference*. Oxford: Blackwell.

———. 1992. "Social Justice, Postmodernism, and the City." *International Journal for Urban and Regional Research* 16: 588–601.

———. 1985a. *The Urbanization of Capital*. Baltimore: Johns Hopkins University Press; Oxford: Basil Blackwell.

———. 1985b. *Consciousness and the Urban Experience*. Baltimore: Johns Hopkins University Press; Oxford: Basil Blackwell.

———. 1982. *The Limits to Capital*. Oxford: Blackwell.

———. 1981. "The Spatial Fix: Hegel, von Thunen, and Marx." *Antipode* 13: 1–12.

———. 1978. "The Urban Process under Capitalism." *International Journal of Urban and Regional Research* 2: 101–31.

———. 1977. "Labor, Capital, and Class Struggle around the Built Environment in Advanced Capitalist Societies." *Politics and Society* 6: 265–95.

———. 1975. "The Geography of Capitalist Accumulation: A Reconstruction of Marxist Theory." *Antipode* 7: 9–21.

———. 1973. *Social Justice and the City*. Baltimore: Johns Hopkins University Press.

Merrifield, Andy, and Erik Swyngedouw, eds. 1997. *The Urbanization of Injustice.* New York: New York University Press.

Mitchell, D. 2003. *The Right to the City: Social Justice and the Fight for Public Space.* New York: Guildford Press.

Lefebvre and the Right to the City

It is interesting to note that about the time Lefebvre was writing about the right to the city and the related need for an "urban revolution," one of the leading urban thinkers on the other side of the Atlantic, Jane Jacobs, was writing her now widely influential book *The Economy of Cities* (1969), in which she identified precisely that generative "spark" that arises from cities, from what can be called the stimulus of urban agglomeration. See the discussion of Jacobs in the notes for chapter 1. For more on Lefebvre, see *Thirdspace* (1996), especially chapter 1.

In the discussion of the new spatial consciousness, I do not discuss the contributions made by others during the period between the early 1970s and the mid-1990s, when the original ideas of Lefebvre and Foucault were buried under misunderstanding and accusations of fetishism and reification. Perhaps the most interesting and influential breakthrough during this period came from the time-space structuration theory of Anthony Giddens, an attempt to create a new social ontology that at least nominally kept a balance between temporal-historical and spatial-geographical influences.

For a link to new movements in London related to the right to the city, see Jane Wills (2004). East London has become an active center for community organizing, especially in preparation for the Olympic Games. At one local symposium I attended in 2006, a Latina activist involved in organizing office cleaners ("janitors" is not commonly used in British English) in the financial City of London spoke about her experience in the Justice for Janitors movement in Los Angeles. The new organization, called Justice for Cleaners, played a prominent role in recent (June 2009) demonstrations in London over the arrest and threatened deportation of immigrant workers at the School of Oriental and African Studies (SOAS). The workers were employed by ISS, Integrated Services Solutions, the same multinational firm lobbied by the Los Angeles Justice for Janitors coalition in 1990, when its headquarters were in Copenhagen. ISS is now under different corporate ownership but still a dominant force in providing cleaning services worldwide. Adding to the L.A. connection was Ken Loach, a vigorous protester in London and director of *Bread and Roses,* the film on Justice for Janitors. For more on these recent events, see solomonsmindfield.net.

Conferences on the right to the city were held in Toronto at York University in 1998, connected to citizenship studies and the work of the geographer-planner Engin Isin; in Rome at the Home of Geography, the Archives and Study Centre of the International Geographical Union in 2001, with a book "*Rights to the City*" (in quotes) published a year later (Wastl-Walter, Staeheli, and Dowler 2003); in Porto Alegre, Brazil, as part of the World Social Forum in 2002 (Worldwide Conference on the Right to Cities Free From Discrimination and Inequality); in Paris organized by UNESCO in 2006 (International Public Debates: Urban Policies and the Right to the City); another organized by UNESCO and the Habitat International Coalition in Lyon in 2006 to assess the European Charter for the Safeguarding of Human Rights in the City; in Los Angeles to inaugurate a new national coalition of activist organizations and intellectuals focused on the right to the city (2007); in Berlin on "The Right to the City: Prospects for Critical Urban Theory and Practice" in 2008; and in the same year at Linköping, Sweden, on "The Right to the City: New Challenges, New Issues," sponsored by the European Science Foundation and UNESCO. I am sure there are several others I have missed.

Contributing to the explicit recognition of the right to the city idea in Athens has been Costis Hadjimichalis, chair of the Department of Geography at Harokopio University in Athens, and Dina Vaiou, professor in the Department of Urban and Regional Planning at the National Technical University. Both are graduates of the School of Architecture and Urban Planning at UCLA, and I thank them both for helping me understand the writings of Henri Lefebvre while they were students working with me in the late 1970s. See Vaiou (2000) and D. Vaiou and Rouli Lykogianni (2006). Very special thanks to Konstantina Soureli for keeping me up-to-date on the citizens' movements in Athens, including an English translation of an article in Greek by Nikos Belavilas on "City Movements in Athens and Piraeus, Greece, 1960–2009," which discusses the Pan-Attic regional expansion of the right to the city movement. Between 2007 and 2009, 140 collective initiatives have been organized in association with the Pan-Attic Network, an increase described as unprecedented in Greek history.

Don Mitchell's earlier book is *Lie of the Land: Migrant Workers and the California Landscape,* published in 1996 by University of Minnesota Press. There is also an interview with Mitchell by the Critical Spatial Practice Reading Group in the special spatial justice issue of *Critical Planning* (2007).

I worked with Purcell, Brenner, and Dikec while they were students at UCLA. I describe them as geographer-planners for several reasons, including the fact that all three studied in both departments. Combining geography and planning provides certain advantages. If one is only a geographer, radical or liberal, there are many temptations to theorize without concern for innovative application. If one remains only an urban planner, again radical or liberal, there is pressure to become a practitioner with little value given to innovative theorizing. I hasten to add that there are exceptions, but I nonetheless believe there is something special in the combination geographer-planner.

Bishara, Suhad, and Hana Hamdan. 2006. Review of *Makan: The Right to the City and New Ways of Understanding Space*, special issue of *Makan*, a journal published by Adalah, the Legal Center for Arab Minority Rights in Israel, in ArabStudiesJournal.org.

Brenner, Neil. 2005. *New State Spaces: Urban Government and the Rescaling of Statehood*. New York: Oxford University Press.

———. 2000. "The Urban Question as a Scale Question: Reflections on Henri Lefebvre, Urban Theory, and the Politics of Scale." *International Journal of Urban and Regional Research* 24, 2: 361–78.

Brenner, Neil, and Nik Theodore. 2002. "Cities and the Geographies of 'Actually Existing Neoliberalism,'" *Antipode* 34, 3: 349–79.

Dikec, Mustafa. 2003. "Police, Politics, and the Right to the City." *GeoJournal* 58: 91–98.

———. 2001. "Justice and the Spatial Imagination." *Environment and Planning A* 33: 1785–805.

Dikec, Mustafa, and Liette Gilbert. 2002. "Right to the City: Homage or a New Social Ethics." *Capitalism, Nature, Socialism* 13, 2: 58–74.

Friedmann, John. 1995. "The Right to the City." *Society and Nature* 1: 71–84.

Habitat International Coalition. 2007. *Right to the City*. Paris: UNESCO (excerpts from the Habitat Agenda).

———. 2005a. *Urban Policies and the Right to the City*. Paris: UNESCO-UN-HABITAT.

———. 2005b. *World Charter for the Right to the City*. Paris: UNESCO, after Social Forum of the Americas, Quito (2004); World Urban Forum, Barcelona (2004); World Social Forum, Porto Alegre (2005 and 2002).

———. 2005c. *Proposal for a Charter for Women's Right to the City*. Paris: UNESCO.

Harvey, David. 2009. [untitled] Opening speech at the World Social Forum, Belém, Brazil, January 29, 2009. http://www.reclaiming-spaces.org/crisis/archives/245.

———. 2008. "The Right to the City." *New Left Review* 53: 23–40.

———. 2006. "The Right to the City." In *Divided Cities: The Oxford Amnesty Lectures 2003*, ed. Richard Scholar, 83–103. Oxford: Oxford University Press.

———. 2003. "A Right to the City." *International Journal of Urban and Regional Research* 27, 4: 939–41.

Lefebvre, Henri. 2003. *The Urban Revolution*. Trans. R. Bononno. Minneapolis: University of Minnesota Press.

———. 1996. *Writings on Cities/Henri Lefebvre*. Selected, trans., and introduction by Eleanore Kaufman and Elizabeth Lebas. Oxford, UK, and Cambridge, Mass.: Blackwell.

———. 1991. *The Production of Space*. Trans. D. Nicholson-Smith. Oxford, UK, and Cambridge, Mass.: Blackwell.

———. 1976. *The Survival of Capitalism*. Trans. F. Bryanit. London: Allison and Busby.

———. 1974. *La production de l'espace*. Paris: Anthropos.

———. 1968. *Le Droit à la Ville*. Paris: Anthropos.

Mitchell, Don. 2003. *The Right to the City: Social Justice and the Fight for Public Space*. New York: Guildford Press.

Nicholls, Beaumont. 2004. "The Urbanization of Justice Movements? Possibilities and Constraints for the City as a Space of Contentious Struggle." *Space and Polity* 2: 119–35.

Ortiz, Enrique. 2006. "Toward a World Charter for the Right to the City." Paris: UNESCO-Habitat International Coalition.

Painter, Joe. 2005. "Urban Citizenship and Rights to the City." International Centre for Regional Regeneration and Development Studies (ICRRDS), Durham University.

Purcell, Mark. 2008. *Recapturing Democracy: Neoliberalization and the Struggle for Alternative Urban Futures*. New York: Routledge.

———. 2006. "Urban Democracy and the Local Trap." *Urban Studies* 43: 1921–41.

———. 2003. "Citizenship and the Right to the Global City." *International Journal of Urban and Regional Research* 27, 3: 564–90.

———. 2002. "Excavating Lefebvre: The Right to the City and Its Urban Politics of the Inhabitant." *GeoJournal* 58: 99–108.

Vaiou, Dina. 2000. "Cities and Citizens: Everyday Life and the Right to the City." In *The Sustainable City*, ed. M. Modinos and E. Efthymiopoulos. Athens: Stochastis/DIPE [in Greek].

Vaiou, Dina, and Rouli Lykogianni. 2006. "Women, Neighborhoods and Everyday Life." *Urban Studies* 43, 4: 731–43.

Wastl-Walter, D., Lynn Staeheli, and Lorraine Dowler, eds. 2003. *"Rights to the City."* Rome: Societa Geografica Italiana.

Wills, Jane. 2004. "Campaigning for Low Paid Workers: The East London Communities Organization (TELCO)." In *The Future of Worker Representation*, ed. W. Brown, G. Healy, E. Henry, and P. Taylor, 264–82. Oxford: Oxford University Press.

4. Seeking Spatial Justice in Los Angeles

Setting the Scene

One of the earliest uses of the term *urban restructuring*—and a significant portion of the subsequent literature on this topic—came from an article published in 1983 that analyzed the crisis-driven spatial restructuring of Los Angeles after the Watts Riots in 1965. This study, which I coauthored with Rebecca Morales and Goetz Wolff, originated from a project initiated by one of the earliest labor–community–university coalitions in the region, the Coalition to Stop Plant Closings (CSPC). This research project aimed at assisting the CSPC in understanding the rapidly changing regional economy and in mobilizing resistance to the factory closures that were devastating many local communities at the time. It was an early example of the lasting relationship that would develop between labor and community groups and the students and faculty in the Urban Planning and Geography departments at UCLA. It was also one of the earliest examples of the effort to translate contemporary spatial theory into effective spatial practice.

For the discussion of rising economic inequalities in the United States, I have relied primarily on the work of the Nobel prize–winning geographical economist Paul Krugman and in particular his 2002 essay in the *New York Times Magazine*, "For Richer: How the Permissive Capitalism of the Boom Destroyed American Equality."

Except for some references to Castells, Krugman, and Sassen, the following bibliography refers specifically to the Los Angeles research cluster as defined in the text. It can also be seen as representative of what some define as the L.A. school. It does not include the many relevant writings of sociologists and others whose approach is not assertively spatial, nor does it contain the critiques that have been written about its allegedly exaggerated claims and omissions. Again, the emphasis is on the application of a critical spatial perspective.

Castells, Manuel. 1998. *End of Millennium*. Vol. 3, The Information Age: Economy, Society, and Culture. Malden, Mass.: Blackwell.

———. 1997. *The Power of Identity*. Vol. 2, The Information Age: Economy, Society, and Culture. Malden, Mass.: Blackwell.

———. 1996. *The Rise of the Network Society*. Vol. 1, The Information Age: Economy, Society, and Culture. Malden, Mass.: Blackwell.

———. 1989. *The Informational City: Information, Technology, Economic Restructuring, and the Urban-Regional Process*. Berkeley and Los Angeles: University of California Press.

Cenzatti, Marco. 1993. *Los Angeles and the L.A. School*. West Hollywood, Calif.: Los Angeles Forum for Architecture and Design.

Davis, Mike. 1998. *Ecology of Fear*. New York: Metropolitan Books.

———. 1990. *City of Quartz: Excavating the Future in Los Angeles*. London: Verso.

Dear, Michael. 2008. "Urban Politics and the Los Angeles School of Urbanism." *Urban Affairs* 44, 2: 266–79.

———. 2005. "Los Angeles and the Chicago School: Invitation to a Debate." In

The Urban Sociology Reader, ed. J. Lin and C. Mele. New York: Routledge. Originally published in the inaugural issue of *City and Community* in 2002 with critical responses.

————. 2003. "The Los Angeles School of Urbanism: An Intellectual History." *Urban Geography* 24, 6: 493–509.

Dear, Michael, and J. Dallas Dishman, eds. 2001. *From Chicago to L.A.: Making Sense of Urban Theory.* Thousand Oaks, Calif.: Sage Publications.

Dear, Michael, H. Eric Schockman, and Greg Hise, eds. 1996. *Rethinking Los Angeles.* Thousand Oaks, Calif.: Sage Publications.

Dear, Michael, and Allen J. Scott, eds. 1981. *Urbanization and Urban Planning in Capitalist Society.* New York: Methuen.

Dear, Michael, and Jennifer Wolch. 1987. *Landscapes of Despair: From Deinstitutionalization to Homelessness.* Princeton, N.J.: Princeton University Press.

Flusty, Steven. 1994. *Building Paranoia: The Proliferation of Interdictory Space and the Erosion of Spatial Justice.* West Hollywood, Calif.: Los Angeles Forum for Architecture and Urban Design.

Friedmann, John. 1986. "The World City Hypothesis." *Development and Change* 17: 69–83.

Friedmann, John, and Goetz Wolff. 1982. "World City Formation: An Agenda for Research and Action." *International Journal for Urban and Regional Research* 6: 309–41.

Keil, Roger. 1998. *Los Angeles: Globalization, Urbanization, and Social Struggles.* New York: John Wiley and Sons.

Krugman, Paul. 2008. *The Return of Depression Economics and the Crisis of 2008.* New York: W. W. Norton.

————. 2007. *The Conscience of a Liberal.* New York: W. W. Norton.

————. 2003. *The Great Unraveling: Losing Our Way in the New Century.* New York: W. W. Norton.

————. 2002. "For Richer: How the Permissive Capitalism of the Boom Destroyed American Equality." *New York Times Magazine,* October 20, 2002.

Miller, D. W. 2000. "The New Urban Studies: Los Angeles Scholars Use Their Region and Their Ideas to End the Dominance of the 'Chicago School.'" *Chronicle of Higher Education,* August 18, 2000. Online version contains numerous reactions and debates.

Ong, Paul, and Evelyn Blumenberg. 1996. "Income and Racial Inequality in Los Angeles." In *The City: Los Angeles and Urban Theory at the End of the Twentieth Century,* ed. Allen J. Scott and Edward W. Soja, 311–35. Berkeley and Los Angeles: University of California Press.

Ruddick, Susan. 1996. *Young and Restless in Hollywood: Mapping Social Identities.* New York: Routledge.

Sassen, Saskia. 1991. *The Global City: New York, London, Tokyo*. Princeton, N.J.: Princeton University Press.

Scott, Allen J. 2008. *Social Economy of the Metropolis: Cognitive-Cultural Capitalism and the Global Resurgence of Cities*. Oxford: Oxford University Press.

———. 2006. *Geography and Economy*. Clarendon Lectures in Geography and Environmental Studies. Oxford: Oxford University Press.

———. 2005. *On Hollywood: The Place, the Industry*. Princeton, N.J.: Princeton University Press.

———, ed. 2001. *Global City-Regions: Trends, Theory, Policy*. Oxford: Oxford University Press.

———. 2000. *The Cultural Economy of Cities*. London: Sage.

———. 1998. *Regions and the World Economy*. Oxford: Oxford University Press.

———. 1993. *Technopolis: High-Technology Industry and Regional Development in Southern California*. Berkeley and Los Angeles: University of California Press.

———. 1992. "Low-Wage Workers in a High-Technology Manufacturing Complex: The Southern California Electronics Assembly Industry." *Urban Studies* 29: 1231–46.

———. 1988a. *Metropolis: From the Division of Labor to Urban Form*. Berkeley and Los Angeles: University of California Press.

———. 1988b. *New Industrial Spaces: Flexible Production Organization and Regional Development in North America and Western Europe*. London: Pion.

———. 1984. "Territorial Reproduction and Transformation in a Local Labor Market: The Animated Film Workers of Los Angeles." *Environment and Planning D: Society and Space* 2: 277–307.

Scott, Allen J., John Agnew, Edward Soja, and Michael Storper. 2004. "Global City-Regions." In *Global City-Regions*, ed. Scott.

Scott, Allen J., and Edward Soja. 1986. "Editorial Essay: Los Angeles: Capital of the Late Twentieth Century." *Environment and Planning D: Society and Space* 4: 249–54.

———, eds. 1996. *The City: Los Angeles and Urban Theory at the End of the Twentieth Century*. Berkeley and Los Angeles: University of California Press.

Scott, Allen J., and Michael Storper, eds. 1986. *Production, Work, Territory: The Geographical Anatomy of Industrial Capitalism*. London: Allen and Unwin.

Soja, Edward. 2003a. "Writing the City Spatially." *City* 7, 3: 269–80.

———. 2003b. "Tales of a Geographer-Planner." In *Story and Sustainability: Planning, Practice, and Possibility in American Cities*, ed. Barbara Eckstein and James A. Throgmorton, 207–24. Cambridge, Mass.: MIT Press.

———. 2003c. "Urban Tensions: Globalization, Economic Restructuring, and the Postmetropolitan Transition." In *Global Tensions: Challenges and Opportunities in the World Economy,* ed. Lourdes Beneria and Savitri Bisnath, 275–90. New York: Routledge.

———. 2000. *Postmetropolis: Critical Studies of Cities and Regions.* Oxford, UK, and Malden, Mass.: Blackwell Publishers.

———. 1997. "Six Discourses on the Postmetropolis." In *Imagining Cities,* ed. Sallie Westwood and John Williams, 19–30. London: Routledge.

———. 1996a. *Thirdspace: Journeys to Los Angeles and Other Real-and-Imagined Places.* Oxford, UK, and Malden, Mass.: Blackwell Publishers.

———. 1996b. "Los Angeles 1965–1992: From Restructuring-Generated Crisis to Crisis-Generated Restructuring." In *The City,* ed. Scott and Soja, 426–62.

———. 1995. "Postmodern Urbanization: The Six Restructurings of Los Angeles." In *Postmodern Cities and Spaces,* ed. Sophie Watson and Kathy Gibson, 125–37. Oxford, UK, and Cambridge, Mass.: Blackwell.

———. 1992. "Inside Exopolis: Scenes from Orange County." In *Variations on a Theme Park: The New American City and the End of Public Space,* ed. M. Sorkin, 94–122. New York: Hill and Wang.

———. 1991. "Poles Apart: New York and Los Angeles." In *Dual City: The Restructuring of New York,* ed. J. Mollenkopf and M. Castells, 361–76. New York: Russell Sage Foundation.

———. 1990. "Heterotopologies: A Remembrance of Other Spaces in the Citadel-LA." *Strategies: A Journal of Theory, Culture and Politics* 3: 6–39.

———. 1989. *Postmodern Geographies: The Reassertion of Space in Critical Social Theory.* London: Verso.

———. 1987. "Economic Restructuring and the Internationalization of the Los Angeles Region." In *The Capitalist City,* ed. M. P. Smith and J. Feagin, 178–98. Oxford: Basil Blackwell.

———. 1986. "Taking Los Angeles Apart: Some Fragments of a Critical Human Geography." *Environment and Planning D: Society and Space* 4: 255–72.

———. 1980. "The Socio-Spatial Dialectic." *Annals of the Association of American Geographers* 70: 207–25.

Soja, Edward, Alan Heskin, and Marco Cenzatti. 1984 and 1985. "Los Angeles nel caleidoscopio della restrutturazione." *Urbanistica* 80: 55–60. "Los Angeles through the Kaleidoscope of Urban Restructuring." Los Angeles: Graduate School of Architecture and Urban Planning, UCLA, Special Publication.

Soja, Edward, Rebecca Morales, and Goetz Wolff. 1983. "Urban Restructuring: An Analysis of Social and Spatial Change in Los Angeles." *Economic Geography* 59: 195–230.

Storper, Michael. 1997. *The Regional World: Territorial Development in a Global Economy.* New York and London: Guilford Press.

Storper, Michael, and Susan Christopherson. 1989. "The Effects of Flexible

Specialization on Industrial Politics and the Labor Market: The Motion Picture Industry." *Industrial and Labor Relations Review*: 331–48.

Storper, Michael, and Susan Christopherson. 1987. "Flexible Specialization and Regional Industrial Agglomerations." *Annals of the Association of American Geographers* 77: 104–17.

Storper, Michael, and Allen J. Scott, eds. 1992. *Pathways to Industrialization and Regional Development*. London: Routledge.

A History of Social Activism in Los Angeles

The best work on the United Farm Workers (UFW), its influence on the development of community unionism, and its continuing impact on justice struggles in Los Angeles and throughout the country is by Randy Shaw. Shaw brings the discussion of the UFW up to the present, noting the direct link between the UFW motto of *Si Se Puede* and the campaign promise that "Yes, We Can" of former community organizer, now President Barack Obama.

The following is a list of more general references on the labor, community, and environmental justice movements in Los Angeles. Particularly noteworthy for their acute spatial perspective and sharply critical reflections on the environmental justice movement are the writings of Laura Pulido. Pulido received her PhD in urban planning at UCLA and has for many years been professor of American studies and ethnicity and geography at the University of Southern California. References on specific organizations such as the Bus Riders Union, Justice for Janitors, and the Los Angeles Alliance for a New Economy are listed separately.

Chang, Edward T., and Russell C. Leong, eds. 1993. *Los Angeles—Struggles toward Multiethnic Community*. Seattle: University of Washington Press.

Chavez, John R. 1998. *Eastside Landmark: A History of the East Los Angeles Community Union, 1968–1993*. Palo Alto, Calif.: Stanford University Press.

Gottlieb, Robert. 2007. *Reinventing Los Angeles: Nature and Community in the Global City*. Cambridge, Mass.: MIT Press.

Gottlieb, Robert, Mark Vallianatos, Regina Freer, and Peter Dreier. 2005. *The Next Los Angeles: The Struggle for a Livable City*. Berkeley and Los Angeles: University of California Press.

Houston, D., and Laura Pulido. 2001. "The Work of Performativity: Staging Social Justice at the University of Southern California." *Environment and Planning D: Society and Space* 20: 401–24.

Mann, Eric. 1987. *Taking On General Motors: A Case Study of the UAW Campaign to Keep GM Van Nuys Open*. Los Angeles: UCLA Institute of Industrial Relations, Center for Labor Research and Education.

Merrifield, Andy. 2000. "Living Wage Activism in the American City." *Social Text* 62, 18-1: 31–54.

Milkman, Ruth. 2007. "Los Angeles Exceptionalism and Beyond: A Response to the Critics." *Industrial Relations* 46: 691–98.

———. 2006. *L.A. Story: Immigrant Workers and the Future of the U.S. Labor Movement.* New York: Russell Sage Foundation.

———, ed. 2000. *Organizing Immigrants: The Challenge for Unions in Contemporary California.* Ithaca, N.Y.: Cornell University Press.

Milkman, Ruth, and Kent Wong. 2000. *Voices from the Front Lines: Organizing Immigrant Workers in Los Angeles.* Los Angeles: UCLA Center for Labor Research and Education.

Nicholls, W. 2003. "Forging a 'New' Organizational Infrastructure for Los Angeles' Progressive Community." *IJURR* 27: 881–96.

Pincetl, Stephanie. 1994. "Challenges to Latino Immigrants and Political Organizing in the Los Angeles Area." *Environment and Planning A* 26, 6: 895–914.

Pulido, Laura. 2006. *Black, Brown, Yellow, and Left: Radical Activism in Los Angeles.* Los Angeles and Berkeley: University of California Press.

———. 2001. "Race, Class, and Political Activism: Black, Chicano/a and Japanese American Leftists in Southern California." *Antipode* 34, 4: 762–88.

———. 2000. "Rethinking Environmental Racism: White Privilege and Urban Development in Los Angeles." *Annals of the Association of American Geographers* 90, 1: 12–40.

———. 1996a. "A Critical Review of the Methodology of Environmental Racism Research." *Antipode* 28, 2: 142–59.

———. 1996b. "Multiracial Organizing among Environmental Justice Activists in Los Angeles." In *Rethinking Los Angeles,* ed. Michael Dear, Eric Schockman, and Greg Hise, 171–89. Thousand Oaks, Calif.: Sage Publications.

———. 1994. "Restructuring and the Contraction and Expansion of Environmental Rights in the United States." *Environment and Planning A* 26: 915–36.

Shaw, Randy. 2008. *Beyond the Fields: Cesar Chavez, the UFW, and the Struggle for Justice in the 21st Century.* Berkeley and Los Angeles: University of California Press.

———. 2001. *The Activist's Handbook: A Primer.* Berkeley: University of California Press.

Webber, Melvin M. 1964. "The Urban Place and Non-Place Urban Realm." In *Explorations into Urban Structure,* ed. Melvin M. Webber et al., 19–41. Philadelphia: University of Pennsylvania Press.

Wilton, Robert D., and Cynthia Cranford. 2002. "Toward an Understanding of the Spatiality of Social Movements: Labor Organizing at a Private University in Los Angeles." *Social Problems* 49, 3: 374–94.

The Birth of Community Unionism: 1965–79

A good general reference on social activism for this period and the next is Robert Gottlieb et al. (2005), listed above. Gottlieb was formerly a lecturer in Urban Planning at UCLA and is now Henry R. Luce Professor of Urban and Environmental Policy and director of the Urban and Environmental Policy Institute at Occidental College. He and his colleague Peter Dreier have written extensively on local politics and social movements in Los Angeles, helping to establish Occidental College as an important center for action-oriented urban and environmental research. References to Webber (1964) and Chavez (1998) are also included in the above list.

The Beginnings of Justice-Based Coalitions: 1979–92

The labor sociologist Ruth Milkman has written extensively on the labor movement in Los Angeles during this period. She was director of the UCLA Institute for Research on Labor and Education (IRLE, formerly the Institute for Industrial Relations) from 2001 to 2008. Milkman has written extensively on the difficulties and successes in organizing immigrants (2006; see the reference list for chapter 1) and on gender issues in the labor movement. Kent Wong, her coauthor in several publications (see Milkman and Wong 2001), is a longtime labor activist and currently director of the UCLA Center for Labor Research and Education.

The name of the IRLE has been slightly revised to become the Institute for Research on Labor and Employment. Its current director is Chris Tilly, a member of the Urban Planning faculty, and its associate director is Christopher Erickson (see Erickson et al. 1997, 2002). The early research for *Seeking Spatial Justice* was funded by a small grant from IRLE under Milkman's leadership. The IRLE under its various names and directorships has been a core educational and research force in the Los Angeles labor movement for more than thirty years.

The bibliography for this period includes references to the events of 1992, the Coalition to Stop Plant Closings, and Justice for Janitors. On Richard Gillett, see Davey (2002).

Baldassare, Mark. 1998. *Los Angeles Riots: Lessons for the Urban Future.* Boulder, Colo.: Westview Press.

Davey, Andrew. 2002. *Urban Christianity and the Global Order: Theological Resources for an Urban Future.* Peabody, Mass.: Hendrickson Publishers.

Davis, Mike. 1993a. "Who Killed Los Angeles? A Political Autopsy." *New Left Review* 197: 3–28.

———. 1993b. "Who Killed Los Angeles? The Verdict Is Given." *New Left Review* 199: 29–54.

———. 1990. "Police Riot in Century City—Just Like Old Times: Cops Beat Up Demonstrators, Unionists, and Latinos." *L.A. Weekly,* June 22–28.

Erickson, Christopher, Catherine Fisk, Ruth Milkman, Daniel Mitchell, and Kent Wong. 2002. "Justice for Janitors in Los Angeles: Lessons from Three Rounds of Negotiations." *British Journal of Industrial Relations* 40: 543–67.

Erickson, Christopher, Ruth Milkman, Daniel Mitchell, Abel Valenzuela, Roger Waldinger, Kent Wong, and Maurice Zeitlin. 1997. "Helots No More: A Case Study of the Justice for Janitors Campaign in Los Angeles." In *Organizing to Win*, ed. Kate Bronfenbrenner, Sheldon Friedman, Richard Hurd, Rudy Oswald, and Ronald Seeber, 102–22. Ithaca, N.Y.: Cornell University Press. A shorter version can be found in "Justice for Janitors: Organizing in Difficult Times." *Dissent* (winter 1997): 37–44.

Gooding-Williams, Robert, ed. 1993. *Reading Rodney King/Reading Urban Uprising*. New York: Routledge.

Gottlieb, Robert. 2001. *Environmentalism Unbound: Exploring New Pathways for Change*. Cambridge, Mass.: MIT Press.

Haas, Gilda. 1985. *Plant Closures: Myths, Realities, and Responses*. Pamphlet. Boston: South End Press.

Haas, Gilda, and Rebecca Morales. 1986. "Plant Closures and the Grassroots Response to Economic Crisis in the United States." Working paper. Los Angeles: UCLA Graduate School of Architecture and Urban Planning.

Howley, John. 1990. "Justice for Janitors: The Challenges of Organizing in Contract Services." *Labor Research Review* 15: 61–72.

Hurd, Richard W., and William Rouse. 1989. "Progressive Union Organizing: The SEIU Justice for Janitors Campaign." *Review of Radical Political Economics* 21, 3: 70–75.

Hurst Mann, Lian, and the Urban Strategies Group. 1993. *Reconstructing Los Angeles from the Bottom Up*. Los Angeles: Strategy Center Publications.

Klein, Norman M. 1997. *The History of Forgetting: Los Angeles and the Erasure of Memory*. London: Verso.

Madhubuti, Haki R. 1993. *Why L.A. Happened: Implications of the '92 Los Angeles Rebellion*. Chicago: Third World Press.

Mahdesian, Michael, et al. 1981. *Report to the Coalition to Stop Plant Closings*. Los Angeles: UCLA Graduate School of Architecture and Urban Planning. Includes copy of pamphlet prepared for the Electricians Union on "Early Warning Signs of Plant Closing."

Mann, Eric. 1993. "Los Angeles—A Year After: (I) The Poverty of Capitalism; (II) The Left and the City's Future." *The Nation*, March 29, 406–11, and May 3, 586–90.

Meyerson, Harold. 2000. "The Red Sea: How the Janitors Won Their Strike." *L.A. Weekly*, April 28, 2000.

Milkman, Ruth, and Kent Wong. 2001. "Organizing Immigrant Workers: Case Studies from Southern California." In *Rekindling the Movement: Labor's Quest for Relevance in the Twenty-first Century,* ed. Lowell Turner, Harry Katz, and Richard Hurd, 99–128. Ithaca, N.Y.: Cornell University Press.

Morales, Rebecca. 1986. "The Los Angeles Automobile Industry in Historical Perspective." *Environment and Planning D: Society and Space* 4: 289–303.

————. 1983. "Transnational Labor: Undocumented Workers in the Los Angeles Automobile Industry." *International Migration Review* 17: 570–96.

Morales, Rebecca, and Goetz Wolff. 1985. "Plant Closings and the Immigrant Labor Force in Los Angeles." Working paper. Los Angeles: UCLA Institute of Industrial Relations.

Pastor, Manuel, Jr. 1995. "Economic Inequality, Latino Poverty, and the Civil Unrest in Los Angeles." *Economic Development Quarterly* 9: 238–58.

Savage, Lydia. 2006. "Justice for Janitors: Scales of Organizing and Representing Workers." *Antipode* 38, 3: 648–67.

————. 1998. "Geographies of Organizing: Justice for Janitors in Los Angeles." In *Organizing the Landscape: Geographical Perspectives on Labor Unionism,* ed. Andrew Herod, 225–52. Minneapolis: University of Minnesota Press.

Savage, Lydia, and Jane Wills. 2004. "New Geographies of Trade Unionism." Editorial introduction, *Geoforum* 35, 1: 5–7.

Smith, Anna Deavere. 1994. *Twilight—Los Angeles, 1992 on the Road.* New York: Doubleday Anchor Books.

Coalition Building and the Search for Spatial Justice: 1992 to 9/11/2001

Many of the details on the specific organizations and coalitions presented here and in the previous discussion are taken from a remarkable document in the form of a two-sided poster titled *Connecting L.A.'s Community Organizations and Labor: Toward a Social and Economic Justice Landscape.* The poster, with several maps and detailed discussions of Justice for Janitors, the Living Wage Campaign, Metropolitan Alliance, and many other organizations and campaigns, was prepared by the UCLA Community Scholars Program (CSP) in 2002. Jacqueline Leavitt was a project manager and director of the CSP at the time. Also participating were Kent Wong, director of the Center for Labor Research and Education, and two research associates, Francisco Garcia and Martha Matsuoka. The CSP is discussed further in chapter 5. It can be accessed at http://www.spa.ucla.edu/dup.

A student assistant for the CSP in 2002, Martha Matsuoka has become a leading community development and labor networker in Los Angeles and elsewhere in California. She received her PhD in urban planning at UCLA, currently teaches in the Urban and Environmental Policy Department at Occidental College, and is involved in many organizations, especially in the area of environmental justice. Her dissertation (Matsuoka 2005) and subsequent writings provide an informative introduction to the important concept of community-based regionalism, a key component in the search for spatial justice. See also Pastor, Benner, and Matsuoka (2009), the best reference for understanding the concept of community-based regionalism and the development of regional coalitions in Los Angeles. Manuel Pastor Jr. has been a key figure writing about the regional coalitions and social movements in Los Angeles from a critical spatial perspective. Pastor is currently professor of geography and American studies and ethnicity at the University of Southern California, where he directs the Program for Environmental and Regional Equity (PERE). Abel Valenzuela Jr., who holds a joint appointment in Urban Planning and the Cesar Chavez Center for Chicana and Chicano Studies at UCLA, has been particularly active in studying day laborers in Los Angeles. See Valenzuela (2003) and Valenzuela et al. (2006). References for Pastor, Valenzuela, and Matsuoka are listed in this section's bibliography.

LAANE's broader accomplishments are many. Between 1992 and 2001, for example, it helped to pass the first service contract workers retention ordinance, increasing job security for workers employed by city contractors; led the way in the successful passing of the city's groundbreaking living wage ordinance in 1997, resulting in higher wages and health benefits for ten thousand workers and providing a model for the rest of the country; helped win a precedent-setting agreement (with the same company that developed Times Square in Manhattan) for the redevelopment of Hollywood Boulevard that included provisions for living wage employment and seed money for a workers' health care center and trust fund; joined with SEIU in 1999 to extend the living wage law to Los Angeles County; allied with Santa Monicans Allied for Responsible Tourism (SMART) to win a landslide victory against passage of a ballot initiative aimed at eliminating the living wage ordinance; and worked with SMART to help pass in 2001 the first living wage ordinance in the country covering businesses that do not receive direct benefits from local government.

Also notable are several published reports from LAANE, such as *Who Benefits from Redevelopment in Los Angeles? An Evaluation of Commercial Redevelopment Activities in the 1990s* (1999), cowritten with the UCLA Center for Labor Research and Education, led by Paul More and four other students from Urban Planning; *The Other Los Angeles: The Working Poor in the City of the 21st Century* (2000), again headed by Paul More and Urban Planning students; and *A Study in Corporate Irresponsibility: McDonalds Corporation's Operations at LAX* (2002). A full list of publications, including some executive summaries and text, is available at the LAANE Web site: laane.org.

Matsuoka, Martha. 2005. "From Neighborhood to Global: Community-Based Regionalism and Shifting Concepts of Place in Community and Regional Development." PhD diss., Urban Planning, UCLA.

Pastor, Manuel, Jr. 2008. "Poverty, Work, and Public Policy: Latinos in California's New Economy." In *Mexicanos in California: Transformations and Challenge,* ed. Patricia Zavella and Ramón Gutiérrez. Chicago: University of Illinois Press.

―――. 2007. "Environmental Justice: Reflections from the United States." In *Reclaiming Nature: Environmental Justice and Ecological Restoration,* ed. James K. Boyce, Sunita Narain, and Elizabeth A. Stanton. London: Anthem Press.

―――. 2001a. "Looking for Regionalism in All the Wrong Places: Demography, Geography, and Community in Los Angeles County." *Urban Affairs Review* 36, 6: 747–82.

―――. 2001b. "Common Ground at Ground Zero? The New Economy and the New Organizing in Los Angeles." *Antipode* 33, 2: 260–89.

Pastor, Manuel, Jr., Chris Benner, and Laura Leete. 2007. *Staircases or Treadmills: Labor Market Intermediaries and Economic Opportunity in a Changing Economy.* New York: Russell Sage Foundation.

Pastor, Manuel, Jr., Chris Benner, and Martha Matsuoka. 2009. *This Could Be the Start of Something Big: How Social Movements for Regional Equity are Reshaping Metropolitan America.* Ithaca, N.Y.: Cornell University Press.

―――. 2006. "The Regional Nexus: The Promise and Risk of Community-Based Approaches to Metropolitan Equity." In *Jobs and Economic Development in Minority Communities,* ed. Paul Ong and Anastasia Loukaitou-Sideris. Philadelphia: Temple University Press.

Pastor, Manuel, Jr., Peter Dreier, Eugene Grigsby, and Marta López-Garza. 2000. *Regions That Work: How Cities and Suburbs Can Grow Together.* Minneapolis: University of Minnesota Press.

Pastor, Manuel, Jr., James L. Sadd, and Rachel Morello-Frosch. 2007. "LULUs of the Field: Research and Activism for Environmental Justice." In *Professional Advocacy for Social Justice,* ed. Andrew Barlow. Lanham, Md.: Rowman and Littlefield.

Valenzuela, Abel, Jr. 2003. "Day-Labor Work." *Annual Review of Sociology* 29, 1: 307–33.

Valenzuela, Abel, Jr., Nik Theodore, Edwin Melendez, and Ana Luz Gonzales. 2006. *On the Corner: Day Labor in the United States.* Technical Report, UCLA Center for the Study of Urban Poverty.

5. Translating Theory into Practice

Geographers, sociologists, and others at UCLA and other major universities in the region played an important role in building an unusually rich literature on urban and regional development in Los Angeles. But I do want to suggest that urban planning as an academic and professional discipline, and the particular form it took at UCLA, had a number of features that made it exceptionally fertile ground, especially for critical spatial thinking. In comparison with geography and the social sciences, urban planning was less encumbered by entrenched disciplinary traditions and somewhat freer to explore interdisciplinary perspectives. The necessary link to practice and principles of social justice, maintained by students willing to be theoretically informed but demanding some attention to how these ideas might prove useful in actual planning activities, sharpened both theoretical and empirical scholarship. As noted in chapter 5, working in Urban Planning at UCLA significantly helped me to develop my own critical spatial perspective and approach to spatial theory and practice.

Creating a Graduate School for Activists

Particularly influential in the early years was John Friedmann's book *Retracking America: A Theory of Transactive Planning* (1973), which promoted a renewed vision of participatory democracy and the empowerment of civil society. See also Allan D. Heskin, "From Theory to Practice: Professional Development at UCLA," *Journal of the American Institute of Planners* 1978: 436–51.

A selected list of the titles of comprehensive projects includes:

Dilemmas of Municipal Solid Waste Management (1987)
Income Inequality and Poverty in Los Angeles (1989)
Paths for Tomorrow: Nickerson Gardens—Neighbors Leading the Way (1991)
Planning for Cultural Equity in Los Angeles (1992)
Running on Empty: Transportation Patterns of the Very Poor in Los Angeles (1992)
A Comprehensive Perspective on Tourism in Los Angeles (1993)
Seeds of Change: Strategies for Food Security in the Inner City (1995)
The Los Angeles Manufacturing Action Project: A Feasibility Study for Organizing Strategies in the Alameda Corridor (1995)
Putting Capital in Its Place: The Los Angeles Worker Ownership Project (1996)
Asian Pacific American Entrepreneurship and Community Economic Development (1997)
The Byzantine-Latino Quarter (1998)
Banking on Blight: Redevelopment in Post-Proposition 13 in California (1999)
Cornfield of Dreams: A Resource Guide of Facts, Issues, and Principles (2000)

Rent Control and Tenants' Rights Movement

Heskin's summative interpretation of these developments was published in *Tenants and the American Dream* (1983). Indicative of the prevailing spatial perspective within Urban Planning and the existing ties between planners and geographers were two journal articles assessing the impact of rent control: Heskin, Levine, and Garrett (2000), analyzing spatially the effects of vacancy control; and Clark and

Heskin (1982), on tenure discounts and residential mobility. The geographer W. A. V. Clark is well known for his work on residential mobility; Levine, a specialist in spatial statistics programs, was lecturer and researcher in Urban Planning from 1980 to 1994; Mark Garrett, like Heskin, a trained lawyer, has been involved in many research projects in Urban Planning since the mid-1980s. His dissertation, "The Struggle for Transit Justice: Race, Space, and Social Equity" (2006), is both a lengthy history of transit politics in Los Angeles and the most detailed analysis and interpretation of the Bus Riders Union court case.

Urban Planning faculty and students participated in various ways in the emergence of more democratic governance and planning in what signs on the freeway at the time, produced by angry landlords, called the "People's Republic of Santa Monica." In 1980, for example, a comprehensive project under the direction of myself and Derek Shearer prepared a report on *An Urban Self-Management Strategy for Santa Monica*. The report drew on Yugoslavia's self-management experiences and explored ways of democratizing the planning process and enhancing the economic and social power of neighborhoods and communities. Shearer, who would later become ambassador to Finland in the Clinton administration, was at that time the husband of Ruth Yanatta Goldway, the future mayor of Santa Monica and a leading figure in Santa Monicans for Renters' Rights.

Baar, Kenneth. 1983. "Guidelines for Drafting Rent Control Laws: Lessons of a Decade." *Rutgers Law Review* 35, 4: 721–885.

Boggs, Carl. 1989. *Social Movements and Political Power: Forms of Radicalism in the West*. Philadelphia: Temple University Press.

Clark, William A. V., and Alan D. Heskin. 1982. "The Impact of Rent Control on Tenure Discounts and Residential Mobility." *Land Economics* 58, 1: 109–17.

Clark, William A. V., Alan D. Heskin, and Louise Manuel. 1980. *Rental Housing in the City of Los Angeles*. Los Angeles: UCLA Institute for Social Science Research.

Haas, Gilda, and Allan Heskin. 1981. "Community Struggles in Los Angeles." *International Journal of Urban and Regional Research* 5, 4: 546–63.

Heskin, Allan D. 1991. *The Struggle for Community*. Boulder, Colo.: Westview Press.

———. 1983. *Tenants and the American Dream: Ideology and the Tenant Movement*. New York: Praeger.

———. 1980. "Crisis and Response: An Historical Perspective on Advocacy Planning." *Journal of the American Planning Association* 46: 50–63.

Heskin, Allan D., J. Eugene Grigsby, and Ned Levine. 1990. "Who Benefits from Rent Control? Effects on Tenants in Santa Monica, California." *Journal of the American Planning Association* 56, 2: 140–52.

Heskin, Allan D., Ned Levine, and Mark Garrett. 2000. "The Effects of Vacancy Control: A Spatial Analysis of Four California Cities." *Journal of the American Planning Association* 66, 2: 162–76.

Spatial Feminism and Environmental Justice

The award-winning environmental policy projects are listed below as Gottlieb et al. 1988 and 1989. For more on the LANCER project, see Gottlieb et al. (2005), listed earlier, and Blumberg and Gottlieb (1989).

Blumberg, Louis, and Robert Gottlieb. 1989. *War on Waste: Can America Win Its Battle with Garbage?* Washington, D.C.: Island Press.

FitzSimmons, Margaret, and Robert Gottlieb. 1996. "Bounding and Binding Metropolitan Space: The Ambiguous Politics of Nature in Los Angeles." In *The City,* ed. Allen J. Scott and Edward Soja, 186–224. Los Angeles and Berkeley: University of California Press.

Gottlieb, Robert. 1993. *Forcing the Spring: The Transformation of the American Environmental Movement.* Washington, D.C.: Island Press.

———. 1989. *A Life of Its Own: The Politics and Power of Water.* New York: Harcourt Brace Jovanovich.

Gottlieb, Robert, and Margaret FitzSimmons. 1991. *Thirst for Growth: Water Agencies as Hidden Government in California.* Tucson: University of Arizona Press.

Gottlieb, Robert, et al. 1995. *Seeds of Change: Struggles for Food Security in the Inner City.* UCLA Comprehensive Project.

Gottlieb, Robert, et al. 1989. *In Our Backyard: Environmental Issues at UCLA, Proposals for Change, and the Institution's Potential as a Model.* UCLA Comprehensive Project.

Gottlieb, Robert, et al. 1988. *The Dilemma of Municipal Solid Waste Managements: An Examination of the Rise of Incineration, Its Health and Air Impacts, the LANCER Project and the Feasibility of Alternatives.* UCLA Comprehensive Project.

Hayden, Dolores. 1985. *The Power of Place: Urban Landscape as Public History.* Cambridge, Mass.: MIT Press.

———. 1984. *Redesigning the American Dream: Gender, Housing, and Family Life.* New York: W. W. Norton.

———. 1981. *The Grand Domestic Revolution: A History of Feminist Designs for Homes, Neighborhoods, and Cities.* Cambridge, Mass.: MIT Press.

———. 1979. *Seven American Utopias: The Architecture of Communitarian Socialism, 1790–1975.* Cambridge, Mass.: MIT Press.

Innovative Research on Urban and Regional Restructuring

A bibliography for the so-called Los Angeles school is contained in the notes for chapter 4.

Joining me in my early thinking about spatial praxis was Gary Gaile, then a doctoral student in geography. Together we planned a project that would theorize nodality, the clustering of activities and people in space, and form the foundations for achieving through spatial planning what he called "effiquity," the combination of efficient as well as equitable development. Nothing was ever published from this early collaboration, but Gary would, curiously paralleling what I had done in the early 1960s, go on to conduct research in Kenya on development geography and spatial planning. He and his wife, Susan Clarke, became lifelong friends, and I chose to publish this book with the University of Minnesota Press through the series on Globalization and Community they coedited. Sadly, Gary suddenly passed away in February 2009 as I was completing the final draft of *Seeking Spatial Justice.* I dedicate whatever value this book might have to his memory and creative geographical imagination.

Goetz Wolff was a doctoral student in the early 1980s when he coauthored a widely cited work on the "world city hypothesis" with John Friedmann. He played a prominent role in the Coalition to Stop Plant Closings and was a key figure in the early research project on urban restructuring in Los Angeles (Soja, Morales, and Wolff 1983), conducting much of the detailed research. After developing close ties with the regional labor movement, Wolff dropped out of the doctoral program to found his own labor-oriented consulting firm, Resources for Employment and Economic Development. He was later appointed as part of the UCLA Urban Planning practitioner faculty and has remained as its primary connecting link to local labor organizations. Wolff was cofounder of the Los Angeles Manufacturing Action Project (LAMAP) and later became research director from 1999 to 2005 of the 800,000-strong Los Angeles County Federation of Labor, the most influential labor organization in Southern California. He also served as director of the Center for Regional Employment Studies and is currently executive director of the labor-oriented Harry Bridges Institute based in San Pedro. There are few scholar-activists anywhere who better combine his theoretical sophistication, critical regional perspective, leadership experience, research capabilities, and commitment to social activism and justice for workers of the world.

The use of immigrant labor as a corporate strategy for adapting to the new economy was illustrated in a visit by Rebecca Morales, then professor of urban planning, to a small sweatshop manufacturing automobile parts south of downtown Los Angeles. As she walked around, with a protective mask against the choking dust, she noticed the final products being piled up. On them was stamped "Made in Brazil." Evidently, labor costs in L.A. were so low and market proximity so short that some industries could compete with offshore producers.

As a new commitment to theoretically informed labor education grew in Urban Planning, several comprehensive projects were organized around topics related to the economic restructuring of Los Angeles and the U.S. economy, including one on the "Widening Divide," chaired by planning professor Paul Ong, which examined in detail the expanding income gap in Los Angeles. This work and its offshoots helped to expand national attention, then focused primarily on the so-called permanent urban underclass and the welfare-dependent, mainly African American population, to include the immigrant and predominantly Latino *working poor* as central to the problems of poverty and inequality in America. Ong's research continued to focus on social and spatial justice issues, particularly with regard to the Asian Pacific Islander population and various aspects of residential accessibility to welfare and related services.

Michael Dear's version of the L.A. research cluster and its transcendence of the Chicago school has attracted widespread attention among geographers and sociologists so that perhaps most outsiders believe it to represent the collective view. This has created some antagonism and confusion, making it difficult to present an alternative interpretation. Especially disturbing are Dear's claims that the core of the Los Angeles–based research denies the importance of centrality and agglomeration, with sprawling peripheral development now the determinative factor. This topsy-turvy view ignores what many local contributors consider the most important achievement of the larger Los Angeles cluster of researchers: focusing on the dynamic forces arising from urban agglomeration and propulsive regional economies.

Urban Planning Restructured

Project reports of the Community Scholars Program from 1991 to 2001 include in approximate order *Accidental Tourism, Manufacturing L.A.'s Future, Banking on Communities, Los Angeles Manufacturing Action Project, Worker Ownership: A Strategy for Job Creation and Retention, Learning for Change: Experiences in Popular Education, Banking on Blight: Redevelopment in Post-Proposition 13 California, Models of L.A. Organizing for Social Justice: Pushing the Boundaries, Crossing the Isms, Participatory Democracy and Coalition Building—Organizing for Social Change in L.A.'s Communities and Workplaces.*

In 2002, the Community Scholars group produced the informative two-sided poster mentioned in the notes for chapter 4, *Connecting L.A.'s Community Organizations and Labor: Toward a Social and Economic Justice Landscape.* Not only does the title signify the many connections between the labor and community development movements, but the use of the term *justice landscape* illustrates both a strategic facility with geographic information systems technologies and the serious attention given to spatial justice–related struggles.

6. Seeking Spatial Justice after 9/11

The growing national movement promoting Community Benefits Agreements is now well documented online. In addition to LAANE's own informative discussion of its involvement in the historical development of CBAs, two major reports are available that recognize LAANE's and Madeline Janis's efforts and present information on the continuing national diffusion of these innovative redevelopment tools. Appearing in 2005, *Community Benefits Agreements: Making Development Projects Accountable* has as its lead author Julian Gross, legal director of the California Partnership for Working Families, a key part of the national coalition. Assisting in preparing the report was Greg Leroy of the Good Jobs First organization based in Washington, D.C., and Janis of LAANE. The second report (2007), which includes an extensive commentary by Janis as well as a keynote address by Manuel Pastor, is titled *Community Benefits Agreements: The Power, Practice, and Promise of a Responsible Redevelopment Tool.* It was part of a monograph series on neighborhood redevelopment sponsored by the Annie E. Casey Foundation.

LAANE now publishes annual reports on poverty, jobs, and the Los Angeles economy and has been involved in new reports not just on CBAs but also on such topics as assessing the impact of living wage ordinances, the outsourcing of security jobs at LAX, the regional economic benefits derived from the Clean Trucks Program at the Port of Los Angeles, and in another example of how local struggles have been having a national impact, *Wal-Mart and Beyond: The Battle for Good Jobs and Strong Communities in Urban America* (2007).

Wikipedia has an excellent entry for South Central Farm, reputed to have been the country's largest urban farm before its closure. See also Henrik Lebuhn, "Entrepreneurial Urban Politics and Urban Social Movements in Los Angeles: The Struggle for Urban Farmland in South Central," *Eurozine* (online journal), 2006.

The documentary film *The Garden* was produced and directed by Scott Hamilton Kennedy and released in 2008 by Black Valley Films in association with Katahdin Productions.

A summary of the proceedings of the first meeting of the Right to the City Alliance can be found in *Right to the City: Notes from the Inaugural Convening,* 2007, available from Right to the City, 152 W. Thirty-second Street, Los Angeles, CA 90007. See also www.righttothecity.org. The regional networks and their participating organizations in the Right to the City Alliance as of August 2008 include Boston/Providence (Alternatives for Community and Environment, Centro Presente, Chinese Progressive Association, City Life/Vida Urbana, Direct Action for Rights and Equality, Olneyville Neighborhood Association); D.C. Metro—Washington D.C./Northern Virginia (ONE DC, Tenants and Workers United); Los Angeles (East LA Community Corporation, Esperanza Community Housing Corporation, Koreatown Immigrant Workers Association, South Asian Network, Strategic Action for a Just Economy, Union de Vecinos); Miami (Miami Workers Center, Power U, Vecinos Unidos); New Orleans (Safe Streets/Strong Communities); New York City (CAAAV Organizing Asian Communities, Community Voices Heard, Fabulous

Independent Educated Radicals for Community Empowerment-FIERCE, Families United for Racial and Economic Equality, Good Old Lower East Side, Make the Road NY, Mothers on the Move/Madres en Movimiento, New York City Aids Housing Network, Picture the Homeless, WE ACT for Environmental Justice); San Francisco/Bay Area (Chinese Progressive Association, Just Cause Oakland, People Organized to Demand Environmental and Economic Rights, People Organized to Win Employment Rights, St. Peter's Housing Committee, South of Market Community Action Network). Each of these organizations has a Web page, address, and invitation to donate to its efforts listed in *Right to the City Alliance: A Funder's Guide*, edited by David Staples, 2008, available online.

Another informative online publication is *The Right to the City: Reclaiming Our Urban Centers, Reframing Human Rights, and Redefining Citizenship* (a conversation between donor activist Connie Cagampang Heller and Gihan Perera of the Miami Workers Center), San Francisco, Tides Foundation, 2007. The Poitevin quote is taken from *Right to the City: Notes from the Inaugural Convening*. Another academic representative at the conference, Harmony Goldberg from CUNY, presents her view on the meeting in "Building Power in the City: Reflections on the Emergence of the Right to the City Alliance and the National Domestic Worker's Alliance," www.inthemiddleofthewhirlwind.wordpress.com/building-power-in-the-city/.

For a full bibliography on the right to the city, see the notes for chapter 3.

David Harvey's lecture at the World Social Forum, Belém, can be found at http://www.hic-net.org/news.asp?PID=913.

Index

EDWARD W. SOJA is Distinguished Professor of Urban Planning at the UCLA School of Public Affairs, and for many years was Centennial Visiting Professor in the Cities Programme, London School of Economics. He is the author of *Postmodern Geographies: The Reassertion of Space in Critical Theory, Thirdspace: Journeys to Los Angeles and Other Real-and-Imagined Places,* and *Postmetropolis: Critical Studies of Cities and Regions.*